Countering Terrorism

HOOVER STUDIES
IN POLITICS, ECONOMICS,
AND SOCIETY

General Editors
Peter Berkowitz and Tod Lindberg

Countering Terrorism

Blurred Focus, Halting Steps

Richard A. Posner

HOOVER STUDIES
IN POLITICS, ECONOMICS,
AND SOCIETY

Published in cooperation with
HOOVER INSTITUTION
Stanford University • Stanford, California

ROWMAN & LITTLEFIELD PUBLISHERS, INC.
Lanham • Boulder • New York • Toronto • Plymouth, UK

ROWMAN & LITTLEFIELD PUBLISHERS, INC.

The Hoover Institution on War, Revolution and Peace, founded at Stanford University in 1919 by Herbert Hoover, who went on to become the thirty-first president of the United States, is an interdisciplinary research center for advanced study on domestic and international affairs. The views expressed in its publications are entirely those of the authors and do not necessarily reflect the views of the staff, officers, or Board of Overseers of the Hoover Institution.

www.hoover.org

Published in the United States of America
by Rowman & Littlefield Publishers, Inc.
A wholly owned subsidary of The Rowman & Littlefield Publishing Group, Inc.
4501 Forbes Boulevard, Suite 200, Lanham, Maryland 20706
www.rowmanlittlefield.com
Estover Road
Plymouth PL6 7PY
United Kingdom
Distributed by National Book Network

First printing, 2006
14 13 12 11 10 09 08 07   9 8 7 6 5 4 3 2 1
Manufactured in the United States of America

British Library Cataloguing in Publication Information Available

Library of Congress Cataloging-in-Publication Data
Posner, Richard A.
Countering terrorism : blurred focus, halting steps / Richard A. Posner.
    p.   cm. — (Hoover studies in politics, economics, and society)
    "Published in cooperation with Hoover Institution."
    Includes bibliographical references and index.
    ISBN-13: 978-0-7425-5883-0 (hardback : alk. paper)
    ISBN-10: 0-7425-5883-5 (hardback : alk. paper)
    1. Terrorism—United States—Prevention.   2. Terrorism—Government policy—United States. I. Hoover Institution on War, Revolution, and Peace. II. Title.
HV6432.P674 2007
363.325'170973—dc22   2007011044

Contents

Introduction

This book completes an unplanned trilogy on the reform of the United States intelligence system since the terrorist attacks of September 11, 2001. It places even greater emphasis on counterterrorism intelligence than the previous books did, and Part Two of the book examines some counterterrorism measures other than intelligence.[1]

At this writing (February 2007), it is almost five and a half years since the 9/11 attacks; four years since the creation of the Department of Homeland Security; more than two years since Congress, in response to the attacks and to the 9/11 Commission's analysis and recommendations,[2] prescribed an ambitious reorganization of the system in the Intelligence Reform and Terrorism Prevention Act of 2004;

1. The two previous books are *Preventing Surprise Attacks: Intelligence Reform in the Wake of 9/11* (2005), and *Uncertain Shield: The U.S. Intelligence System in the Throes of Reform* (2006). My book on the constitutional dimensions of national security—*Not a Suicide Pact: The Constitution in a Time of National Emergency* (2006)—also bears on intelligence issues.

2. National Commission on Terrorist Attacks Upon the United States, *The 9/11 Commission Report* (2004).

22 months since the appointment of John Negroponte as the first Director of National Intelligence—and one month since the announcement that he was resigning the post to become Deputy Secretary of State.[3]

It is also 16 months since I finished the second book of the trilogy, *Uncertain Shield*, and much has happened that bears on my subject. We are now deep in the implementation phase of the reorganization. In addition, the appointment of a former Director of Central Intelligence, Robert Gates, as Secretary of Defense may portend a change in the balance between civilian and military control of intelligence, while the Democrats' control of Congress may lead to tougher legislative oversight of the intelligence community.[4] The crisis in Iraq, though it may distract policymakers from attention to the shortcomings of the intelligence system, instead may redouble attention to those shortcomings because of the Iraq Study Group's pointed criticism of the inability of our intelligence agencies to penetrate Iraq's warring sects.[5] And the replacement of Negroponte as Director

3. All references in this book to the Director of National Intelligence as an individual (as distinct from as a position) are to Negroponte because, as of this writing, his designated successor, John M. McConnell, has not yet taken office. On the changing of the guard, see the interesting discussion in Shane Harris, "The Return of the Grown-Ups: President Bush Has Put Four Men at the Top of the Military and Intelligence Establishments Who Know One Another Well and Have Worked Together since the 1990s," *National Journal*, Jan. 13, 2007, p. 52. Besides Gates and McConnell, they are Lieutenant General James Clapper, newly appointed as Undersecretary of Defense for Intelligence, and General Michael Hayden, who became the Director of the Central Intelligence Agency on May 30, 2006.

4. The Speaker of the House of Representatives, Nancy Pelosi, has announced the formation of the Select Intelligence Oversight Panel, to be composed of members of the House intelligence and appropriations committees. David Rogers, "Pelosi Plans Panel to Oversee Spy-Agency Funds: 'Hybrid' Committee Spans Oversight and Budget Work, Fulfilling 9/11 Panel's Call," *Wall Street Journal*, Dec. 14, 2006, p. A3.

5. Iraq Study Group, *The Iraq Study Group Report: The Way Forward—A New Approach* 94–95 (2006): James Risen, "Sunni and Shiite Insurgents Remain Mystery to U.S., Iraq Report Charges: Violence in Baghdad Has Hobbled Intelligence Gathering, Officials Say," *New York Times*, Dec. 11, 2006, p. A14.

of National Intelligence invites reconsideration of the pace and direction of intelligence reform. In short, it is an opportune time to take stock, to update,[6] and to rethink. Those are my aims in this book.

It may seem presumptuous for a federal judge, with no background in national security and no access to classified materials (other than those leaked materials published by journalists!), to be writing about intelligence and counterterrorism. But an outsider's perspective can be valuable—I have always welcomed outsider perspectives on law.[7] Insiders know more, but are hobbled. If former national security officials, they will be under psychological pressure to defend the positions they took when they were in government. If current officials, career concerns and loyalty to their superiors will preclude candor. Both sorts of official may, moreover, have a parochial outlook because of their particular niche in the national security establishment. And both sorts may be reluctant to express in public views that might be thought based on classified information.

This is not to deny the primacy of the insider perspectives. It is merely to suggest that someone who has no commitments to a particular position in the debate and who is therefore able to cast a cold eye on the contending positions may be worth listening to by those who, pooling all sources of insight, must decide on the structure and focus of our counterterrorism efforts. The outsider may be as worth listening to as the naïf who watches the emperor on parade and notices something missing. But no doubt my lack of insider knowledge limits my ability to address issues such as the insertion and control of undercover agents abroad and the strengths and limits of technical intelligence (satellite imaging, electronic surveillance, and "measurement and signatures intelligence"—intelligence derived from radia-

6. I have not, however, attempted to update my discussions (in *Uncertain Shield*, note 1 above, chs. 6–8) of the intelligence system's computer woes or Congress's deficient oversight.

7. See, for example, Richard A. Posner, *Frontiers of Legal Theory* (2001).

tion, seismic waves, and other sources of information that are remote from looking and listening), as these are especially secretive areas of intelligence.

Part One of this book, much the longer of the two parts, continues my examination of intelligence reform, with emphasis on implementation. After sketching a simple theoretical framework that emphasizes the importance of probabilistic analysis, and after raising doubts about the conception of intelligence reform that guided Congress in enacting the Intelligence Reform Act, I suggest a number of benchmarks for evaluating progress in implementing the act and improving the intelligence system more generally. Evaluation of that progress dominates the discussion in the rest of Part One.

I note several successes, including improved coordination of the 18,000 intelligence analysts scattered across the intelligence community. And I applaud the new emphasis that the community is placing on "open source" intelligence data—that is, data that are publicly accessible, for example by searching the World Wide Web. But I also express a number of concerns. One is with the trend—now happily arrested, at least for the moment—toward decentering the Central Intelligence Agency. Another is the assumption by Director of National Intelligence Negroponte of the role of the President's senior *substantive* intelligence adviser, in addition to his role as the intelligence system's coordinator, monitor, and overall supervisor. All that is too much for one person; I hope Negroponte's sucessor will realize this and be able to do something about it. A related concern is Negroponte's failure to have made more rapid progress toward solving fundamental problems of structure and performance of the intelligence community. It is related because he and his staff allowed themselves to become immersed in responding to the daily crisis rather than leaving that to the agencies. System-wide problems have not gotten the attention they require. My overarching concern is with the slow pace at which plans for solving these problems are being turned into action.

Among the system-wide problems that continue to defy solution are the following, all interrelated: overclassification of sensitive information; "need to know" as an impediment to the sharing of data among intelligence agencies; antiquated and incompatible computer software; and lack of standardization both of security protocols that limit access to digital databases and of the criteria and procedures for issuing security clearances. The last two of these problems are the consequence of what I call the "tyranny of the security officers"—their refusal to take even the tiniest risk of a security breach.

The most serious of the neglected system-wide problems, however, is that of domestic intelligence, which seeks to detect and foil terrorist attacks inside the United States as well as espionage by foreign nations. Our system of domestic intelligence is in disarray, with many gaps. This disarray is related to the broader problem of divergent organizational cultures within the intelligence community. The failure to separate the national intelligence agencies[8] from the Department of Defense has contributed to the continuing imbalance in the principal competing intelligence cultures—those of the department, the Central Intelligence Agency, and the Federal Bureau of Investigation—an imbalance that has given the department disproportionate influence over intelligence. The national agencies have large staffs and expensive equipment, and together with the Defense Intelligence Agency (also, of course, a part of the Defense Department) account for about 75 to 80 percent of the total federal intelligence budget, excluding expenditures for tactical military intelligence. The agencies engage in both military and nonmilitary intelligence, operating in the latter capacity as suppliers of data to the CIA, FBI, and other agencies engaged in civilian intelligence.[9]

8. That is, the National Security Agency, the National Reconnaissance Office, and the National Geospatial-Intelligence Agency. They are called the "national" intelligence agencies because of the word "national" in their names. They engage exclusively in technical intelligence, such as satellite mapping and electronic interception.

9. I do not discuss military intelligence in this book.

The intelligence *Kulturkampf* is also a factor in the embattlement of the CIA. And it is the biggest impediment to improving domestic intelligence, dominated by the FBI despite the bureau's permeation by a culture of criminal investigations that is incompatible with the effective conduct of national security intelligence. We need a domestic intelligence agency separate from the FBI, an agency like Britain's Security Service (MI5) or the Canadian Security Intelligence Service (CSIS). Those are agencies that have no arrest or other police powers but use purely intelligence techniques to detect and disrupt activities inimical to national security that take place inside the nation rather than abroad. The need for such an agency is underscored by the growing danger of homegrown terrorism, which finds us with most of our intelligence capabilities focused on terrorist activities abroad, and by the mounting evidence of the FBI's inability, despite the efforts of its last two directors, to reinvent itself as an intelligence service.

Part Two looks at counterterrorism from a broader perspective than merely that of intelligence, which is after all only one of the tools for fighting terrorists, although it may be the most useful one. Another tool, of course, is criminal law enforcement. But experience with its use since 9/11 has shown that it has only limited value against terrorism because it is designed for dealing with ordinary criminal behavior, which terrorism doesn't much resemble. Our overuse of the criminal justice system in the struggle against terrorism is a product of a hyperlegalistic American culture that teaches that for every problem there is a legal solution. Our legalistic attitudes also lead to exaggerating the legal obstacles to effective counterterrorism. I argue that we can resolve the continuing controversy over the National Security Agency's domestic surveillance activity without fetishizing warrants. The warrant fetish is an example of our overinvestment in criminal prosecutions (for which warrants are designed, and to which the FBI is oriented) as a tool of counterterrorism.

Part Two also considers how to think about counterterrorist methods alternative to intelligence, such as hardening potential terrorist targets, and how to allocate counterterrorist resources between federal and local government and, within the latter category, among different cities. I am led by reflection on these difficult questions to expand my conception of a domestic intelligence agency to include other counterterrorist roles so that it would be a full-fledged domestic security service, like MI5. One of those roles would be that of an honest broker creating a two-way information pipeline between federal and local counterterrorism personnel and offering politically neutral advice on counterterrorist resource allocation. I point out that still another reason for creating such an agency is that the feasibility of target hardening and of other measures to backstop intelligence failures is severely limited because of the immense number of potential targets.

If my preoccupation with domestic intelligence seems excessive, I remind the reader that by all accounts the key intelligence failing that enabled the 9/11 attacks to succeed was the failure of the FBI and the CIA to share information with each other about al Qaeda. One root of that failure, in turn, was that the FBI is not an intelligence agency but a criminal-investigation agency. We'll see in Chapters 5 and 6 that little progress has been made in changing the bureau's culture of criminal investigation and that complete success in that endeavor is unlikely to be achieved in time to avert the next attack. A successful fusion of foreign and domestic intelligence would require that the CIA work closely with what the United States still does not have—an American counterpart to MI5.

Although there is much criticism in this book of the pace and efficacy of efforts to reform the intelligence system, I do not intend criticism of the reformers. At the present juncture in American history, federal officials (including such quasi-officials as the members of ad hoc commissions, like the 9/11 and Silberman-Robb commissions, that have been influential in intelligence reform) are forced to operate in an environment of unrealistic expectations, intense political partisanship, obsessive blaming, stifling bureaucracy, crushing information overload, insatiable media, and an eighteenth-century governmental structure straining to cope with twenty-first-century challenges of unprecedented variety and complexity, and probably gravity as well. It is no surprise that few senior officials leave government with their reputations intact, let alone enhanced. They deserve our sympathy (not all of them!).

1

Thinking in Probabilities

Let us admit it, we have had no end of a lesson: anthrax in the United States, sarin in Japan, a Pakistani mail-order business for nuclear weapons components, scientific papers on the Internet explaining how to engineer lethal viruses. We can hear the distant thunder, we can see the dark clouds, we feel the chill in the air that precedes the approaching storm, and yet we are grasping for reasons to deny what our knowledge is telling us.

—Fred Charles Iklé[1]

This is a practical book; but a simple theoretical point is fundamental to an understanding of the struggle against terrorism. It is that analysis of terrorist threats and counterterrorist responses must be framed in terms of probabilities—even when probabilities cannot be computed.[2] We do not know the probability of another major terrorist attack on the United States, or its likely magnitude, or the consequences if there is an attack. Or the probability that if we allow a terrorist plot to unfold in the hope of learning more about the aims, methods, suppliers, and accomplices of the plotters we'll lose track of them and they'll attack us—or that if we take that risk we will be compensated by our fuller knowledge of the plot's scope. We do not know the probability of detecting a terrorist attack in advance and of thus being able to prevent it, or, if it is not detected, of being able

---

1. Fred Charles Iklé, *Annihilation from Within: The Ultimate Threat to Nations* 64–65 (2006).
2. This is a principal theme of my book *Catastrophe: Risk and Response* (2004), where I first wrote about the terrorist threat.

to defeat it or at least reduce the damage caused by it. Another un-known is the probability that a terrorist plot we manage to thwart would actually have succeeded; there are more plots than there are attacks. We also can't compute the probability that measures to com-bat terrorism will cause serious harm to civil liberties.

Rational analysis has the general form of cost-benefit analysis: if you have a choice among several courses of action, you compare the costs and benefits of each and choose the one that produces the greatest surplus of benefits over costs. Often you do this intuitively, using various cognitive shortcuts,[3] rather than quantitatively because quantification is infeasible, too costly, too slow, or too unfamiliar. But if you are rational, your procedure will at least approximate that of explicit cost-benefit analysis. When the costs or benefits are not cer-tain to materialize, therefore, you will want to discount (multiply) them by the probability that they will materialize (and again your procedure may be rigorous or intuitive). The results of such discount-ing are "expected" values. If an investment that will cost $750,000 will yield a $1 million return with a probability of 85 percent, your expected return will be $850,000, and that is the figure you'll compare to the $750,000 cost in deciding whether the investment is worth-while.[4]

Often, it is true, the probability of an event cannot be quantified. Yet it may still be possible to make coarse but useful distinctions, for example between "high" and "low" probability events. The intelligence community is beginning to understand the importance of thinking in probabilities even when quantification is impossible. Thus we read in a recent National Intelligence Estimate on Iraq that

---

3. See, for example, Eduard Brandstätter, Gerd Gigerenzer, and Ralph Hertwig, "The Priority Heuristic: Making Choices without Trade-Offs," 113 *Psychological Review* 409 (2006).

4. There are complexities, such as risk preference and risk aversion, that can be ignored for the moment; risk aversion will figure in later chapters.

Intelligence judgments pertaining to likelihood are intended to re-flect the [Intelligence] Community's sense of the probability of a development or event. Assigning precise numerical ratings to such judgments would imply more rigor than we intend . . . We do not intend the term "unlikely" to imply an event will not happen. We use "probably" and "likely" to indicate there is a greater than even chance. We use words such as "we cannot dismiss," "we cannot rule out," and "we cannot discount" to reflect an unlikely—or even remote—event whose consequences are such it warrants mention-ing. Words such as "may be" and "suggest" are used to reflect sit-uations in which we are unable to assess the likelihood generally because relevant information is nonexistent, sketchy, or fragmented. In addition to using words within a judgment to convey degrees of likelihood, we also ascribe "high," "moderate," or "low" confidence levels based on the scope and quality of information supporting our judgments.[5]

It's an uphill fight to get people to think in terms of probabilities, especially quantified probabilities.[6] (And hence the intelligence com-munity's struggle, reflected in the National Intelligence Estimate that I just quoted, to devise a vocabulary in which to express probability judgments without using percentages, which in any event would often convey a delusive sense of exactness.) Our brains evolved to their present biological state many thousands of years before there was much survival value to being able to compute probabilities and so before there was evolutionary pressure to acquire such an ability. The pressure, rather, was to avoid doubt that might paralyze action. From that pressure comes a tendency to either write up a probability to 1

5. National Intelligence Council, "National Intelligence Estimate: Prospects for Iraq's Stability: A Challenging Road Ahead," Jan. 2007, http://dni.gov/press_releases/20070202_release.pdf.

6. For a lucid introduction to the problem, see Gerd Gigerenzer, *Calculated Risks: How to Know When Numbers Deceive You* (2002). The limitations are both cognitive, as stressed by Gigerenzer and by me (see Posner, note 2 above, at 9–11, 120–121, 248), and emotional, as stressed by Cass R. Sunstein, *Worst-Case Scenarios*, chs. 1–2 (forthcoming, Harvard University Press, 2007).

or write it down to 0, thus moving from uncertainty to certainty. Cognitive psychologists call such a tendency "confirmation bias" ("doubt aversion" would be an alternative term). We lean one way, and look for evidence that will push us all the way, dispelling any doubts that our inclination was correct. We shall see the operation of this tendency with reference to intelligence estimates in Chapter 3.

The harmful effect on national security of failing to think in probabilities is illustrated by a wave of recent assertions that the menace of terrorism is actually slight, even negligible. That is an example of writing a probability down to zero. The political scientist John Mueller tells us that "the lifetime chance of an American being killed by international terrorism is about one in 80,000 . . . The massive and expensive homeland security apparatus erected since 9/11 may be persecuting some, spying on many, inconveniencing most, and taxing all to defend the United States against an enemy that scarcely exists."[7] That "chance" of one in 80,000 is not the odds of a terrorist attack, that is, a probability; it is a frequency. (Mueller appears not to understand the difference.) Frequencies are a record of the past, not a prediction of the future unless there are solid grounds for expecting the future to be like the past. Government is more vigilant about terrorist threats today than it was before the 9/11 attacks and is devoting greater resources to trying to prevent terrorist attacks— hence the "terrorism industry": "The terrorist threat is still small. It's

7. John Mueller, "Is There Still a Terrorist Threat?" *Foreign Affairs*, Sept./Oct. 2006, pp. 2, 8. Mueller elaborates these views in his book *Overblown: How Politicians and the Terrorism Industry Inflate National Security Threats, and Why We Believe Them* (2006). See also John Tierney, "Waiting for Al Qaeda," *New York Times*, Sept. 9, 2006, p. A15, summarizing Mueller's analysis approvingly; Robert E. Goodin, *What's Wrong with Terrorism?* ch. 6 (2006); and references in my book *Catastrophe: Risk and Response*, note 2 above, at 236. Mueller is consistent; a decade ago (and thus before 9/11) he called international terrorism "wildly unimportant in an objective sense." John Mueller, "Fifteen Propositions about American Foreign Policy and Public Opinion in an Era Free of Compelling Threats," Mar. 31, 1996, p. 13, http:// psweb.sbs.ohio-state.edu/faculty/jmueller/isa1996.pdf.

the terrorism industry that got bigger."[8] The claim that "the terrorist threat is still small"—that "in general, terrorism, particularly international terrorism, doesn't do much damage when considered in almost any reasonable context"[9]—is pure assertion.[10] The threat may be large, only not so large as it would be were it not for the growth of the "terrorism industry"—that is, the growth of our defenses against terrorism, which Mueller wants to reverse.

But he is right to criticize national security officials who make groundless claims about the gravity of the terrorist threat.[11] It is not that these officials are exaggerating; since no one knows how great the threat is, it is difficult to know when it is being exaggerated. The objection is to assertions that may be true but for which there is no evidence, such as that the United States is rife with terrorist sleeper cells. In part such assertions reflect the tendency to write probabilities up to 1 or down to 0. The fact that there *could* be sleeper cells, or that terrorists *could* obtain weapons of mass destruction, morphs into the assertion that these things *will* happen (unless we stop them), ignoring that probability is a function of intentions and circumstances as well as of capabilities.

Worse, by continually issuing warnings that turn out to be false alarms, such as the color-coded alerts issued by the Department of

8. Tierney, note 7 above.

9. Mueller, *Overblown*, note 7 above, at 4.

10. Mueller goes way overboard in defending his thesis, as when he remarks that "in World War I only some 2 or 3 percent of those gassed on the Western Front died." Mueller, *Overblown*, note 7 above, at 18. (Imagine 2 or 3 percent of the American population killed in a bioterror attack—that would be 6 to 9 million people.) Or when he remarks, anent dirty bombs, that "some scientists, in fact, think it [raising radiation levels slightly above background levels] may actually be good for health." Id. at 22. Or when he equates the total number of deaths from wars and other state violence in the twentieth century to the death toll from automobile accidents. Id. at 153. Mueller compares 9/11 to the attack on Pearl Harbor—and questions whether we were right to go to war with Japan in response to the Pearl Harbor attack rather than adopting a policy of containment. Id., ch. 3 and p. 170.

11. Id., ch. 2, and pp. 161–164.

Homeland Security, security officials, wanting to be able if there is an attack to claim that they warned us it was coming,[12] *systematically* reduce threat alertness. Human beings are programmed to economize on their attention (a scarce resource) by discounting—to the point of ignoring completely—warnings that have previously proved false.[13] Our wolf-crying security officials play into Mueller's hands. With no attack on the United States having occurred in more than five years despite all the (false) alarms, alertness fatigue has set in and vigilance is giving way to complacency.[14] This tendency is difficult to resist, because its roots are emotional rather than intellectual. I, too, *feel* safer than I did for several years after the 9/11 attacks waiting for the other shoe to drop, though my reasoning self tells me that the danger of terrorism probably has grown. Overwarning was a factor in the failure to anticipate both the Pearl Harbor attack and the Tet Offensive, two of the nation's worst intelligence failures.[15] It's time we learned to fight our instincts.

12. An egregious example is the Department of Homeland Security's recent warning of a possible terrorist attack on the stock market and on banking sites on the web. The department stated that there was no corroboration of the threat, that the warning was being issued "as a routine matter and out of an abundance of caution. There is no immediate threat to our homeland at this time." The reassurance negated the warning. Nor did the warning provide any guidance to what financial institutions might do that they're not already doing to protect themselves from terrorist attacks. See John L. McCreary, "NightWatch," Nov. 30, 2006, nightwatch.afcea.org/ NightWatch_20061115.htm. On the chronic ineptitude of efforts by governments to warn the public about terrorism risks, see Lawrence Freedman, "The Politics of Warning: Terrorism and Risk Communication," 20 *Intelligence and National Security* 379 (2005).

13. See, for example, Shlomo Breznitz, *Cry Wolf: The Psychology of False Alarms* 11 (1984); James P. Bliss et al., "Human Probability Matching Behaviour in Response to Alarms of Varying Reliability," 38 *Ergonomics* 2300 (1995); David J. Getty et al., "System Operator Response to Warnings of Danger: A Laboratory Investigation of the Effects of the Predictive Value of a Warning on Human Response Time," 1 *Journal of Experimental Psychology: Applied* 19 (1995). On the "economy of attention," see also Posner, note 2 above, at 120–122.

14. Mueller *commends* complacency. Mueller, note 7 above, at 143.

15. On the first, see Richard A. Posner, *Preventing Surprise Attacks: Intelligence Reform in the Wake of 9/11* 77–78 (2005). On the second, see Don Oberdorfer, *Tet!*

Just days before the revelation of the plot to use liquid bombs to destroy airliners flying to the United States from London's Heathrow Airport, the *Atlantic Monthly* published an article declaring victory over Islamist terrorism.[16] The author claimed that by depriving bin Laden of his Afghanistan sanctuary, we had defeated al Qaeda and now the only danger was that of overreacting to a diminished terrorist threat. Bin Laden was indeed deprived of his Afghanistan sanctuary. But he and his second in command, Ayman al-Zawahiri, promptly found another one, in Pakistan. And though the Heathrow plotters were British citizens, the plot in its scope and objective had al Qaeda written all over it. Al Qaeda is the high-end terrorist group. It is not content with bombing a subway or a train. Its hallmark is the spectacular attack. Had the Heathrow plot succeeded, it would have rivaled the 9/11 attacks in its effect on the United States. Whether al Qaeda's role in that plot was directive or merely inspirational is not critical.[17] What is significant is the shrewdness of al Qaeda or those inspired by it in continuing to focus destructive efforts on civil aviation, which remains highly vulnerable despite strenuous efforts to protect it against terrorism.[18] The vulnerability is psychological as well

---

The Turning Point in the Vietnam War 9 (1971): "The Tet truce had been cancelled the morning before the Embassy attack and U.S. forces throughout the country placed on 'maximum alert' . . . The alert order . . . did not cause great alarm, because alerts had become routine . . . By the time of Tet, 'maximum alert' orders and predictions of attack were widely viewed in the field as 'cover your ass' papers for the protection of headquarters officers."

16. James Fallows, "Declaring Victory: The United States Is Succeeding in Its Struggle against Terrorism. The Time Has Come to Declare the War on Terror Over, So That an Even More Effective Military and Diplomatic Campaign Can Begin," *Atlantic Monthly*, Sept. 2006, p. 60.

17. Marc Sageman, an astute student of Islamist terrorism, argues in his book *Understanding Terror Networks* 51–54 (2004), that al Qaeda is no longer capable of mounting attacks on the scale of the 9/11 attacks, and that without such spectaculars its influence will fade. But his book was written before the Heathrow plot, and before al Qaeda's intensified activities in Iraq, Afghanistan, and Pakistan suggested that the group was regaining its footing.

18. See the superb discussion in Shane Harris, "Five Years after 9/11, Question

as physical. Death in a plane crash is one of the "dreaded" forms of death that psychologists remind us arouse far more anticipatory fear than more humdrum forms of death. This explains the extraordinary safety of air travel compared to gas heaters, which kill with a much higher probability.

The concern with airline safety, coupled with the fact that protection against terrorist attacks on aviation can be strengthened only at a substantial cost in inconvenience to travelers, makes the foiled Heathrow plot a merely partial failure for terrorism. The episode has made air travel more costly. The added costs are no less real for being largely nonpecuniary (fear, restrictions on carry-on luggage, anger at rude, confiscation-happy security checkers, and loss of time—effects that ironically will induce a further substitution of less safe forms of travel, namely automobile travel[19]). Notice, too, how longer lines of people waiting to go through airport security checkpoints increase airport vulnerability. A homemade bomb tossed into a crowd in an airline terminal might have a devastating effect on air travel because of the background anxiety about flying. Such an attack would be the catalyst for enhanced security measures that would further increase the cost of air travel, including airport delay.

The potential supply of terrorists is larger than it has ever been. It consists of a small percentage of the world's 1.3 billion Muslims, but a minute percentage of a huge number can be a large number. The number of willing recruits to terrorism, male and female, Arab and non-Arab, including recent converts to Islam, has grown since 9/11 because of increased anger at the United States and the West felt throughout the Muslim world. (Think of how the two million Iraqi refugees must view us.) Has that growth been offset by the success of the United States and other nations in eliminating a number of terrorist leaders? Only if the eliminated leaders had skills or charisma

---

Is: Could It Happen Again?" *Gov.Exec.com*, Sept. 1, 2006, http://govexec.com/dailyfed/0906/090106nj1.htm.

19. See Chapter 8.

that cannot be found elsewhere in an expanding terrorist community. Judging from the rapid replacement of captured or killed terrorist leaders, al Qaeda and cognate terrorist groups have a deep bench.

Think of Iran, Iraq, Pakistan, Afghanistan, Lebanon, the Toronto and Heathrow plots, the Pope's apology for accurately noting the correlation between Islam and violence—the Islamist extremists are on a roll.[20] Europe, the penetration of which by Muslim immigrants may remind some Europeans of the infiltration of the Roman Empire by barbarian populations in the era of its decline, is cringing. The United States is fixated on what at this writing is a losing war in Iraq that has greatly diminished the popularity and effectiveness of a lame-duck President confronting a Congress controlled by the opposition party. In the current atmosphere of Western distraction, indecision, fumbling, and disarray—of fear married to complacency, incompetence, and political timidity—the selection, recruitment, emboldening, and promotion of terrorist leaders may well be proceeding apace. We cannot afford to think otherwise and let down our guard.

Not only are there more potential terrorists than ever before; the lethality and availability of highly destructive weaponry are growing. The North Korean nuclear test in October 2006 and Iran's seemingly inexorable march toward the acquisition of nuclear weapons are reminders that proliferation is a growing danger and that no policy to counter it has emerged.[21]

20. See, for example, Robert S. Leiken, "Europe's Angry Muslims," *Foreign Affairs*, Jul./Aug. 2005, p. 120. Their only recent reversal is the defeat of the Islamic Union of Courts in Somalia.

21. On the vulnerability of the U.S. homeland, see, for example, Derek Smith, *Deterring America: Rogue States and the Proliferation of Weapons of Mass Destruction* 105–107 (2006), and references cited there; Richard A. Falkenrath, Robert D. Newman, and Bradley A. Thayer, *America's Achilles Heel: Nuclear, Biological, and Chemical Terrorism and Covert Attack* (1998); Dany Shoham and Stuart M. Jacobsen, "Technical Intelligence in Retrospect: The 2001 Anthrax Letters Powder," *20 International Journal of Intelligence and CounterIntelligence* 79 (2007); William J. Broad and David E. Sanger, "Restraints Fray and Risks Grow as Nuclear Club Gains Members," *New York Times*, Oct. 15, 2006, § 1, p. 1. On the feasibility of terrorists'

We have had successes against al Qaeda, and as a result it is dispersed and fragmented and so presents a more diffuse target. More diffuse—and therefore more elusive, and not necessarily less dangerous.[22] The terrorist danger to the United States and its allies may have increased rather than receded since the 9/11 attacks, as argued in a National Intelligence Estimate[23] prepared by the National Intelligence Council that gains credibility from the fact that its finding that the war on Iraq has increased the terrorist danger goes counter to the position of the Bush Administration. The interesting argument

---

stealing fissile material and building a Hiroshima-style atomic bomb from it, see William Langewiesche, "How to Get a Nuclear Bomb," *Atlantic Monthly*, Dec. 2006, p. 80. And we have something new to worry about: terrorists introducing the radioactive isotope polonium 210 into the food supply or using it in a dirty bomb. See Karen Kaplan and Thomas H. Maugh II, "A Restless Killer Radiates Intrigue: Polonium-210's Past Is Strewn with Deaths: A Former Russian Spy is the Latest Victim of This Potent Substance," *Los Angeles Times*, Jan. 1, 2007, p. A1; Peter D. Zimmerman, "The Smoky Bomb Threat," *New York Times*, Dec. 19, 2006, p. A33; William J. Broad, "U.S. and Foreign Regulators Consider Tightening Controls on Deadly Polonium 210," *New York Times*, Dec. 10, 2006, § 1, p. 16.

22. See, for example, "On the March, Not on the Run: Global Terrorism" *Economist*, Jan. 20, 2007, p. 72. See also Peter Bergen, "The Return of Al Qaeda: Where You Bin?" *New Republic*, Jan. 29, 2007, p. 16—a responsible article, despite the juvenile subtitle, more likely an editor's invention than the author's. Bergen marshals evidence that al Qaeda's strength is growing, though he notes potentially disabling long-run weaknesses.

23. See Mark Mazzetti, "Spy Agencies Say Iraq War Worsens Terrorism Threat: U.S. Intelligence Assessment Is Said to Find a Rise in Global Islamic Radicalism," *New York Times*, Sept. 24, 2006, § 1, p. 1. The National Intelligence Estimate is classified, but a summary of its key findings has been released: "Declassified Key Judgments of the National Intelligence Estimate on Global Terrorism," *New York Times*, Sept. 27, 2006, p. A6. For other expressions of concern that the danger of terrorism is growing rather than receding despite our efforts to combat it, see, besides Bergen's article, note 22 above, Council on Global Terrorism, "Preliminary Report: State of the Struggle against Global Terrorism" (Sept. 2006), http://councilonglo balterrorism.org/pdf/A06_265_cgt_report_final.pdf; "Al-Qaeda: The Many Faces of an Islamist Extremist Threat," Report of the U.S. House Permanent Select Committee on Intelligence, 109th Cong., 2d Sess. (U.S. Government Printing Office, Sept. 6, 2006); Richard A. Falkenrath, "Prepared Statement of Testimony before the Committee on Homeland Security and Governmental Affairs, United States Senate" 13–16 (Sept. 12, 2006).

that terrorists will eventually learn that terrorist attacks on civilians rarely promote terrorists' political goals[24] is weakened by the failure to explain why terrorists haven't learned yet (terrorist attacks on civilians are not a recent invention) and by the tumult created by the 9/11 attacks—attacks on civilians that may succeed in driving the United States out of the Middle East. They've already led us to withdraw our troops from Saudi Arabia, which was one of the aims of the attacks.

At most, all that our good fortune in not being attacked since 9/11 implies is that the annual probability of a terrorist attack on the United States is low. Suppose it is 1 percent, the approximate annual probability of a Katrina-scale hurricane's hitting New Orleans and causing the flooding it did. Then the 10-year probability is 9.6 percent.[25] And the next attack, if it comes, may do much more damage to life and property than the 9/11 attacks did.

We may be lucky and escape attack even if we let our guard down, as Professor Mueller and others recommend. But it would be reckless to gamble in this fashion, confusing frequencies (the past) with probabilities (the future) and irrationally writing down an unknown probability to a zero probability and on that basis refusing to take feasible measures to avert disasters that may occur though they are not certain to do so.

The highly politicized debate over whether we are "safer" as a result of the administration's efforts since 9/11 to combat terrorism has caused further confusion. Not only is the debate indeterminate; it confuses relative with absolute safety, neglecting the fact that the latter is much more important. As the chief of the New York City Police Department's counterterrorism bureau has explained,

24. Max Abrahms, "Why Terrorism Does Not Work," 31 *International Security*, Fall 2006, p. 42.
25. The formula for the probability that an event of annual probability p will occur sometime in the next n years (provided that the annual probabilities are independent of each other) is $1 - (1 - p)^n$. See Chapter 8 for a further discussion of cumulative probability.

> Because of continued offensive operations by the United States and its allies against some known international terrorist networks, as well as significant improvements in U.S. border security, the ability of any international or foreign terrorist organization to launch an attack into the United States from abroad appears to have diminished somewhat since late 2001. The NYPD takes no comfort in this analytic conclusion, however, *because our baseline vulnerability was enormous.*[26]

It matters little whether the annual probability of a terrorist attack has fallen from 1 percent to .8 percent; the 10—year cumulative probability would remain a terrifying 7.7 percent. Claims that we are safer—bragging by officials that we haven't been attacked since 9/11 because of our vigilance—merely feed complacency on the part of the public and commentators.

One criticism of the proposal to create a domestic intelligence agency separate from the Federal Bureau of Investigation is that because we are "at war" with the terrorists (a characterization that I resist, as it obscures the unique character of the current terrorist threat), we simply don't have time to establish a new national security agency. It is an odd criticism on several grounds. One is that we *have* established new national security agencies in wartime, notably the Office of Strategic Services during World War II and the National Security Agency during the Korean War. We have even established new national security agencies since 9/11, such as the National Counterterrorism Center, not to mention the Department of Homeland Security and the Office of the Director of National Intelligence. But what is germane to the present discussion is the criticism's neglect of probabilities over time. Were the terrorist menace about to vanish, it would indeed be dumb to establish a new agency to cope with it. But the menace extends into the future, and whether it is increasing or not the probability of an attack is greater the further out the horizon of our concern.

26. Falkenrath, note 23 above, at 14 (emphasis added).

A good planning horizon for intelligence reform would be five years (and it should not take that long to create an effective domestic intelligence agency) because scientists expect to be able to synthesize the smallpox virus within five years. With that triumph of science, the menace of terrorism will take a leap upwards. We should not squander our five years of lead time, if that is what we have.

Apparently it is the administration's policy that any probability of a terrorist attack that equals or exceeds 1 percent is to be treated as a certainty and is to be prevented at all costs.[27] That makes no sense. It ignores both costs and benefits. If an attack would cause $1 million in damage, and the probability of the attack over some interval if efforts were not made to prevent it would be 2 percent and the cost of preventing it $50 million, then the expected benefit of prevention, $20,000 ($1 million $\times$ .02), would be much less than the cost of prevention. Conversely, if the attack if it occurred would cause $100 billion in damage—a gross underestimate of the damage caused by the 9/11 attacks[28]—and the probability of its occurring was one-tenth of 1 percent, the expected loss ($100 billion $\times$ .001 = $100 million) would exceed the $50 million cost of prevention.

We shall see in Chapter 5 how the purblind thinking behind the one percent doctrine has fathered a policy of arresting terrorist suspects prematurely because there can be no certainty that there is less than a 1 percent chance that if not arrested immediately they would commit a terrorist crime. The policy may increase the risk of terrorist attacks by tipping the government's hand, so that an opportunity to learn more about the terrorist group and maybe even penetrate it is lost, and by alerting accomplices of the persons arrested, enabling

27. See Ron Suskind, *The One Percent Doctrine: Deep Inside America's Pursuit of Its Enemies Since 9/11* 62 (2006); Matthew Purdy and Lowell Bergman, "Where the Trial Led: Between Evidence and Suspicion; Unclear Danger: Inside the Lackawanna Terror Case," *New York Times*, Oct. 12, 2003, § 1, p. 1.

28. Even $500 billion would be an underestimate. See K. A. Taipale, "The Ear of Dionysus: Rethinking Foreign Intelligence Surveillance" 5 n. 26 (Jan. 26, 2007; forthcoming in *Yale Journal of Law and Technology*).

them to avoid arrest. The one percent doctrine is a further example of how failing to think intelligently about the probabilistic nature of the terrorist threat, and of responses to it, can undermine national security.

The doctrine is an egregious example of writing up a probability to a certainty, but not an isolated one. Security officers strive to prevent, at whatever cost, any loss of secrets, rather than comparing the cost of such a loss (discounted by its probability) to the cost of prevention, which, as we'll see in Chapter 4, can be considerable. In effect, they treat small or unknown probabilities of security leaks as certainties. (They also exaggerate the harm to national security that such leaks are likely to cause and understate the costs of preventing them.) Likewise, critics of the Transportation Security Administration think it a scandal that tests of airport security that involve attempting to conceal guns in carry-on bags miss a significant percentage of the attempts. The critics do not realize that terrorists are unlikely to gamble on succeeding in such attempts as long as the probability of success, though not zero, is low. Given the other obstacles to trying to smuggle a gun on board an airliner, the screening of carry-on bags for guns, though imperfect, makes hijacking a plane at gunpoint an unpromising terrorist project. Insistence on perfect security would be unsound.

Professor Mueller writes serious risks down to zero; the one percenters, the security officers, and the critics of the TSA write them up to one. These equal and opposite mistakes are forceful reminders of the need to think in probabilities when considerating how to respond to the threat of terrorism.

Part One

The Role of
Intelligence

2

The Road from 9/11;
Benchmarking the
Intelligence
Reorganization

The 9/11 attacks, like the Pearl Harbor attack 60 years earlier, were immediately pronounced (in both cases inaccurately) the consequence of a culpable, an inexcusable, intelligence failure. Yet in the first three years after the attacks, only incremental changes in the structure, as distinct from the operational methods, focus, and resources, of the nation's intelligence system were made. The FBI hired many intelligence analysts and reassigned a number of special agents from ordinary criminal investigations to counterterrorism. An undersecretary for intelligence was appointed in the Defense Department. The Terrorist Threat Integration Center (later the National Counterterrorism Center) was created inside the CIA to integrate foreign and domestic counterterrorist intelligence analysis. The "wall" between domestic and foreign intelligence was further weakened by the USA PATRIOT Act and by the relaxation of the Attorney General's guidelines on terrorism investigations; these measures were long overdue. The CIA was expanded, and reoriented (a process that had begun before 9/11) toward intelligence about and covert action against Islamist terrorism; these were overdue measures as well. An intelligence division was established in the newly created Department of Homeland Security.

Not until the fall of 2004 did Congress, in the Intelligence Reform and Terrorism Prevention Act, decree an ambitious reorganization of the nation's intelligence system. The most important thing the act did was split apart the job of intelligence-system coordinator— Director of Central Intelligence—from that of Director of the Central Intelligence Agency. Previously the two jobs had been required by law to be held by the same person; now the CIA's director would report to the DCI, renamed the DNI—Director of National Intelligence. The DNI was to be not only the system coordinator (and with enhanced powers and duties) but also, as the DCI had been, the nation's senior intelligence adviser. To enable the DNI to perform the adviser function, Congress gave him significant analytic assets, both strategic (the National Intelligence Council) and operational (the National Counterterrorism Center). The general thrust of the act, then, was toward greater centralization of intelligence.

The spring and summer of 2005 saw further, though modest, organizational changes, without new legislation. The principal changes were the formation of a National Security Branch in the Federal Bureau of Investigation, consolidating the bureau's three divisions concerned with national security (the Directorate of Intelligence and the Counterterrorism and Counterintelligence Divisions), and a reorganization of the intelligence structure of the Department of Homeland Security. In April 2005, a month after the President had endorsed most of the organizational recommendations made by the Silberman-Robb Commission,[1] John Negroponte became the nation's first Director of National Intelligence.

Criticisms of the reorganization of intelligence brought about by

---

1. Commission on the Intelligence Capabilities of the United States Regarding Weapons of Mass Destruction, *Report to the President of the United States* (Mar. 31, 2005).

the various legislative and executive measures focused initially on the reorganization's design, which indeed was flawed (see Chapter 3), but soon switched to implementation and have persisted. A typical criticism is that "the [intelligence] agencies—remain troubled by high-level turnover, overlapping responsibilities and bureaucratic rivalry."[2] Members of Congress who have responsibility for oversight of the intelligence community have made similar criticisms.[3] The *Economist* magazine calls the job of Director of National Intelligence "an impossibly sticky wicket" and the reorganized intelligence system a "botched structure" that has created "accountability without power."[4] John Lehman, a member of the 9/11 Commission, has accused the Bush Administration of deciding to "leave this sprawling mess"—the intelligence system as it existed before the Intelligence Reform Act— "untouched."[5] Similar criticisms appear in other articles and studies[6] and have been voiced, sometimes *sotto voce*, by current and former members of the intelligence community.

Many of the criticisms preceded the sudden departure of Porter Goss, the CIA's director, in May 2006, after 19 months in office. (He had been appointed before the Intelligence Reform Act was passed.) The circumstances of his departure and the widespread belief that his performance had been plainly inadequate from the start—raising the question why he was retained in office as long as he was—sparked

2. Scott Shane, "Year into Revamped Spying, Troubles and Some Progress," *New York Times*, Feb. 28, 2006, p. A12.

3. Scott Shane, "In New Job, Spymaster Draws Bipartisan Criticism," *New York Times*, Apr. 20, 2006, p. A1.

4. "A Bad Job: Restructuring Intelligence," *Economist*, Jan. 13, 2007, p. 40.

5. John Lehman, "Are We Any Safer?" *Proceedings of the U.S. Naval Institute*, Sept. 2006, pp. 18, 20.

6. See, for example, Amy B. Zegart, *Failure and Consequence: Understanding U.S. Intelligence and the Origins of 9/11*, ch. 8 (forthcoming, Princeton University Press, 2007), and references cited there; David Ignatius, "Fix the Intelligence Mess," *Washington Post*, Apr. 21, 2006, p. A23; John Brennan, "Is This Intelligence? We Added Players, But Lost Control of the Ball," *Washington Post*, Nov. 20, 2005, p. B1.

fresh doubts about the reorganized intelligence system.[7] But the prompt appointment of General Michael Hayden (Negroponte's principal deputy) to replace Goss, with Stephen Kappes as Hayden's principal deputy, brightened the prospects for the CIA and quieted, for the moment anyway, controversy over the agency.

One is tempted to short-circuit assessment of the reorganization by indulging the comforting thought that all must be well because Negroponte, an able civil servant with long experience in national security, hired able people to staff the Office of the Director of National Intelligence. Indeed he did. But in all likelihood they would be working equally or even more productively back at the individual agencies from which they (largely) came. (It is a subtle, and in the context of intelligence an unexamined, question whether to concentrate the ablest people in central staff or spread them throughout the line agencies.) The reorganization mainly reshuffled rather than augmented the nation's intelligence personnel—and the only benefits that can be attributed to a reorganization are those that could not have been achieved at the same or lower cost without it.

The shift of personnel to the new bureaucracy came at a time when many of the ablest and most experienced intelligence officers were leaving the government. This talent drain (which is continuing) is a consequence mainly of increased demand by private companies, following 9/11, for sophisticated security personnel. But it is also a consequence of serious morale problems at the CIA that are due in part to the reorganization, though more to Porter Goss's management (and to that extent they will fade with time). The exodus of experi-

---

7. See, for example, Editorial, "Gossed Over," *Wall Street Journal*, May 6, 2006, p. A8; Greg Miller, "CIA Chief's Ouster Points to Larger Issues," *Los Angeles Times*, May 7, 2006, p. A4. On Goss's performance as CIA director, see Ken Silverstein, "Gosslings, Bacon, and a Kobe Beef Cow: The Media Misreports the Porter Goss Story," *Harper's Magazine*, May 26, 2006, www.harpers.org/sb-gosslings-23887 238.html.

enced intelligence officers,[8] combined with the rapid expansion of the intelligence community in recognition of the increased challenges that it faces (and in response to steep, short-sighted personnel cuts in the 1990s), has caused a dramatic reduction in the average age and experience of U.S. intelligence officers. Half the community's 18,000 intelligence analysts, for example, have fewer than five years of service.

Another false comfort would be to think the reorganization a tailored response to deep *structural* flaws, revealed by the 9/11 attacks, in the intelligence community. The motivations for the reorganization, especially for the legislative reorganization decreed by the Intelligence Reform Act, lay elsewhere. There was the political imperative to "do something," and the allure of a reorganization as a cheap and dramatic symbol of doing something. There was the proclivity of government officials to emphasize planning over execution because of our government's inability to execute policy competently. And there was confusion between design flaws and performance flaws. The main performance failures leading up to the 9/11 attacks occurred *within* intelligence agencies, notably the CIA, the FBI, the National Intelligence Council, the Defense Intelligence Agency, and the National Security Agency.[9] Such failures were not obviously attributable to faults in the overall design of the intelligence system. The only clear design faults concerned the dual hatting of the Director of Central Intelligence, the lodgment of the national intelligence agencies in the Department of Defense, and the vesting of the FBI with primary responsibility for domestic intelligence. Congress dealt inadequately with all three problems. And rather than address the performance problems directly, Congress layered a new bureaucracy (the Office of the Director of National Intelligence) over the agencies—a measure

8. See, for example, Linda Robinson and Kevin Whitelaw, "Seeking Spies," *U.S. News & World Report*, Feb. 13, 2006, p. 35.

9. Jeffrey R. Cooper, *Curing Analytic Pathologies: Pathways to Improved Intelligence Analysis* 3 (CIA, Center for the Study of Intelligence, Dec. 2005).

at best obliquely responsive to their performance failures. Such failures continue. A recent assessment of the National Security Agency, for example, describes it as "by far the largest and most powerful intelligence agency within the U.S. intelligence community—accounting for the majority of the highest level intelligence information going to the President of the United States. And yet, like the community of which it is an integral part, it remains deeply troubled by a host of problems, many of its own making."[10]

Another spur to the reorganization was a misunderstanding of the limitations of national security intelligence. It is the kind of misunderstanding that the commissioner of baseball might harbor if, distressed that 70 percent of the time even the best hitters fail to get a hit, he resolved to double their batting averages by reorganizing the leagues. Because intelligence is not prophecy but information that often is incomplete or erroneous and assessment that often is speculative, failures of prediction are a constant rather than being a function of the details of the table of organization.[11] Not that intelligence can't be improved.[12] But, continuing with the baseball analogy, we need to distinguish between forced and unforced errors, to accept the inevitability of the latter and focus on reducing the incidence of the former by targeted measures rather than by a wholesale reorganization bound to be disruptive and, if the historical and comparative record can be credited, unlikely to be successful.

10. Matthew M. Aid, "Prometheus Embattled: A Post-9/11 Report Card on the National Security Agency," 21 *Intelligence and National Security* 980, 995 (2006).

11. See Richard A. Posner, *Preventing Surprise Attacks: Intelligence Reform in the Wake of 9/11*, ch. 3 (2005); Joshua Rovner and Austin Long, "The Perils of Shallow Theory: Intelligence Reform and the 9/11 Commission," 18 *International Journal of Intelligence and CounterIntelligence* 609, 620–628 (2005).

12. See, for example, Peter Pirolli, *Assisting People to Become Independent Learners in the Analysis of Intelligence* (Office of Naval Research, Final Technical Report, Contract N00014-02-C-0203, CDRL A002, Feb. 28, 2006); John A. Kringen, "How We've Improved Intelligence: Minimizing the Risk of 'Groupthink,'" *Washington Post*, Apr. 3, 2006, p. A19; Dana Priest, "Foreign Network at Front of CIA's Terror Fight: Joint Facilities in Two Dozen Countries Account for Bulk of Agency's Post–9/11 Successes," *Washington Post*, Nov. 18, 2005, p. A1.

Ephraim Kahana lists Israeli intelligence failures since the nation's founding in 1948.[13] It is a long list. Although many of the failures occurred before Israel's warning-intelligence system was reorganized after the nation's biggest intelligence failure—the Egyptian-Syrian surprise attack of October 1973—as many occurred afterwards. The most recent was the failure to foresee the July 2006 attack by Hezbollah across Israel's northern border, despite Hezbollah's proximity and Israel's long involvement in southern Lebanon. Israel's intelligence system is on continuous high alert because of the threat to the nation's existence posed both by hostile states in its region and by terrorists. Yet it has been fooled repeatedly, with its rate of being fooled seemingly insensitive to changes in its organizational structure.

U.S. intelligence has been fooled repeatedly too.[14] Think of Pearl Harbor, after which we reorganized our intelligence system, the Tet Offensive of 1968, which put us on the road to eventual defeat in Vietnam, and of course the 9/11 attacks. We were fooled in these and other instances not because our intelligence agencies are incompetent but because surprise attacks are extremely difficult to predict. The attacker has a wide range of times and places when and at which to attack and endeavors to conceal his intentions and preparations. When he is a terrorist whose aim is simply to inflict serious harm on the United States, the range of potential targets is well-nigh infinite.

Now it is true that in all these examples avoidable errors contributed to the failure of prediction, as we now know with the clarity of hindsight. But no agency, especially an agency of the United States government, can be expected to turn in a flawless performance. The obstacles to such performance that politics, bureaucracy, and other

13. Ephraim Kahana, "Analyzing Israel's Intelligence Failures," 18 *International Journal of Intelligence and CounterIntelligence* 262 (2005).
14. For excellent discussions, see Peter Gill and Mark Phythian, *Intelligence in an Insecure World*, ch. 6 (2006); John Hollister Hedley, "Learning from Intelligence Failures," 18 *International Journal of Intelligence and CounterIntelligence* 435 (2005); Richard K. Betts, "Analysis, War, and Decision: Why Intelligence Failures Are Inevitable," 31 *World Politics* 61 (1978).

inherent conditions of public service create are too formidable. The causes of intelligence failure include (1) the inherent limitations of organizations in general and governmental organizations in particular, for example their limited ability to adapt to changed circumstances;[15] (2) the structure of the U.S. intelligence community; (3) the quality of the community's leadership and rank and file; (4) the direction and monitoring of the intelligence system by the President and Congress; and (5) the inherent limitations of intelligence. Regarding (1), (4), and (5) little can be done as a practical matter—yet they are the greatest impediments to intelligence success and so place a low ceiling on the intelligence community's attainable performance.

Not being fatalists, Americans resist accepting limits to improvement. They assume that if there is a failure, someone or something must be to blame and therefore *should* be blamed so that matters can be set right for the future. The assumption ignores not only the obstacles that any nation's intelligence services would be bound to encounter but also stubborn features of American national culture that despite our wealth and technological prowess raise barriers to our ability to conduct effective intelligence. These include our provincialism—our ignorance of foreign languages and cultures, especially cultures built around honor, revenge, and intense family and tribal loyalties, and our resulting inability to think our way into the minds of foreigners, especially non-Europeans, and even to understand what they are saying. Related to provincialism is our arrogance—our sense that we have nothing to learn from foreigners. Another handicap is our limited experience with terrorism compared to that of other countries. We haven't had time to evolve institutions tailored to the current terrorist threat, and our chauvinism prevents us from simply copying foreign institutions that have proved effective against terrorism.

Other handicaps under which U.S. intelligence labors are the structural obstacles to governmental efficiency that are inherent in

15. As emphasized in Zegart, note 7 above.

our vaunted "separation of powers," which is actually a system of overlapping and rivalrous powers lodged in the three branches of the federal government;[16] our suspicion and fear of government and, concomitantly, the absolutist conception of civil liberties that many articulate and influential Americans hold; and a sense that spying is un-American because of its furtive, "underhanded" character—it is no accident that James Bond is British rather than American. Another handicap is our commitment to a form of democracy that has political appointees occupying the policymaking jobs in government (perhaps because filling those jobs with civil servants would make the civil service too powerful in a system of divided, as opposed to unitary parliamentary, government—the civil service would play Congress and the President off against each other). The result is to relegate the civil service to a supporting role, and, by doing so, to reduce the level of professionalism in government, both directly and by making a career in the civil service less attractive to people who have good career alternatives. And skepticism about "big government" and the exaltation of free markets have in recent decades sapped the prestige of public service. Finally, the sheer size and complexity of American society, along with the immensity of America's international responsibilities and undertakings, require an intelligence system so vast and complex that it verges on being unmanageable.

Not understanding these things, the public insists that all intelligence failures are blameworthy. Among our intelligence agencies the CIA is the least popular and so is the predestined scapegoat for intelligence failures. It is much less popular than the military services and somewhat less popular than the FBI. One reason for their greater popularity is simply that the armed forces and the FBI have other functions besides intelligence, and so their intelligence failures, while frequent, stand out less. The CIA's only function besides intelligence

16. I emphasized these obstacles in my first book on national security. See Posner, note 11 above, ch. 5. See also Amy B. Zegart, *Flawed by Design: The Evolution of the CIA, JCS, and NSC* (1999).

is covert action.[17] Often that takes the form of clandestine combat, where frequent and occasionally embarrassing failures are unavoidable (especially when the objective is to undermine or overthrow a government), compounding the mistaken impression of the agency as always botching its missions.

So it is the CIA, rather than the Defense Intelligence Agency or the FBI, that has gotten the lion's share of the blame for the failure to have detected the 9/11 plot and the subsequent failure to detect Saddam Hussein's abandonment of his program of weapons of mass destruction, even though the FBI was deeply implicated in the former failure and the Defense Intelligence Agency in the latter. And although the CIA's covert action against Islamist terrorists since 9/11 has been effective, this success tends to be overshadowed by criticisms of the agency by Porter Goss's diehard supporters—and by his critics!

Failure in our society, being unacceptable, requires not only scapegoats but also responses that promise, however quixotically, to prevent future failures. The Intelligence Reform Act is a product of that attitude. The Act bears down hardest on the CIA,[18] consistent with the scapegoat theory. That is not, of course, all the Act does. The separation of the jobs of CIA director and Director of Central Intelligence was not only or mainly a way of punishing, by demoting, the CIA. It was an overdue recognition that the expansion of the

17. An awkward feature of the reorganized intelligence system is that the director of the CIA continues to report to the President regarding covert action, though to the Director of National Intelligence regarding intelligence.

18. "The C.I.A. used to coordinate, write and sign all 'finished national intelligence'—no longer. The C.I.A.'s director used to lead the meetings of the heads of the numerous organizations that make up the 'intelligence community'—no longer. The C.I.A. used to have final say on many aspects of intelligence 'tasking'—no longer. Last to go was the role that made the agency pre-eminent, responsibility for briefing the president. Now that job belongs to Mr. Negroponte, with his $1 billion budget and staff of 1,500." Thomas Powers, "Spy vs. Spy," New York Times, May 10, 2006, p. A25. This is somewhat overstated. The director of the CIA has not always been the President's intelligence briefer. See Chapter 3, note 2.

intelligence community and the novel challenges posed by Islamist terrorism had made the two jobs too much for one person. The jobs could, however, have been separated, without demotion of the CIA and its director, by configuring the DNI's job as strictly one of system management and not of intelligence advice (see Chapter 3). The system needed an effective coordinator,[19] an overall manager or supervisor—a role that Directors of Central Intelligence had been unable to perform adequately. It did not need a new senior intelligence adviser. It had one already in the person of the CIA director. A football team needs a coach and a quarterback, not a coach who doubles as the quarterback. Not that Goss was the right person to head up the CIA and function as the nation's senior intelligence adviser. But reform, if it is to endure, must abstract from the competence of particular officials.

There is no use crying over spilt milk. The Intelligence Reform Act is a brute fact to which the intelligence system must accommodate itself until the act is amended; and as yet there are no moves afoot to amend it. (The administration's lack of a legislative program for intelligence is difficult to understand.) I want to consider how the system has adjusted to the act and how it should do so. But I must not play an irresponsible blame game myself. I must try to determine whether criticisms of the intelligence reorganization reflect merely teething troubles—the inevitable transition costs involved in an ambitious governmental reorganization, and perhaps sour grapes on the part of officials adversely affected by it—or point to deep flaws in the reorganized system.

To do this, I need performance benchmarks. Not the "metrics"

---

19. See, for example, Amy B. Zegart, "'CNN with Secrets:' 9/11, the CIA, and the Organizational Roots of Failure," 20 *International Journal of Intelligence and CounterIntelligence* 18 (2007); Zegart, "An Empirical Analysis of Failed Intelligence Reforms before September 11," 121 *Political Science Quarterly* 33 (2006); Zegart, "September 11 and the Adaptation Failure of U.S. Intelligence Agencies," *International Security*, Spring 2005, p. 78.

(quantitative performance measures) that enable success in business to be evaluated objectively; they are rarely available for evaluating intelligence. And not "bottom line" benchmarks, such as whether we are safer today (and how much safer) than we were five years ago, whether we are penetrating more terrorist cells, and whether the accuracy of intelligence analysis has increased. Those are questions very difficult for an outsider to shed light on, but insiders as well have difficulty answering them. There are too many intangibles, including changes in the size, composition, methods, and aims of our terrorist and other enemies, that bear on such questions and are largely unknown to us. It is the absence of bottom-line benchmarks that makes it so difficult for businessmen to manage government agencies successfully. Academic administrators tend to do better at managing such agencies because they come from another sector in which there are no good performance measures.

Still, qualitative assessments of the intelligence reorganization, focused on internal progress rather than on ultimate effectiveness, can be useful if they are responsive to searching questions, such as the following:

1. Is the reorganized structure an improvement over the previous one? If not, is there pressure for change? Are plans for change, including plans for structural change that Congress rejected (such as the creation of a domestic intelligence agency), being formulated against the day when they may be at once urgently needed and politically feasible?

2. Has the Director of National Intelligence clearly defined his role and that of his staff? Are short-run concerns blotting out long-run concerns? For example, is adequate attention being given to possible emergent and future threats, that is, threats other than those posed by Islamist terrorism and "rogue" nations?

3. Have the right people been appointed to the right senior jobs in the intelligence community, and are mistakes in appointments quickly corrected? The forced resignation of Porter Goss indicates

that the drumbeat of criticisms of his management of the CIA[20] was finally heeded, but after inordinate delay. A parallel case is that of John Russack, the Program Manager of the Information Sharing Environment, a key feature of the Intelligence Reform Act. (See Chapter 4.) A more complex case is that of Negroponte himself. I have no reason to think that dissatisfaction with his performance as DNI, as distinct from the President's preoccupation with the war in Iraq and Negroponte's own preferences and aptitudes, played a role in his being shifted to the job of Deputy Secretary of State. But he was not the President's first choice to be Director of National Intelligence, nor—the analysis in subsequent chapters will suggest—the best choice.

4. Have the right priorities been set for the reorganized intelligence system? Did Negroponte, for example, overemphasize—however understandably given his background as a career foreign-service officer—foreign intelligence at the expense of domestic intelligence? More than five years after the 9/11 attacks revealed the ineptness of the FBI's performance of national security intelligence in the terrorist era, the bureau continues to stumble, as underscored by the surprise resignation of the first director, appointed only eight months earlier, of the bureau's National Security Branch. (See Chapter 6.) We shall see that the Office of the Director of National Intelligence must become much more attuned to the needs of domestic intelligence, an area of continued dangerous weakness that the DNI and his senior staff have largely ignored in a signal failure of sound prioritization.

5. Are the senior officials of the reorganized intelligence community proceeding with a proper sense of urgency or are they mired in bureaucratic molasses and "business as usual" attitudes, committed

20. See, for example, Silverstein, note 8 above; Robert Dreyfuss, "The Yes-Man: President Bush Sent Porter Goss to the CIA to Keep the Agency in Line: What He's Really Doing Is Wrecking It," *American Prospect*, Online Edition, Dec. 10, 2005, www.prospect.org/web/page.ww?section oot&name˜iewPrint&articleId 0472;   Priest, note 12 above.

to consensus rather than "take charge" management, and timid in dealing with the White House and Congress? Are they hiding behind the comfortable evasion that Congress gave them their marching orders in the Intelligence Reform Act and march they shall? Actually, despite its numbing detail, the act is quite open-ended. It is not a set of orders; it is a framework.

6. Have senior intelligence officials adopted proper benchmarks for their own performance, and if so, are they meeting them?

7. Is there too much staff in the Office of the Director of National Intelligence or too little? Are sound management practices being followed or flouted? Are the right lessons being drawn from the continued floundering of the Department of Homeland Security? Are officials able to step back from day-to-day management and evaluate structure and progress from perspectives informed by comparative and historical experience and by the social sciences (cognitive psychology, organization theory, statistical theory, economics, political science), which, as I have emphasized in my previous books on intelligence, have much to teach the leaders of our intelligence system?

8. Has good progress been made in addressing other high-priority intelligence needs—the need to improve information technology and the sharing of digitized information, the need to hire officers who have the requisite linguistic abilities, the need to standardize security clearances so that classified information can be shared easily within and across agencies and with experts outside government, the need to classify less and end the tyranny of the security officers, and the need to improve "vertical" information sharing (for example with local police)?

9. Is the community overinvested in criminal law enforcement? In military responses to terrorism? Do policymakers understand the extent to which intelligence methods can be used lawfully not only to detect but also to disrupt plots against the nation—in short, do they understand that intelligence is an alternative as well as an adjunct or precursor to law enforcement and military force?

10. Is the intelligence community getting its message out to the general public? Is it educating the public in the need for but also the limits of intelligence? Is too much revealed or concealed?

11. Is the community demonstrating adequate concern for issues of legality, privacy, civil liberties, and separation of powers? Do senior officials reach out to civil libertarians and other critics? Are they forthright in explaining the dangers of too expansive a conception of civil liberties?

12. Is congressional oversight of the reorganized system competent, continuous, and penetrating?

13. Are politics being kept at bay to the extent consistent with democratic governance? Do policymakers sufficiently respect the professionalism and independence of career intelligence officers? To what extent are so-called intelligence failures actually policy failures?

14. Is intelligence adequately coordinated with the other components of national security?

I try to touch on all these questions in the chapters that follow.

3

Design
Problems

Flaws in the organization of our intelligence system on the eve of
9/11 lent plausibility to the idea that the system needed to be reorganized, though not along the lines drawn by the Intelligence Reform
Act on the advice of the 9/11 Commission. There was was the stack-
ing of too many responsibilities on the Director of Central Intelligence, with insufficient statutory powers. A related flaw was poor
coordination of foreign and domestic intelligence—related because of
widespread resistance to entrusting the Director of the Central Intelligence Agency—the other hat worn by the Director of Central
Intelligence—with responsibility for *domestic* intelligence. That resistance was based on civil libertarians' hostility to the CIA's conducting
intelligence operations inside the United States ("spying on Americans").

A third problem was the Defense Department's ownership and
control of the national intelligence agencies.[1] Being both owner-op-

---

1. See Introduction, note 8.

erator and customer, the department had a conflict of interest when dealing with other customers, such as the CIA and the FBI, for data generated by the national agencies. And because the budget of those agencies greatly exceeded that of all the other intelligence services combined, as it still does, the Defense Department's ownership of them gave the department the lion's share of the total intelligence budget (even excluding tactical military intelligence) and reduced the DCI's authority accordingly. A fourth problem was the FBI's domination of domestic intelligence because the United States had (and has) no counterpart to Britain's MI5 or Canada's Security Intelligence Service.

The Intelligence Reform Act tried to solve the first problem but failed (and the Director of National Intelligence compounded the failure), solved the second problem, did little with the third problem, and did nothing of any consequence about the last problem.

The Director of Central Intelligence was the coordinator of the 15 U.S. intelligence agencies,[2] and this should have been a full-time job—especially since he had limited statutory powers, in particular over the Defense Department's intelligence agencies; as a result he had to operate largely by politicking and cajolery rather than by command. Managing the CIA—the DCI's second job—had long before 2004 become a full-time job because of the agency's size and the sensitivity of many of the missions of its Directorate of Operations,

---

2. Now 16: the Drug Enforcement Administration's intelligence unit has been added to the official list of members of the intelligence community. (The government wants to yoke drug enforcement to the "war on terrorism" in part, I suspect, to increase the number of reported successes in the "war." But there is also a legitimate concern with the financing of terrorist activities by profits from trafficking in illegal drugs.) Actually, there are more than 16 federal intelligence services. The National Counterterrorism Center, the National Counterproliferation Center, and the National Intelligence Council should be added to the count, along with the intelligence services in the Transportation Security Administration, the Border Patrol, and other component agencies of the Department of Homeland Security besides the department's Office of Information and Analysis and the Coast Guard's intelligence service, both of which are counted in the 16.

which runs the spies and does covert action. The DCI also was the President's (and the cabinet's) senior intelligence adviser, itself nearly a full-time job if the President wanted to meet frequently with his senior intelligence adviser, as George W. Bush does.[3] All this had become too much for one person, especially given the enormous challenge to the intelligence system—greater than the challenge the Cold War had posed—that Islamist terrorism poses because of its dispersed character and the increasing accessibility of weapons of mass destruction, particularly biological weapons, to small groups and even individuals.[4] Proliferation may empower other terrorists as well, and has made formerly weak nations such as Iran and North Korea potentially formidable enemies of the United States. Our enemies have multiplied both in number and in destructive potential, thus placing great strain on the intelligence community.

So Congress was right to split the jobs of CIA director and Director of Central Intelligence and to strengthen the powers of the latter (renamed Director of National Intelligence). A further benefit, curiously overlooked in most discussions of the reform, was to enable better management of the CIA. Directors of Central Intelligence had had to devote some attention to their community-wide role, even if much less than they gave to running the CIA. The reform enables CIA directors to give the considerable challenge of managing this large and controversial agency their undivided attention.

Although Congress gave more power to the Director of National Intelligence than the Directors of Central Intelligence had had, it did

---

3. In the Carter Administration, in contrast, the President's daily intelligence briefing was conducted by the National Security Adviser, Zbigniew Brzezinski. In some administrations a CIA analyst brings the President's Daily Brief to the President and remains to answer any questions about it that the President may have.

4. For portents, see James Randerson, "Revealed: The Lax Laws That Could Allow Assembly of Deadly Virus DNA: Urgent Calls for Regulation after Guardian Buys Part of Smallpox Genome through Mail Order," *Guardian*, June 14, 2006, p. 1; Joby Warrick, "Custom-Built Pathogens Raise Bioterror Fears," *Washington Post*, July 31, 2006, p. A1.

not make him the actual administrator, or "czar," of the intelligence community,[5] in the same way that a cabinet secretary is the administrator, the "czar," of his department. That is, unlike the approach taken in the other major post-9/11 structural change, the creation of the Department of Homeland Security, Congress did not create a Department of Intelligence and put the 16 federal intelligence services into it. Wisely—to have done that would have recreated the problem of heaping too many responsibilities on one person.

But Congress still went too far, by designating the Director of National Intelligence the nation's senior intelligence adviser and equipping him with analytic resources to enable him to play that role. His job should have been configured more modestly, as that of co-ordinator, overall supervisor, or board chairman of the intelligence community, preserving the role of the CIA's director as the senior intelligence adviser and thus as the official primarily responsible for the preparation of the President's Daily Brief.[6] Coordinating the overall intelligence system would have been job enough for a Director of National Intelligence.

This solution, which would have moved us in the direction of the British intelligence system, would not have been ideal. In our presidential system of government, in contrast to highly centralized parliamentary systems (which fuse the executive and legislative branches) such as those found in the United Kingdom and Canada, officials

5. The use of the word "czar" in this connection is confusing. The Russian czar was indeed an absolute monarch, but the impotence of the "drug czar" has given the word an ironic undertone when used to describe an American official.

6. I am unclear why the President should want to get a *daily* intelligence update rather than just being updated when important new intelligence is received. A daily update means feeding the President a steady diet of current intelligence, which is bound to be both ephemeral and to a considerable extent inaccurate. (The broader question, which I cannot pursue in this book, is why American officials spend so much time in meetings.) On the evolution of the President's Daily Brief, see the fascinating account in Richard Kovar, "Mr. Current Intelligence: An Interview with Richard Lehman," www.cia.gov/csi/kent_csi/docs/v44i3a05p.htm, visited Jan. 29, 2007.

whose only responsibility is coordination tend to lack sufficient levers to move agencies out of their accustomed grooves. That has been the fate of the "drug czar." The CIA became effective only when it added substantive functions to its coordination role, which is all it had started out with.[7] So an alternative to creating the position of Director of National Intelligence would have been to give the Director of Central Intelligence additional powers over the intelligence community's budget, personnel, and programs while he continued in his role as CIA director[8]—but then the benefits from separating the two jobs would have been lost.

Was the only choice, therefore, the unhappy one between a coordinator too weak to be effective and a coordinator too encumbered with substantive responsibilities to be effective? No. An alternative would have been to give the Director of National Intelligence (relieved of the DCI's responsibility for managing the CIA) more power to manage the intelligence community as a whole than the Directors of Central Intelligence had had. The Intelligence Reform Act did give the DNI more authority than his predecessors to shuffle staff and (in the interval between congressional appropriations) money among intelligence agencies. Congress would have given him still more had it not been for the tenacious opposition of the Defense Department. A further and even more stubborn obstacle to empowering the DNI, however, was the fragmentation of responsibility for approving the intelligence budget among literally dozens of congressional committees. This structure, which has persisted despite intense criticism by the 9/11 Commission, limits the DNI's power over the budget however much authority he is given over other officials of the executive branch.[9]

7. See text at note 23 below.

8. As proposed by Amy Zegart in testimony before the Senate Select Committee on Intelligence, Aug. 18, 2004.

9. As argued in Helen Fessenden, "The Limits of Intelligence Reform," *Foreign Affairs*, Nov./Dec. 2005, pp. 106, 114. As noted in the Preface, however, there are now stirrings of reform of intelligence oversight in Congress.

Although final budget authority rests with Congress, the President's budget requests are influential, even when Congress is in the hands of the opposing party. The DNI's power to shape the intelligence budget request is greatly limited, however, by the fact that he shares authority over most of the intelligence agencies with cabinet officers—the secretaries of the departments in which the agencies are lodged. As for his interim budget authority, that can of course be reversed by the next appropriation.

Instead of giving the Director of National Intelligence adequate powers to enable him to perform his essential role of system coordinator, Congress may have given him excessive responsibilities (related to the substance as distinct from the organization of intelligence—the product rather than the process), thus assuring the inadequacy of his powers. The responsibilities should be lessened, as I have suggested; the powers could be augmented by amending the Intelligence Reform Act.

The Act provides that

> (A) The Director of National Intelligence, with the approval of the Director of the Office of Management and Budget and in accordance with procedures to be developed by the Director of National Intelligence and the heads of the departments and agencies concerned, may transfer personnel authorized for an element of the intelligence community to another such element for a period of not more than 2 years.
>
> (B) A transfer of personnel may be made under this paragraph only if—
>
> (i) the personnel are being transferred to an activity that is a higher priority intelligence activity; and
>
> (ii) the transfer supports an emergent need, improves program effectiveness, or increases efficiency.[10]

The two-year limitation, the stipulations in section (B), and especially the requirement in (A) that the procedures for personnel transfers be

10. 50 U.S.C. § 4031-1(e)(2).

developed jointly with the heads of the affected agencies, are crippling. A broader authority to shift personnel would enhance the DNI's ability to enforce his management decisions—as would greater authority to reprogram funds between appropriations.

Heads of cabinet-level departments, it is true, achieve a measure of authority over the departments' constituent agencies without being able to reprogram budgets or shift personnel, powers that Congress tends jealously to reserve to itself. But they have other levers. The Secretary of Defense, for example, must approve all promotions to three- and four-star rank. Unlike a cabinet officer, the Director of National Intelligence does not "own" the intelligence agencies, other than his several analytic staffs. So he may need the special powers that Congress has been chary about granting him.

The Intelligence Reform Act authorizes the Director of National Intelligence to veto the appointment of the directors of the various intelligence services (for example, the Under Secretary of Defense for Intelligence, the Director of the National Security Branch of the FBI, the Chief Intelligence Officer of the Department of Homeland Security, and the directors of the national intelligence agencies in the Defense Department) when a vacancy occurs. But he should also be authorized to remove those directors. It is true that because the act did not bestow tenure (in the sense in which most civil servants, like most professors, can be removed only for good cause) on the directors of the intelligence agencies—which anyway it could not do, consistent with the separation of powers—there is nothing to prevent the Director of National Intelligence from going to the President and requesting that he order the relevant department head to fire the director of his departmental intelligence service. But there is also nothing to prevent that department head from contesting the request.

It might seem that even with greater statutory powers to manage the components of the intelligence community, the Director of National Intelligence would be ineffectual were he not the President's senior intelligence adviser; the President would turn to him for the answers to critical intelligence questions, such as what will Iran do next?, and he would bite his lip. But this picture, and the inference drawn from it that the Director of National Intelligence must somehow couple advice on substantive issues to his managerial duties, misconceive the nature of enterprise governance. The chief executive officer of Boeing does not design airplanes. What he does do is assure customers that the company has used sound methods and competent personnel to design and produce the product in which they're interested. Similarly, the DNI has to understand the intelligence community thoroughly so that he can assure the President that the intelligence the President is getting is the product of a thoughtful and meticulous process. But he doesn't have to be his own chief intelligence analyst. A high-level manager is not necessarily, or even probably, a person who is well-equipped to filter, assess, and present high-quality intelligence estimates.

Moreover, while Boeing brings out new products only at long intervals, the DNI, even if he could shake himself free of responsibility for the President's Daily Brief, would as senior intelligence adviser still have to weigh in on Iraq, Iran, North Korea, Venezuela, Somalia, proliferation, etc. The range is enormous, and covering it enormously time-consuming. It is a bit like a university president's having to sign off on all the books and articles published by the members of his university's faculty. It is true that the intelligence estimates that the DNI has to vouch for to the President and other senior policymakers are a small fraction of the estimates that the intelligence community produces—but they are still too many for him to be able to study, present, and defend while also governing the large and unruly community.

Renaming the Director of Central Intelligence the Director of National Intelligence was a cosmetic change, but a sensible one. The act gave the DNI authority over domestic as well as foreign intelligence, whereas the DCI had had virtually no authority over domestic intelligence. Congress didn't want anyone to think it was giving this authority to the head of the CIA—"Director of Central Intelligence" and "Director of the Central Intelligence Agency" sound so much alike that they are easily confused (one doubts that many members of the public know the difference)—because of anxiety about the CIA's operating inside the United States.[11] The act thus took a further step toward completing the project begun in the USA PATRIOT Act of dismantling artificial barriers between domestic and foreign intelligence. That was all to the good, though in hindsight it is apparent that the Intelligence Reform Act should also have taken down the wall that the Foreign Intelligence Surveillance Act erects between foreign and domestic intelligence (see Chapter 7).

But the Intelligence Reform Act did little about the Defense Department's control of the national intelligence agencies (not quite nothing, because it did give the DNI greater, though still insufficient,[12] budgetary authority over them than the DCI had possessed). The reason was the department's immense influence, coupled with the natural reluctance of any government agency to relinquish turf and thus signal weakness.

The act also did nothing to alter the FBI's domination of domestic intelligence. That was a tragic failure. As Amy Zegart points out, "design choices made at an agency's birth condition its development from that moment forward. Change is not impossible, but evolution is constrained at the outset; initial structural choices make some ev-

---

11. Actually, the CIA *does* operate in the United States, through its National Resources Division. There are CIA offices and CIA station chiefs in major U.S. cities. But of course the CIA does not operate with the same freedom in the United States with which it operates abroad. Moreover, the National Resources Division's main functions are not domestic intelligence but debriefing American businessmen who have useful foreign contacts and recruiting agents for service abroad. Most civil libertarians sensibly do not seem much concerned nowadays with which agency performs which intelligence functions.

12. Robert D. Vickers Jr., "The Intelligence Reform Quandary," 19 *International Journal of Intelligence and CounterIntelligence* 356, 358 (2006).

olutionary paths more likely while ruling others out."[13] Government agencies lack both the competitive prods of the private sector and the instruments that facilitate organizational changes in that sector (mergers, spin-offs, Chapter 11 reorganizations, tender offers, leveraged buyouts, etc.). Created in 1908, the FBI had been designed to be a superdetective bureau for the investigation of federal crimes. Later, in default of competitors, it had added counterterrorism, counterintelligence, and domestic intelligence to its portfolio, but without altering its basic character as a criminal investigation agency. Its conduct of domestic intelligence had been deemed satisfactory before 9/11, and the powerful inertial forces emphasized by Zegart would have thwarted a reorganization of domestic intelligence in the absence of a big external shock. The 9/11 attacks *were* such a shock, however. They enabled the swift adoption of measures that had languished in Congress for years.[14] But the moment passed without sustained consideration of the need to reorganize domestic intelligence.

It is tempting to think that a mistake in institutional design can be overcome by the appointment of a strong leader. But that is less true in government than elsewhere. The reason is not, as is often thought, that civil servants have tenure and therefore can't be fired if they refuse to accept direction from the top, and that if they are fired they have rights of appeal. Often—in the CIA, for example—they do not have tenure. The reason that forceful leadership is so difficult in government is that the heads of agencies tend to be appointed from outside the agency, to serve for only a brief period, and to have little influence over the appointment of their successor and thus little ability to assure the continuity of whatever reforms they institute. The civil servants can lie low and wait them out. They call themselves "we-bes": "we be here when you got here, we be here when you're gone."

13. Amy B. Zegart, *Flawed by Design: The Evolution of the CIA, JCS, and NSC* 93 (1999).
14. See, for example, id. at 201–205.

While it is true that chief executive officers of private firms are often hired from other companies, they are in the same profession—they are business executives. In contrast, senior government officials come from business, law, politics, academia, and other lines of work remote from that of the government agencies they are put in charge of. Of the 21 CIA directors and two Directors of National Intelligence (including Negroponte's successor) that the nation has had, a total of 23, only 5 had been career intelligence officers before their appointment (Richard Helms, William Colby, Robert Gates, Michael Hayden, and John McConnell). Those who were not tended not to focus on internal reform, though George Tenet was an exception.

Agency heads tend, therefore, to be uncomfortably dependent on the civil servants—strangers whom they they don't know well, don't understand well, have difficulty evaluating, and in consequence may distrust—for the actual management of the agency. If they try to govern without relying on the advice of the career officials, disaster beckons. Yet those officials are heavily invested in the existing culture of their agency, especially as they have no reason to think that changes instituted by their temporary boss will have any sticking power. With the policymakers bold though ignorant and the career officials knowledgeable though timid, there is a potential for fruitful complementarity; but realizing that potential is very difficult.

Congress's designation of the Director of National Intelligence as not only the coordinator, motivator, monitor, and resource allocator of the intelligence community (also the manager of the community's relations with Congress and the cabinet)—the functions that the Director of Central Intelligence had lacked time and clout enough to perform adequately—but also the President's senior intelligence adviser diminished the CIA's role and stature. Diminished them even beyond what was entailed by the agency's having now to report to the DNI (except for covert action) rather than, as before the Intelligence Reform Act, directly to the President. To support his role as senior intelligence officer, the Director of National Intelligence was given the National Intelligence Council, which prepares National Intelligence Estimates, the most authoritative analytic products of the intelligence community, and the National Counterterrorism Center, along with the tiny staff that prepares the final draft of the President's Daily Brief, formerly a responsibility of the CIA. The DNI later created, as the Intelligence Reform Act had authorized him to do, the National Counterproliferation Center. Under its previous name, Terrorist Threat Integration Center, the National Counterterrorism Center had been part of the CIA. The National Intelligence Council, nominally independent, had been dominated by the CIA. And the CIA had and has two counterproliferation centers—WINPAC (Weapons Intelligence, Proliferation, and Arms Control Center) and CPD (Counterproliferation Division)—that are now presumably to take direction from the new National Counterproliferation Center.

At the same time that the CIA was being demoted and its traditional responsibilities trimmed, the military, under its aggressive civilian leadership (Donald Rumsfeld and his undersecretary for intelligence, Stephen Cambone), was making inroads into the CIA, though this will change with the replacement of Rumsfeld by Robert Gates, who is both milder than his predecessor and a former Director of Central Intelligence. (Cambone has also been replaced, as noted in the Introduction; and the Democratic Congress is bound to be less friendly to the conduct of domestic intelligence by the Defense Department than the Republican Congress was.) The FBI also made inroads into the CIA. Squeezed from both sides (the military and the FBI) as well as from above (Congress in the Intelligence Reform Act, and the DNI)—and distrusted by influential White House officials[15]—the CIA became increasingly embattled during Porter Goss's reign.[16]

15. R. Jeffrey Smith, in his article "Fired Officer Believed CIA Lied to Congress: Friends Say McCarthy Learned of Denials about Detainees' Treatment," *Washington Post*, May 14, 2006, p. A1, remarks the "long-standing feud between the CIA and the Bush White House, stoked by friction over the merits of the war in Iraq, over

The agency is now in much stronger hands. General Hayden is the nation's senior intelligence officer. (Negroponte is a career diplomat rather than an intelligence professional. His designated successor, McConnell, is, like Hayden, a career military intelligence officer, although he retired from the military, and went into business, a decade ago.) And Stephen Kappes, Hayden's principal deputy, a former chief of the CIA's Directorate of Operations, is highly respected throughout the intelligence community.[17] Hayden and Kappes should be able to prevent further erosion of the CIA's powers and assure competent performance of its core operational, analytical, and technical functions.[18] The concern expressed in some quarters that because Hayden is a general he will militarize the agency is

whether links existed between Saddam Hussein's government and al-Qaeda, and over the CIA-instigated criminal inquiry of White House officials suspected of leaking the name of covert CIA officer Valerie Plame." The idea that the CIA schemes against Presidents is of long standing. President Johnson "absurdly suspected the Agency of having plotted to make sure he lost the Democratic nomination to Kennedy in 1960." Christopher M. Andrew, "American Presidents and Their Intelligence Communities," in *Intelligence and the National Security Strategist: Enduring Issues and Challenges* 431, 439 (Roger Z. George and Robert D. Kline eds. 2006). Nixon believed that the CIA had engineered Kennedy's victory over him in 1960. Id. at 440. Apparently some people in the White House think that the CIA schemed, albeit this time unsuccessfully, to swing the 2004 election to John Kerry. As far as I can determine, there is no basis for any of these suspicions.

16. See, for example, David Ignatius, "The CIA at Rock Bottom," *Washington Post*, May 7, 2006, p. B7.

17. Shane Harris, "Hayden's Horizon," *National Journal*, May 20, 2006, p. 66.

18. As Hayden explained to the CIA workforce his first day on the job, "this agency's got so much connective tissue to the other parts of the intelligence community that if we're competent, and if we're collaborative, both of which are totally within our control, there is no question that we'll be 'central.'" "Q&A: Gen. Michael Hayden," *USNews.com*, Nov. 3, 2006, www.usnews.com/usnews/news/articles/061103/3qahayden.htm. The Hayden-Kappes team is likely to receive the backing of the new Secretary of Defense, Robert Gates, who in strongly supporting Hayden's appointment as CIA director said that he was "unhappy about . . . the decline in the CIA's central role." Robert M. Gates, "An Intelligent CIA Pick: And, Yes, Hayden Will Stand up to the Pentagon," *Washington Post*, May 18, 2006, p. A23. Of course that was before Gates became Secretary of Defense, and the view from his new perch may be different.

specious; he is not a typical general and his entire career has been in intelligence.

A welcome aspect of Hayden's appointment is that it is likely to reduce the *politicization* of intelligence. I must be precise in my use of the term. The intelligence community is not a separate branch of the federal government, like Congress or the federal judiciary. It is part of the executive branch, controlled by and answerable to the President. It is also just one source (actually a cluster of sources) of information on which presidential action is based. But meddling by the political level of government can have deleterious effects on the quality of intelligence.[19] A series of events—the most important of which was the CIA's disagreement with senior officials of the Bush Administration that Saddam Hussein was in cahoots with al Qaeda— persuaded those officials that the agency was hostile to the Bush Administration. Goss, a partisan Republican Congressman, was appointed director and a purge ensued, though in part it was a product of animosity between the staff that he brought with him from Congress and CIA professionals who had crossed swords with that staff in the past.

The Silberman-Robb Commission, in its report on the Iraqi weapons of mass destruction fiasco, found that the administration had not pressured the CIA or other intelligence agencies to bring their intelligence estimates into line with the administration's preconceptions. The commission was politically diverse and its unanimous finding is entitled to respect. Yet it qualified its finding by stating that "it is hard to deny the conclusion that intelligence analysts worked in an environment that did not encourage skepticism about the conventional wisdom [that Iraq had weapons of mass destruction]."[20] And

19. See generally Jack Davis, "Intelligence Analysts and Policymakers: Benefits and Dangers of Tensions in the Relationship," 21 *Intelligence and National Security* 999 (2006).

20. Commission on the Intelligence Capabilities of the United States Regarding Weapons of Mass Destruction, *Report to the President of the United States* 11 (Mar. 31, 2005).

Hayden, in an exchange with Senator Carl Levin at the hearing on Hayden's confirmation as CIA director, explained how the administration had influenced the intelligence community's estimates without having to exert direct pressure:

LEVIN: Now, prior to the war [the invasion of Iraq in 2003], the undersecretary of defense for policy, Mr. Feith, established an intelligence analysis cell within his policy office at the Defense Department. While the intelligence community was consistently dubious about links between Iraq and Al Qaeda, Mr. Feith produced an alternative analysis asserting that there was a strong connection. Were you comfortable with Mr. Feith's office's approach to intelligence analysis?

HAYDEN: . . . No, sir, I wasn't comfortable—There are a lot of things that animate and inform a policy-maker's judgment, and intelligence is one of them, and, you know, world view and—there are a whole bunch of other things that are very legitimate. The role of intelligence—I'd try to say it here by metaphor because it's the best way I can describe it—though is you've got to draw the left- and the right-hand boundaries . . . The tether to your analysis can't be so long, so stretched that it gets out of those left- and right-hand boundaries. Now, with regard to this particular case, it is possible, Senator, if you want to drill down on an issue and just get laser beam focus, and exhaust every possible—ounce of evidence, you can build up a pretty strong body of data, all right? But you have to know what you're doing. All right? I got three great kids, but if you tell me "Go out and find all the bad things they've done, Hayden," I can build you a pretty good dossier and you'd think they were pretty bad people because that's what I was looking for and that's what I built up . . . At the end of the day, when you draw your analysis, you have to recognize that you've really laser-beam focused on one particular data set, and you have to put that factor into the equation before you start drawing macro judgments.[21]

21. "Morning Session of a Hearing of the Senate Select Intelligence Committee: Nomination of General Michael Hayden to be Director of the Central Intelligence Agency," *Federal News Service*, May 18, 2006. For confirmation of Hayden's account,

If a political official tells the intelligence community to look for evidence that confirms the official's preconception, the community is likely to produce a one-sided picture because it is being asked, like a lawyer preparing a case, to concentrate on trying to find evidence that supports rather than challenges the preconceived opinion. This is an example of confirmation bias in action (see Chapter 1). To their credit, the CIA and the other intelligence agencies—including the National Security Agency, which Hayden headed at the time—never budged from their disbelief in a significant linkage between Iraq and al Qaeda. They were less successful in resisting similar indirect pressure to find evidence supporting the belief—which the CIA's own officials shared, however, along with almost everyone else in foreign as well as U.S. intelligence agencies—that Iraq had weapons of mass destruction.

Rightly or wrongly, the influence of the intelligence community on policymakers is undermined by suspicion that intelligence officers have their own political agenda. That suspicion could be allayed, to an extent, if intelligence agencies hired academics on a temporary basis, much as the Council of Economic Advisers does; the pursuit of a political agenda by academics during their temporary government

---

and precedents, see Maria Ryan, "Filling in the 'Unknowns': Hypothesis-Based Intelligence and the Rumsfeld Commission," 21 *Intelligence and National Security* 286 (2006). Hayden himself, under pressure from congressional Republicans, retracted his criticism of Feith, but not his broader concern with pressure exerted on the intelligence community by political officials to find evidence to support those officials' beliefs. See "Hayden Corrects the Record," *Wall Street Journal*, June 27, 2006, p. A14. That, at least, is how I interpret the following excerpt, quoted by the *Journal*, from Hayden's letter: "the issues I attempted to address were focused on broad questions of analytic tradecraft, not characterizing the work of Mr. Feith's office let alone attempting to address questions of lawfulness or even appropriateness. My comments about 'wrong,' 'inaccurate,' and 'misleading' were attached to a broader discussion of analytic challenges and not to any specific activities, including those under Mr. Feith." Other evidence of pressure exerted by political appointees on the intelligence community to support their preconceptions concerning Iraqi weapons of mass destruction is presented in Peter Gill and Mark Phythian, *Intelligence in an Insecure World* 132–136 (2006).

service is limited by their concern with maintaining their reputation in academia.[22]

The names of government agencies often don't mean a great deal. But there is significance to the word "central" in the name of the Central Intelligence Agency. Though intended at its birth in 1947 to perform merely a clearinghouse function,[23] with the action to remain with the existing intelligence agencies (mainly army and navy intelligence and the State Department), the CIA soon became the real center of the U.S. intelligence system. It had most of the spies and analysts, along with responsibility for covert action and substantial technical capabilities. The National Reconnaissance Office and the National Geospatial-Intelligence Agency, which along with the National Security Agency comprise the Defense Department's "national" (technical) intelligence agencies, originated inside the CIA. The CIA retains substantial technical functions in its Directorate of Science and Technology.

With its analysts and techies, the CIA was and is equipped to combine intelligence data obtained by other agencies with the data obtained by its own Directorate of Operations (which runs spies)— so: "all source" data—and to present comprehensive analyses of the data to the President and other high officials. The agency's centrality was symbolized and solidified in its director's *ex officio* appointment as Director of Central Intelligence, and legitimized by the provision (since repealed) of the National Security Act of 1947 that authorized the agency "to perform such additional services as are of common concern to the elements of the intelligence community, which services the Director of Central Intelligence determines can be more efficiently accomplished centrally."[24]

22. Ohad Leslau, "Intelligence and Economics: Two Disciplines with a Common Dilemma," 20 *International Journal of Intelligence and CounterIntelligence* 106, 117 (2007).
23. Zegart, note 13 above, chs. 6–7.
24. 50 U.S.C. § 403-3(d)(4).

The traditional conception of the CIA as the center of the intel-ligence system makes a good deal of sense even today. This is not to exonerate the agency of criticisms of its performance, and of specific practices that may be unwise, such as excessive reliance on lie de-tectors to screen applicants and monitor employees, timidity in hiring applicants who maintain contact with relatives in countries that har-bor terrorists, too-rapid rotation of operations officers between coun-tries (retarding their ability to understand the local scene and recruit and evaluate local agents), underspecialization of analysts (also re-sulting from too-rapid rotation), and underutilization of open source intelligence. But these are not structural problems soluble by decen-tering the agency. Its centrality was a strength.

So the National Counterterrorism Center, which does intelli-gence analysis of terrorist threats but also strategic planning of coun-terterrorist operations,[25] should be part of the CIA (where, remember, it began life as the Terrorist Threat Integration Center) rather than, as it now is, part of the Office of the Director of National Intelli-gence—though awkwardly a part because it doesn't report to him with respect to counterterrorist planning. There may well be a need for an agency that coordinates such planning. For it is not as if covert action, a CIA specialty, were the nation's only counterterrorist tool. We shall see in later chapters that the New York City Police Department has created separate bureaus for intelligence and for counterterrorism— for detection and for response. But insofar as the National Counter-rorism Center does counterterrorist intelligence—and that is what it mainly does—it should be returned to the CIA. That incidentally would minimize friction with the CIA's Counterterrorism Center,[26]

25. See Todd M. Masse, "The National Counterterrorism Center: Implementa-tion Challenges and Issues for Congress" (CRS [Congressional Research Service] Report for Congress, Mar. 24, 2005).

26. The Counterterrorism Center conducts operational intelligence, that is, in-telligence in support of specific missions, as distinct from strategic intelligence. The National Counterterrorism Center, contrary to the original idea behind it, has gotten into the operational-intelligence business as well, exacerbating the friction with the

with which, indeed, the National Counterterrorism Center could be merged.

The present set-up is not only confusing, but also pushes analysts and operations officers too far apart. The National Counterterrorism Center has no operations officers, that is, officers who run spies; more broadly, officers who collect intelligence, as distinct from those who analyze it. It is purely an analytic center. Now much of the information that operations officers forward to analysts is of uncertain provenance and questionable reliability, coming as it does from agents recruited in foreign, often disordered, countries. The motives, loyalty, skill, and opportunities of such agents are often questionable. Yet to protect their safety, the officers who recruit and run them are reluctant to give an analyst enough information to enable him to identify an agent, and this may prevent the analyst from evaluating the information that he is getting from the operations officer. Despite the assistance provided by "source descriptions" furnished by those officers, and the role of "report officers" in mediating between operations officers and analysts, the analyst may have trouble getting complete answers to such questions as: Do multiple reports come from many sources or one? Did the source actually have access to the information that he reported to the operations officer? Is the source honest, or is he perhaps a fabricator or even a double agent? When analysts and operations officers work closely together, which is facilitated by placing them in the same agency, information gleaned by analysts from other sources can more easily (quickly, accurately) be conveyed to operations officers to help them decide whether their agents are reliable. For example, an analyst might obtain from an open source or another agency information that suggested that a trusted agent's report was actually a fabrication.

Counterterrorism Center. For strong criticism of the concept of the National Counterterrorism Center, see Paul R. Pillar, "Good Literature and Bad History: The 9/11 Commission's Tale of Strategic Intelligence," 21 *Intelligence and National Security* 1022, 1040 (2006) ("a confusing entity with multiple missions and multiple lines of responsibility").

Restoring the National Counterterrorism Center to the CIA would, it is true, give the latter a significant domestic role. But it would be one of analysis rather than of conducting operations; and no one was much troubled that the formation of the Terrorist Threat Integration Center put the CIA in the domestic intelligence business. Like the Foreign Intelligence Surveillance Act (see Chapter 7), the taboo against mixing foreign and domestic intelligence was a legacy of the 1970s and a casualty of 9/11. Not only was there little resistance to placing the Director of National Intelligence in charge of both foreign and domestic intelligence; but when in October 2005 the creation of a National Clandestine Service within the CIA (absorbing the CIA's Directorate of Operations) was announced, there was not a peep of protest even though the service and thus the CIA would now be responsible for coordinating the human intelligence conducted by all parts of the intelligence community, including the FBI's National Security Branch, which does domestic intelligence. The National Clandestine Service gives the CIA an indirect but potentially significant role in the conduct of intelligence operations in the United States, as distinct from a role merely in analyzing domestic intelligence data. I say "potentially" significant because the service is new and its effectiveness yet to be proved.

Restoring the National Counterterrorism Center to the CIA would alleviate concerns that analysts are being drained from the CIA into the Office of the Director of National Intelligence, since the NCTC is a part of the office. More than a hundred of the center's analysts are detailees from the CIA.[27] (The center's entire staff consists of detailees from other agencies, which is a separate problem— see Chapter 4.)

The biggest obstacle to the restoration is that the FBI, which dominates domestic intelligence, is less likely to cooperate with the

27. Kevin Whitelaw, "The Eye of the Storm: In a Secret, High-Tech Spy Hub near Washington, the War on Terror Is 24-7," *U.S. News & World Report*, Nov. 6, 2006, pp. 48, 50.

CIA than with a separate entity, because of the long history of rivalry between the two agencies. That is part of the larger problem of our incoherent domestic intelligence architecture, of which more in later chapters.

The newly created National Counterproliferation Center likewise belongs in the CIA rather than in the Office of the Director of National Intelligence (where it is)—if it belongs anywhere. The multiplication of intelligence centers signals a tendency to bureaucratic hypertrophy that could eventually strangle the intelligence community. There is also a danger that intelligence tasks that do not fall within the scope of some center will be slighted, and a further danger that centers will survive after the need that gave rise to them has waned.

The National Counterproliferation Center is itself an example of proliferation, since there are two counterproliferation centers in the CIA, and the NCPC is too small to do much more than kibbutz.

A sensible restructuring of the Office of the Director of National Intelligence would leave the DNI with, at most, only two small analytic units, the National Intelligence Council and the President's Daily Brief staff (which is not merely small, but tiny). National Intelligence Estimates, the principal output of the National Intelligence Council, traditionally were bland consensus documents adopted by vote of the council's members,[28] who are representatives of the different intelligence agencies. This mode of adoption was unsound, because the agencies have very different areas of expertise and so their votes should not be weighted equally. (It's as if defense policies were determined by a vote of the cabinet.) Dissenters would sometimes add footnotes to a National Intelligence Estimate expressing their disagreement, but the footnotes tended to be ignored by readers. The DNI's deputy for analysis, Thomas Fingar, who doubles as the

28. For a notorious example, see Glenn Hastedt, "Public Intelligence: Leaks as Policy Instruments—The Case of the Iraq War," 20 *Intelligence and National Security* 419, 431 (2005).

chairman of the National Intelligence Council, is deemphasizing consensus and making the National Intelligence Estimates shorter and crisper. These are excellent reforms.

I said that "at most" the Director of National Intelligence should retain the National Intelligence Council and the President's Daily Brief staff, and the qualification requires emphasis. If, as I believe, the Director of National Intelligence should not be his own chief intelligence officer, this implies removing both the council and the PDB staff from the Office of the DNI, presumably returning them to the CIA.

Before the reorganization, however, the President's Daily Brief was criticized as overrepresenting the views of the CIA, which prepared the brief and naturally wanted the President and cabinet to believe that the most valuable analysis emanates from the CIA. That view had some grounding in the fact that the other intelligence agencies belong to cabinet-level departments, which have policy agendas that can influence their intelligence assessments. The National Intelligence Council is not a departmental service. It is intended to speak for the entire intelligence community rather than just for one agency, and so to be a neutral in the policy wars, like the CIA. The President's Daily Brief could be made the joint responsibility of the CIA's director, who should be designated the intelligence community's senior intelligence officer (as distinct from the community's overall manager, the DNI), and of the Director of the National Intelligence Council. The council should be made independent (which also means not dominated by the CIA, as was inevitable when the head of the CIA was the Director of Central Intelligence, but needn't be under the new regime). For if it remains lodged in the Office of the Director of National Intelligence, it will tend to provide analytic support to the DNI, which he wouldn't need if his role was that of full-time manager, not part-time manager and part-time (in the case of Negroponte almost full-time) intelligence adviser.

The suggested solution may seem awkward because the President's Daily Brief focuses on current intelligence and the National Intelligence Estimates on longer-term strategic assessments. But the PDB's emphasis on current intelligence is excessive, and input from the Director of the National Intelligence Council might help to correct that excess.

I am suggesting, in short, that the DNI be strictly a managerial job; that the CIA's director be the President's senior intelligence adviser, but with significant assistance from an independent National Intelligence Council. But would this structure be legal, workable, an improvement over what we have? For example, would designating the CIA's director senior intelligence adviser (thus making his relation to the Director of National Intelligence approximate that of the Chairman of the Joint Chiefs of Staff to the Secretary of Defense) violate the Intelligence Reform Act, which assigns the role of senior intelligence adviser to the Director of National Intelligence? It would not. That assignment does not preclude the DNI's delegating the advisory role to a subordinate official—almost all the powers vested by statutes in agency heads are delegated to subordinates. Despite its length and detail, the Intelligence Reform Act is vague and in many respects open-ended. It cries out for bold interpretation by the officials charged with making a success of it. It should not be regarded as if it were a wartime military order to be blindly obeyed (theirs not to reason why, theirs but to do or die).

A better argument for the DNI's retaining the role of senior intelligence adviser is that he needs as much "face time" with the President as he can get in order to strengthen his hold over the intelligence agencies that are "owned" by cabinet secretaries, notably the Secretary of State, the Secretary of Defense, the Secretary of Homeland Security, and the Attorney General. There are, however, substitutes for face time: the strengthening of the DNI's statutory powers, as I suggested earlier; a commitment by the President to back the DNI; and the appointment of a senior presidential assistant whose only duty would be national security intelligence, or perhaps the appointment of dual assistants—one for intelligence and the other for counterterrorism, which are distinct though overlapping national security functions. (See Chapter 8.) It is a sad commentary on American government that senior officials should feel they must climb over one another to get into the President's visual field in order to be effective, as if they were Louis XIV's noblemen, forced to live with the king at Versailles.

I have heard it suggested that the real significance of "face time" is that it helps the Director of National Intelligence understand where the President's concerns lie. But a President ought to be able to indicate his concerns to a subordinate without meeting with him six times a week.

Another unpersuasive argument is that if the DNI relinquishes the role of senior intelligence adviser, the intelligence community will not respect him. It will not respect him on that ground only if it misunderstands his role. The Secretary of Defense is not supposed to be a military strategist; if he assumes that role, he is heading for trouble.

The difference between an overall manager and a chief intelligence officer can be illustrated with reference to intelligence analysis (as distinct from collection). Unless the DNI is the nation's senior intelligence officer in a substantive sense, he doesn't need a large number of analysts. What he needs as a manager, and what the able deputy DNI for analysis (Thomas Fingar) is in the process of acquiring for the Office of the DNI, is the ability to coordinate intelligence analysts across agencies. The intelligence community employs some 18,000 analysts scattered across the agencies that make up the community. Enabling analysts to work better with their counterparts in other agencies (to know what they're doing, what their areas of expertise are, how to exchange information with them, and so forth) is just the kind of coordination function on which a Director of National Intelligence and his staff should concentrate.

That staff is mounting toward 1,500—a number that is misleadingly small, however, because it excludes numerous contract employees—and the annual budget of the Office of the Director of National Intelligence toward $1 billion. Neither figure is likely to be a ceiling. The staff, which already exceeds the number of CIA operations officers, is a new bureaucracy layered on top of the intelligence community's existing agencies. True, it is not entirely new. For among the bureaucracies that the Intelligence Reform Act ordered transferred to the Office of the Director of National Intelligence was the 300-person Community Management Staff, the principal staff of the Director of Central Intelligence for coordinating the intelligence community; and also the staff of the National Counterintelligence Executive (NCIX), about whom more later. In fact, some two-thirds of the employees of the Office of the Director of National Intelligence are there as a direct result of provisions of the Intelligence Reform Act. In part this is a consequence of the act's having tasked the Director of National Intelligence not only with coordinating the intelligence system but also with managing his own intelligence agency, consisting of the National Counterterrorism Center, the National Counterproliferation Center (though its creation was authorized rather than commanded by the act), the National Counterintelligence Executive's staff, the National Intelligence Council, and the President's Daily Brief staff. But the result is that the reorganization may have perpetuated the main organizational flaw—an overburdened Director of Central Intelligence—that it sought to correct, while doing nothing to correct the other two pre-9/11 design flaws—the Defense Department's control of the national intelligence agencies and the FBI's domination of domestic intelligence. This is the essence of the case against the reorganization.

Negroponte's background in diplomacy (of which we were continually reminded by his preferred style of address—"Ambassador" Negroponte), and his assignment as the President's chief intelligence briefer, led him to delegate as much as he could of his managerial responsibilities to his principal deputy, General Hayden.[29] A highly experienced intelligence manager, Hayden had spent six years as director of the National Security Agency, the largest of the intelligence agencies with some 30,000 employees. His departure from the Office of the Director of National Intelligence to become the head of the Central Intelligence Agency in the summer of 2006 created a vacuum only partially filled by the appointment of Lieutenant General Ronald L. Burgess, Jr. as acting principal deputy DNI. At this writing there is no permanent replacement for Hayden. The delay in filling this critical job is typical of the slow motion in which our government operates even at a time declared by the President to be one of war. And it is not as if Burgess had been nominated and the Senate had dawdled in confirming him. Apparently he was never intended to be Hayden's replacement; for he was never nominated. Momentum was lost by the departure of the DNI's principal deputy after only a year in office without a permanent replacement having been found. It was only because the CIA was such a troubled agency that an executive of Hayden's caliber had to be shifted so soon from a vital post to head it up—and the CIA was troubled in part because of the reorganization that Congress had decreed.

Given Negroponte's focus on substantive intelligence issues, and hence the importance of his principal deputy to the performance of the coordination role, it is surprising not only that General Burgess was never nominated but also that he is a rank below Hayden—a three-star general rather than a four-star one. That is a big difference in the military pecking order (conceivably it could affect the relations between McConnell, who retired as a three star, and Hayden), and

29. "The DNI's chief job, in addition to briefing the president every morning, is largely managerial and takes an enormous amount of time and personal energy. Negroponte rarely showed himself to be interested in or suited to such tasks, observers said." Shane Harris, "The Return of the Grown-Ups: President Bush Has Put Four Men at the Top of the Military and Intelligence Establishments Who Know One Another Well and Have Worked Together since the 1990s," *National Journal*, Jan. 13, 2007, pp. 52, 53.

weakened the DNI's ability to exert control over the Defense Department's intelligence apparatus, which in budget and in personnel dwarfs the rest of the intelligence community.

Rumor has it that Hayden's permanent replacement will be Thomas Fingar, the deputy DNI for analysis. Should this happen it will reverse the job descriptions of the intelligence community's two senior officers. Instead of the DNI's being the substantive intelligence officer and his deputy the system manager, the DNI (Vice Admiral McConnell, whose resumé is similar to Hayden's) will be the system manager (if the President lets him!)—and his deputy will be the substantive officer.

That would be an improvement over the present set-up, because no matter how able the principal deputy, the extent of managerial responsibility that the DNI can delegate consistent with effective management of the intelligence community is limited. Because the heads of the intelligence services (other than the CIA and the services that are in the Office of the Director of National Intelligence) report to superiors in cabinet-level departments as well as to the DNI, and because the services' personnel are therefore departmental employees rather than employees of the Office of the Director of National Intelligence, the services are inclined to pay greater heed to their departmental superiors than to officials in the DNI's office. No one in that office except the Director of National Intelligence himself can go head to head with a cabinet secretary, especially as powerful a one as the Secretary of Defense, the Attorney General, the Secretary of State, or the Secretary of Homeland Security.

When Negroponte leaves the directorship of national intelligence to become Deputy Secretary of State and is succeeded by McConnell, the Bush Administration will have succeeded—22 months late—in placing the round peg in the round hole and the square peg in the square hole. Negroponte is qualified to be a senior State Department official, and McConnell—a career intelligence professional with high-level managerial experience (like Hayden a former Director of the

National Security Agency)—is qualified to be Director of National Intelligence if I am correct that the job is properly considered one of managing the intelligence community rather than of being the nation's senior intelligence analyst. But should his deputy be a substantive intelligence officer with limited managerial experience? I think not. This is not a criticism of Fingar, but merely reflects my conception of the proper role of the Director of National Intelligence and his staff. If the number two person in the Office of the DNI functions primarily as a substantive intelligence officer, the office's focus on management will be blurred.

The appointment of a strong CIA director highlighted the awkwardness of the command structure that Congress created. Ask yourself who (before Negroponte's recent resignation) *was* the nation's intelligence chief. Was it in fact Negroponte, a diplomat rather than an intelligence professional, charged with a coordination role as well as an intelligence-advisory role? Will it be Negroponte's successor, an intelligence professional with substantial management experience, in both respects unlike Negroponte? Will it perhaps be Hayden, as the strong chief of what is still the principal, if diminished, U.S. intelligence agency? But is Hayden the CIA's *real* chief or is it the Director of National Intelligence, because the CIA reports to him? Is it the DNI's principal deputy, should he turn out to be Thomas Fingar?

Questions such as these (which return us to the earlier issue of how properly to conceptualize the role of a Director of National Intelligence) are raised in a recent book by Efraim Halevy, a former head of Israel's foreign intelligence service.[30] Halevy points out that "authority and responsibility must go together and the chain of command must ensure that he who shoulders the responsibility for the product, for the assessment, or for the procurement of information has direct command of the troops. It is impossible to hold an intel-

30. Efraim Halevy, *Man in the Shadows: Inside the Middle East Crisis with a Man Who Led the Mossad* 254–255 (2006).

ligence chief accountable if he does not have full command of his subordinates."[31] Halevy goes on to argue that a nation's intelligence chief must both "have his ear to the ground," that is, be intimately involved in the intelligence process, and have a close relationship with his political superiors.[32] It is unclear whether there is such a person in the reorganized U.S. intelligence system. I think it should be the Director of the Central Intelligence Agency.

Another way to understand the issue of leadership is to distinguish between two senses of "coordination" of intelligence. In one, the coordinator deals with systemic issues, such as standardizing (to the extent appropriate) recruitment, training, compensation, promotion, and other personnel policies, creating clear channels among analysts, overhauling information technology,[33] identifying gaps and overlaps, establishing rational standards for classification and security clearances, parceling out responsibilities among the different agencies, setting priorities, allocating funding, resolving interagency disputes, monitoring performance, and appointing senior staff. Some of these issues are being addressed. For example, the DNI has designated the CIA's Open Source Center (of which more in Chapter 4) to be the intelligence system's open source nucleus, charged with developing methods and standards and disseminating them throughout the system. The creation of the National Clandestine Service in the CIA is a parallel example; it is to human intelligence roughly as the Open Source Center is to open source intelligence. These measures cast into sharp relief the anomaly of situating the National Counterterrorism Center and the National Counterproliferation Center within the Office of the Director of National Intelligence rather than within the CIA.

In its other sense, "coordination" refers to the coordination of

31. Id. at 254.
32. Id. at 255.
33. Which is in dreadful shape. See Richard A. Posner, *Uncertain Shield: The U.S. Intelligence System in the Throes of Reform*, ch. 6 (2006).

specific operations, such as surveillance and analysis of North Korea's nuclear and missile programs. Improving system coordination tends to be a long-term endeavor without a fixed deadline or a sense of urgency. Operational coordination is short term; it responds to immediate concerns. In government, attention to short-term problems crowds out attention to long-term ones because of the election cycle, the natural impatience of officials, the pressure of emergency, hectoring by the media, the demand for palpable "results" and the consequent emphasis on performance measures even when meaningless or distorted (an emphasis observable in the Iraq war as earlier in Vietnam), and the sheer stubbornness of long-term problems—which is why their solution tends to be continuously deferred; why, in short, they are "long term" problems. Solutions to such problems, being postponable until they turn critical, *are* postponed, often indefinitely, while officials at the political level of government wrestle with the daily crisis and compel the intelligence agencies to do likewise.

Distracting the Director of National Intelligence and his staff from their system-wide coordination functions would be a less serious problem if he had separate staffs for systemic and operational coordination. Instead the same staff is trying to do both. So, to exaggerate somewhat, when North Korea conducts its first nuclear test, the staff drops everything in favor of assessing the test and interpreting to the President its significance. The pressure on the staff is particularly intense because policymakers and intelligence officers are on different time tracks. Intelligence is not updated daily, so when a crisis hits and the policymaker asks for an intelligence estimate, the intelligence community has to scramble to provide him with current rather than stale data and interpretation. In light of the crisis in Iraq and the criticisms of our intelligence performance there by the Iraq Study Group (see Introduction), I imagine that Negroponte and much of his staff were in the last few months of his tenure preoccupied with Iraq to the virtual exclusion of other concerns, especially concerns relating to structural or managerial rather than substantive issues.

Better than creating separate staffs would be confining the Office of the Director of National Intelligence to system management, leaving operational coordination to the Central Intelligence Agency. Were the Director of National Intelligence to limit his role so, the benefits that Congress sought from separating overall system management from command of the CIA would have a better prospect of being achieved. To the extent that the Director of National Intelligence and his staff become immersed in operational coordination, not only are projects for increasing the coherence of the intelligence system deferred but lines of command are blurred because coordination blends insensibly into command.

The prospects for systemic coordination were dimmed by two decisions by Negroponte, neither decreed in the Intelligence Reform Act but both recommended by the Silberman-Robb Commission and approved by the White House. The first was the appointment of mission managers to coordinate intelligence in specific areas, geographical or subject-matter: Iran, North Korea, Cuba-Venezuela, proliferation, and counterintelligence. The idea of mission managers may be a good one, though there is a problem of duplication; for there is both a Counterproliferation Center and a counterproliferation mission manager, although the center director and the mission manager are one and the same person, and likewise there is both a National Counterintelligence Executive and a counterintelligence mission manager and again they are the same person. Besides such redundancies, there is a risk that missions that are not assigned a mission manager will be neglected.

If mission managers are good things to have, still they should not be appointees of the Director of National Intelligence. Not that he should play no role. Part of the role of a system manager is to identify gaps in the system and take steps to fill them, and mission managers may be a good method of gap filling. But rather than pick the mission managers, the DNI should designate the agency most familiar with the mission and let that agency take the lead in overseeing the collection and analysis of pertinent intelligence data—be responsible, in short, for accomplishing the mission, including appointing the manager. The DNI would play an important role beyond designating the lead agency; for he would monitor performance and, of particular importance, see to it that the other agencies accepted the authority of the mission manager.

But because the DNI appoints the mission managers, who are responsible for the success of specific intelligence operations (in other words, they are more like line officers than staff officers),[34] he becomes directly responsible for the success or failure of their missions. This makes him a *director* of intelligence operations as well as a coordinator of them, as well as being responsible for the President's Daily Brief. And so most of his time will be occupied in attending to substantive intelligence questions, just as the time of his predecessor, the Director of Central Intelligence, was consumed by substantive matters as a result of his doubling as the CIA's director.

The daily briefing of the President is time-consuming all by itself. Negroponte met six days a week with the President when the latter was in Washington. That this is indeed a time-consuming assignment was suggested in an interview with General Hayden, who, in noting that his predecessors as directors of the CIA had that job and he does not, remarked:

> My workday starts here; they pick me up at 6:45; I'm reading the [President's Daily Brief], all right? I've read through the PDB book, which is more than just what the president gets, but all the other cables I should be looking at, and I'm done before [DNI] John Negroponte goes into the Oval Office. So, I am now the director of an agency, in mind as well as body, by 8 o'clock, whereas George

34. "In the days after North Korea's recent nuclear test, the DNI put mission manager and CIA veteran Joseph DeTrani at the center of the developing crisis. Along with issuing a twice-daily intelligence summary, DeTrani served as a 'traffic cop,' coordinating analysis, briefing the White House, and tasking spies on what to target." David E. Kaplan and Kevin Whitelaw, "Playing Defense," *U.S. News & World Report*, Nov. 10, 2006, pp. 44, 48–49.

[Tenet] when he was doing this or Porter [Goss], couldn't turn his attention to the smooth functioning of this agency until much later in the day . . . So, it really is, I've used the word, *liberating*.[35]

This implies that the Director of National Intelligence can't turn *his* attention to the management of his enterprise until much later in the day (though one insider has told me that Hayden was exaggerating, and that Negroponte averaged only two hours a day in preparing for and attending the briefing—not that two hours is a trivial fraction of a workday). In addition, the DNI is responsible for the analysts who produce the intelligence estimates reported in the President's Daily Brief, and discharging that responsibility takes time as well, as does supervision of the mission managers.

The plight of the Director of National Intelligence thus resembles that of the chief executive officers of large corporations. "They feel like Gulliver bound by a thousand ropes. It is extremely difficult for public company CEOs and their management teams to focus and execute long-term strategies that require fundamental changes in business practices at the same time as they are responding to the cacophony of their many, multiple constituencies."[36] The only difference is that the DNI's plight is much worse. He has fewer powers than a corporate CEO and operates in an even more challenging environment. He must conciliate Congress, a more demanding and unruly set of overseers than a corporate board of directors. He must negotiate with the White House and the cabinet, a collection of willful peers and imperious masters that has no counterpart in the corporate world (the closest counterparts are the securities analysts). His legal and regulatory environment is as harrowing as that of a corporate CEO, and he is entangled in a denser bureaucratic web. He must cultivate the media even more assiduously than a corporate CEO must. And he has less control over his subordinates. Facing a her-

35. "Q&A: Gen. Michael Hayden," note 18 above (emphasis in original).

36. Donald J. Gogel, "What's So Great about Private Equity," *Wall Street Journal*, Nov. 27, 2006, p. A13.

culean management challenge, he cannot afford to waste his time speculating about Fidel Castro's life expectancy.[37] Let us hope that the President does not demand a daily briefing from Negroponte's successor.

Negroponte's second questionable (though less so) structural decision was to organize his staff along functional lines—particularly collection, customer relations, analysis, information technology, and science—rather than along substantive lines, such as domestic, foreign, and military intelligence, or, more realistically, a combination of substantive and functional lines. (An exception to the functional organization is the National Counterintelligence Executive. His role is substantive. But he was foisted on the DNI by the Intelligence Reform Act.) One result of the functional organization is that multiple officials in the agencies report to multiple officials in the Office of the Director of National Intelligence, which makes it difficult for that office to evaluate the performance of individual agencies as a whole. Another result may be that the agencies' officials will become subordinates taking directions from the officials in the DNI's office (and not only the mission managers), who will thereby become supervisors rather than staffers. Third, no official has full-time responsibility for domestic intelligence, even though it is the weakest link in the intelligence chain.

The last of these consequences could be avoided by redefining the role of the National Counterintelligence Executive. The position was created to improve counterintelligence in its narrow sense of preventing the penetration of our own intelligence operations by our enemies, in the wake of the Aldrich Ames and Robert Hansen spy scandals and growing concern about Chinese espionage. The NCIX's

37. "Cuban President Fidel Castro is very ill and close to death, Director of National Intelligence John D. Negroponte said yesterday. 'Everything we see indicates it will not be much longer—months, not years,' Negroponte told a meeting of Washington Post editors and reporters." Karen DeYoung, "Castro Near Death, U.S. Intelligence Chief Says," *Washington Post*, Dec. 15, 2006, p. A23.

mandate could be broadened to include all domestic intelligence. Counterintelligence is like domestic counterterrorist intelligence in being oriented toward defending the U.S. homeland against covert activity, albeit by foreign spies rather than by terrorists.

Might having deputy DNIs for collection and analysis lead ultimately to combining the collection units in the various intelligence agencies into one division and the analysis units into another, reducing the current 16-plus intelligence agencies to just two? That is the logic, though not the likely destiny, of the functional organization of the DNI's staff. It is a logic of centralization. Centralization is not a good formula for the management of an enterprise engaged in the production of knowledge, whether it is a university, a newspaper, a software producer, or the intelligence community. It has benefits in reducing gaps and overlaps but retards innovation and diversity, which are basic to so uncertain an activity as national security intelligence. In contrast, competition fosters those goods.[38] Imagine a university in which professors' research papers had to be approved by the university's president before they could be submitted for publication in a scholarly journal.

So some of the frictions, the turf wars, the information hoarding that critics of the intelligence community (including myself!) deplore may actually be indispensable to the optimal performance of the intelligence system. The challenge of coordination is to strike the right balance between overcentralization and anarchy. The system must be managed, but managed with a light touch. Each intelligence agency, like each department in a university, should be allowed considerable autonomy so that it can develop and exploit a distinctive perspective and culture of inquiry.

Adopting the horizontal, substantive rather than functional, management structure that is the preferred organizational form for knowl-

38. See, for example, Yingyi Qian, Gérard Roland, and Chenggang Xu, "Coordination and Experimentation in M-Form and U-Form Organizations," 114 *Journal of Political Economy* 366 (2006).

edge producers would require the Director of National Intelligence to replace the deputy DNIs for collection, analysis, and other functions by deputies for domestic, foreign, and military intelligence. These deputies would coordinate, with the aid of small staffs, groupings of autonomous, largely self-sufficient, fiercely independent agencies. No thick bureaucratic layer would cover, and maybe smother, the agencies. The need for coordination of the three substantive fields would remain—would in fact be urgent. But it would be a defined and limited need, enabling a sharp focus on system-wide issues, such as information sharing, standardizing security clearances, modernizing computer technology, and improving the training (including language training), recruitment, incentives, evaluation, and compensation of intelligence officers. The staff responsible for carrying out these tasks of system management could be kept small.

I don't have a great deal of confidence in this proposal, however; maybe a mixed system is best. It may be more important and more manageable to coordinate collection across agencies, and analysis across agencies, than to coordinate entire agencies with each other, and then groups of agencies with other groups of agencies. (The most important area for coordinating agencies is, as we'll see in subsequent chapters, domestic intelligence.)

And despite what I have been urging, maybe the problem isn't overcentralization (as distinct from overstaffing at the top, which is to say in the Office of the Director of National Intelligence). Maybe the problem is that there isn't *enough* hierarchy in the intelligence community today. Think back to the question of who really is the nation's intelligence chief. The question underscores the chain-of-command problem that besets the relationship (however good on a personal level) between the Director of National Intelligence and the Director of the Central Intelligence Agency. The latter official remains in charge of most human-intelligence collection by virtue of "owning" the National Clandestine Service, and he still has, in the agency's Directorate of Intelligence, the lion's share of the analysts.

The chain of command for operations used to run from the CIA chief of station in the field to the division chief or center chief in CIA headquarters, then to the CIA's deputy director for operations, next to the CIA's director, and finally to the President. The chain of command for analysis ran from the operating level to the deputy director for intelligence (that is, for analysis), to the CIA's director, and to the President. Now it is the Director of National Intelligence who has charge of analysis and advice to the President; he has been slotted in between the CIA's director and the President. The chief of station reports directly to the DNI on strategic issues, but up the normal CIA chain of command on human spying operations ("human intelligence") and on relations with the intelligence services of the country in which the chief of station resides. So if the DNI wants to have a full picture of the intelligence situation in, say, Egypt, he may have to ask both the Cairo chief of station directly and the CIA's director.

Although supposed to be the nation's intelligence leader, the Director of National Intelligence leads nothing at the Defense Department, has only limited influence on the lagging domestic-collection efforts of the FBI, the Department of Homeland Security, and other domestic agencies, and is not in direct charge of the National Clandestine Service. Maybe he should have more authority or less authority, but he should not be left with the uncertain authority that the tangle ordained by Congress, and accepted as marching orders rather than fought by the Director of National Intelligence, has created. I think he should have more authority. But it should be authority to coordinate at the system level, not authority (and the staff needed to enable him to exercise that authority) to make intelligence assessments.

4

Successes
and
Failures

It is impossible for an outsider, such as myself, to give a balanced assessment of the successes and failures of our reorganized intelligence system, because intelligence failures invariably are better publicized than intelligence successes. Not only are the successes less dramatic—indeed, they usually are nonevents—and therefore less newsworthy; they are also more likely to remain securely classified. This is partly because revelation might compromise their success, partly because failures are more likely to generate self-serving leaks as employees involved in the failure seek to shift blame to others, and partly because policymakers like to blame policy failures on poor intelligence but to take credit for policy successes enabled by good intelligence. It is of no help in correcting this imbalance between the good news and the bad that the intelligence community has been awful at getting its message out. An example is John Negroponte's virtual silence (taken in some quarters as signaling disapproval) during the debate over the surveillance that the National Security Agency was conducting in apparent violation of the Foreign Intelligence Surveillance Act. General Hayden was left to defend it more or less by himself—which he did articulately; but having created the program when he was the head of NSA, he could not seem as impartial a defender as Negroponte might have seemed. The debate stirred up a storm that after subsiding burst out anew because of further revelations concerning the program's scope.[1]

Nothing new here: think of the astonishing failure of the intelligence community to obtain any credit from either the general public or influential opinion makers for its contribution to the U.S. victory in the Cold War. Or, coming back to the present, think of how the Bush Administration consistently seems surprised by the inevitable leaks concerning intelligence programs (such as the National Security Agency's warrantless surveillance program—see Chapter 7) and evaluations (such as the National Intelligence Estimate that said the war in Iraq was increasing the terrorist threat to the United States) and unprepared to respond to them.

Yet there have been identifiable successes in implementing the reorganization decreed by the Intelligence Reform Act, although success must not be confused with activity—there is no question that the DNI and his staff have been extremely active.[2]

I mentioned in Chapter 3 the improved coordination of the scattered intelligence analysts. Here I add that Thomas Fingar—who besides being the deputy DNI for analysis doubles as chairman of the National Intelligence Council—is experimenting with an ingenious

1. See, for example, Eric Lichtblau and Scott Shane, "Bush Is Pressed over New Report on Surveillance: Complaints in Congress: Pick to Lead C.I.A. Could Have Trouble Because of New Disclosures," *New York Times*, May 12, 2006, p. A1; Walter Pincus and Charles Babington, "Specter Wants More Debate on Spying: Senator to Try to Block Program's Funding," *Washington Post*, Apr. 28, 2006, p. A4. For the latest episode in the surveillance saga, see Chapter 7.

2. See Office of the Director of National Intelligence, "Report on the Progress of the Director of National Intelligence in Implementing the 'Intelligence Reform and Terrorism Prevention Act of 2004,'" May 2006, www.fas.org/irp/dni/implement.html.

method of evaluating analysts' performance: giving the same question on which the National Intelligence Council has been asked to prepare a National Intelligence Estimate to a panel of uncleared academics. (Fingar has an academic background.) Should they produce equally good or even better estimates, this may suggest that some high-level intelligence analysis should be privatized, as well as casting doubt on the value of classified data as a source of intelligence analysis.

I also mentioned the Open Source Center, created in November 2005. With the staggering amount of data now publicly available on the web, open source intelligence has assumed enormous importance,[3] though it is difficult to do well because of the volume of data to be searched.

The open source "movement"—it is appropriately called that[4]— has a significance that transcends the wealth of information that the Internet has made available to search:

1. It is a reminder that secrets—the information that our adversaries seek to conceal from us—are only a small part, and often not the most important part, of the information that the intelligence community needs in order to be able to give good advice to policymakers.[5]

3. See, for example, Stephen C. Mercado, "Reexamining the Distinction between Open Information and Secrets," *Studies in Intelligence*, 2005, www.cia.gov/csi/studies/Vol49no2/index.html; Patience Wait, "Intelligence Units Mine the Benefits of Public Sources: Open Source Center Draws, Analyzes Info from a Variety of Public Databases," *Government Computer News*, Mar. 20, 2006, www.gcn.com/print/25_6/40152-1.html; Bill Gertz, "CIA Mines 'Rich' Content from Blogs: Policy-makers Turn to Internet, Other Open Sources for Intelligence," *Washington Times*, Apr. 19, 2006, p A4 (reporting that "China built its first Yuan-class attack submarine at an underground factory that was unknown to U.S. intelligence until a photo of the submarine appeared on the Internet"). For an excellent discussion of the Open Source Center, see Robert K. Ackerman, "Intelligence Center Mines Open Sources," *SIGNAL Magazine*, Mar. 2006, www.afcea.org/signal/articles/templates/SIGNAL_Article_Template.asp?articleid=1102&zoneid=31.
4. But it must not be confused with the open source *software* movement.
5. See Gregory F. Treverton, *Reshaping National Intelligence for an Age of Information*, ch.1 (2003); and, for a good popular treatment, Malcolm Gladwell, "Open Secrets: Enron and the Perils of Full Disclosure," *New Yorker*, Jan. 8, 2007, p. 44.

The fact that information is not concealed does not mean we have it. We are woefully ignorant of the aims, attitudes, values, sensitivities, and personalities of our enemies, whether they are state enemies like Iran and North Korea, potential enemies like China and Russia, contending factions in Iraq, or foreign (or for that matter homegrown) terrorists. But our ignorance is not due primarily to efforts at concealment. Much of the information that we need in order to make good intelligence estimates is hiding in the open—which doesn't mean it isn't well hidden. Winnowing it from the billions of web (and conventional library or archive) pages of irrelevant material in which it is embedded is a formidable undertaking, specially since conventional search engines, such as Google, provide access to only about 20 percent of all web pages, creating a need for more advanced technologies to enable searches of the rest (the "deep web," as it is called).[6] But these technologies, in turn, increase the difficulty of winnowing; there is more to be winnowed the more comprehensive the search.

The open source movement thus complements Fingar's effort to expand the intelligence community's "analytic outreach" program—an effort to make better use of the enormous reservoir of knowledge bearing on intelligence issues that is found in universities, think tanks, the media, and other nongovernmental institutions.[7]

2. Open source intelligence offers a means of improving communication between federal and local authorities. Being with rare

6. See, for example, Marcus P. Zillman, "Deep Web Research 2007," LRRX.com, Dec. 17, 2006, www.llrx.com/features/deepweb2007.htm.

7. The complentarity of outreach and open source is explicit in Office of the Director of National Security, National Intelligence Analysis and Production Board, Subcommittee on Analytic Outreach, "A Strategy for Analytic Outreach: Seeking Expertise 'Wherever It Resides!'" (Office of the Director of National Intelligence, June 19, 2006)—an uncommonly lucid, straightforward program statement. Greater outreach, expanded use of open source materials, and better sharing of information among intelligence analysts across the intelligence community are three complementary goals of Fingar's effort to improve intelligence analysis.

exceptions unclassified (the exceptions are mainly for when disclosure would reveal a target, source, or method not believed to be known to our enemies—for the fact that something is in an open source doesn't mean that it's known to them), open source materials can be shared with local police and other local public-safety officers without their having to obtain security clearances.

3. It thus alleviates the problem of overclassification, an enormous problem, as we'll see shortly. The more intelligence data that can be obtained from open sources, the more that can be shared without need to dismantle the barriers to sharing that are created by classification.

4. Open source intelligence provides a benchmark for judging the value of intelligence obtained by conventional means (conventional in the intelligence community, that is), such as human and signals intelligence. If most of the intelligence data that our intelligence services need are in open sources, this suggests that we may be overinvested in clandestine data gathering—may be, not are, because the more securely protected the enemy's secrets and therefore the costlier it is to steal them, the more valuable they are likely to be, repaying the cost.

5. Open source is a reminder that intelligence failures are more often failures of understanding than failures of information. Pearl Harbor, Vietnam, and Iraq are all examples of this point. This insight is obscured by a preoccupation with digging information out of secretive adversaries and using it as the principal raw material for analysis. But the vastness of open source enforces an even more important lesson for intelligence analysis: there is too much information for it to be possible to base analysis on systematic sweepings of databases. Analysis must to a great extent be based on intuitions honed by long experience in specialized areas of knowledge, intuitions that enable the handful of tiny nuggets to be spotted amidst the dross.[8] Recog-

8. See, for example, Elbridge A. Colby, "A Lighter Burden: Taking Stock of Intelligence Reform" (Dec. 2006, forthcoming in *Policy Review*).

nition of this point—a point that was obscured during the Cold War, when priority was given to locating and counting our adversaries' weapons and forces—brings into focus the weakness of an intelligence system in which most analysts are young and inexperienced and in which rapid rotation, both in response to changes in policymakers' priorities and as a method of structuring an analyst's career, prevents analysts from obtaining deep knowledge of any area.

6. Open source is also a reminder of the need to be attentive to signals sent by our adversaries. By definition, signals are not secrets—they are deliberate, though oblique, implicit, and often enigmatic, efforts to communicate. Preoccupation with secrets can lead intelligence agencies to neglect signals by assuming erroneously that our adversaries are trying to conceal everything that is of interest to us.

7. Open source intelligence facilitates the recruitment, motivation, and retention of intelligence analysts. Remember that half the intelligence community's 18,000 analysts have been employed for fewer than five years. Most of them are quite young. The young are Internet addicts and proficient and habitual searchers of the web. By encouraging them to use the Internet in their work, the intelligence community can not only play to their strengths but also enable them to be collectors of intelligence as well as analysts. That is an efficient fusion, particularly if the ratio of open to clandestine intelligence data is indeed very high, as it clearly is in the case of political intelligence.

8. The open source movement brings the Internet into the heart of intelligence analysis, enabling novel forms of analysis, such as intelligence blogging. There are two models of intelligence analysis. One is the academic model, a variant of which is the standard model for intelligence analysts. In it the results of analysis are embodied in reports that are carefully vetted, in advance of publication or other circulation, by peers (in the case of academic research) or supervisors (in the case of intelligence analysis). The other model is the blogging (or blogging plus wiki) model, in which the analytical product is informal, collaborative, and dispersed. By enabling the pooling of knowl-

edge fragments scattered across a far-flung community of inquirers, blogging has proved a rapid-fire method of error correction. It should work for intelligence analysis—in fact, there are beginning to be analysts' blogs.[9] Intelligence blogging has the further virtue of preserving the diverse perspectives of the different agencies that make up the intelligence community, because blog postings are not filtered by an agency. Such diversity has its downside (see Chapter 5), but it is essential for maximizing the production of useful knowledge. And finally what I am calling the "academic" model is imperfectly approximated in a system in which review is by supervisors rather than peers, since supervisors may impose a biased organizational perspective on the analysts.

The open source movement is resisted by some intelligence officers who, heavily invested from a psychological as well as a career standpoint in clandestine data gathering, tend to think that the only information worth having is information that the adversary tries to hide.[10] They do not want to see their scope and influence curtailed by the web-powered rise of a competing mode of intelligence that might in time dominate the more traditional forms of intelligence— human intelligence (spies) and intelligence gathered by electronic surveillance, photography, and other technical means. It is bad enough that policymakers often rely on open source materials to by-

---

9. D. Calvin Andrus, "Toward a Complex Adaptive Intelligence Community: The Wiki and the Blog," *Studies in Intelligence*, Sept. 2005, p. 63; David E. Kaplan, "Wikis and Blogs, Oh My! Spooks Catch Up with the Internet Age," *U.S. News & World Report*, Nov. 6, 2006, p. 52; Clive Thompson, "Open-Source Spying," *New York Times*, Dec. 17, 2006, § 6 (magazine section), p. 54. Wikis are online sites in which visitors can add and edit content. *Wikipedia* is the best-known example. I suggest in Chapter 5 using analyst blogs to evaluate intelligence analysts.

10. See United States Congress, *Joint Inquiry into the Intelligence Activities before and after the Terrorist Attacks of September 11, 2001* 6 (2002); Rob Johnston, "Analytic Culture in the U.S. Intelligence Community: An Ethnographic Study" 24 (2005); Office of the Undersecretary of Defense for Intelligence and Warfighting Support, "Defense Open Source Council Assessment" 12 (May 2005); Wait, note 3 above.

pass the intelligence agencies. The government did not decide to invade Iraq on the basis of information obtained by intelligence, but rather used that information to convince skeptics of the soundness of a decision already reached on other grounds.

The resistance to open source intelligence is thus institutional as well as individual. Open source saps the intelligence community's ability to control the policymakers' access to information to prevent the community's function from shrinking to mere provision of information and analysis to bolster policymakers' preconceptions. Policymakers cannot do open source research as well as experts can, but they can do some, and to the extent that they become their own collectors as well as their own analysts the intelligence professionals are bypassed.

Because of internal resistance to open source intelligence, the jury is out on the success of the Open Source Center. A bad omen is that the center was created by renaming the CIA's Foreign Broadcast Intelligence Service and retaining its director as director of the center. FBIS was an open source unit, but devoted mainly to translation. The open source action has moved from broadcasting to the Internet. To build an Open Source Center on an archaic open source operation seems mistaken, even if it did save the few months that would have been required to create a brand-new center.

Open source intelligence has been designated a part of collection rather than of analysis, and so has been placed under the supervision of the deputy DNI for collection. I am concerned about separating collection from analysis in the open source world, where neither the recruitment, management, and protection of agents, nor the financing, deployment, and operation of pricy and supersophisticated technical facilities, are factors. Separating analysis and collection of data often is inefficient. If you want to know something, you'll usually prefer to go directly to the sources where the information resides—especially if you're a proficient researcher—rather than having to ask librarians or other custodians of the sources to do the searching for you. You may not even be able to formulate your request without some searching around, and in the process you are likely to learn things that will enable you to refine your search. Scholars collect their own data unless the data are found in compilations that the scholar cannot readily duplicate. Intelligence analysts should be able to collect from open sources most of the data they need, relying on operations officers for clandestine and technical data. An analyst who wants to look for information on the web should not have to ask the Open Source Center to do the looking for him.

The Office of the Director of National Intelligence is aware of this issue and so has withheld from the new center a monopoly of open source collection. Long before the center was created, every intelligence agency did some open source research, and this will continue and even accelerate. One problem has been that agencies tend to incorporate open source materials into reports that also contain classified materials; the entire reports are classified, and thus their open source components secreted. The Open Source Center hopes to receive copies of such open source materials before they are merged with classified materials and thus drop out of the open source world. As well as conducting its own open source research in response to standing requirements or ad hoc requests, the center has system-wide responsibilities: training open source officers in other parts of the CIA and in other intelligence agencies, monitoring the use of open source materials by intelligence analysts throughout the intelligence community, promoting the best open source practices, identifying new open sources, researching new search techniques, and buying and compiling open source databases for use by the community. System-wide activity of this character is the more difficult and less immediately rewarding duty of the new center, and it may therefore be slighted. One hopes that any slack will be picked up by the open source officers in the Office of the Director of National Intelligence, to whom the center reports and whose only concerns should be systemic ones. But the hope will be dashed if it's true that the senior open source official in the Office of the DNI has a staff of only two.[11]

This discussion brings to light an ambiguity in "Information Sharing Environment" and other responses to the need for better pooling of information within and across intelligence agencies. Information sharing can mean just that A gives B information in response to a request by B; yet the real imperative is for B to be able to reach into A's database and search for the information he wants. B may be denied access because the source's gatekeeper has decided that B lacks the "need to know" (or as it is mordantly called by intelligence insiders, "need to 'no'"), and so he may have to content himself with a morsel of information served to him by A. Ideally analysts should have unrestricted access to a digital library containing all the information in the world relevant to U.S. national security, though considerations of security make the ideal unattainable except insofar as it is a library of unclassified data.

The success of the Open Source Center is not yet assured. Our government is much better at ideas and plans and starts than at follow-through and completion and so actual improvement,[12] and most issues of structure are not being addressed by the Office of the DNI with a proper sense of urgency. Nevertheless I consider the center a

---

11. As claimed in Robert David Steele, "Foreign Liaison and Intelligence Reform: Still in Denial," 20 *International Journal of Intelligence and CounterIntelligence* 167, 168 (2007).

12. "Presidents need not be overly concerned about a paucity of good management ideas. Hundreds of them are available for someone with the will and the guts to implement them. Ideas are generated within the bureaucracy or by such external sources as the GAO [General Accounting Office, now the General Accountability Office], client groups, university scholars, and private think tanks. In fact, appraisal of the government's flaws and foibles is so extensive that it is becoming embarrassingly clear that what is lacking is not the ability to study or evaluate *but the ability to take corrective action.*" Charles F. Bingman, "The President as Manager of the Federal Government," in *Control of Federal Spending, Proceedings of the Academy of Political Science*, vol. 35, no. 4, pp. 146, 155 (1985) (emphasis added). That was said more than twenty years ago, but nothing has changed since.

tentative success, and also on the credit side of the ledger is the DNI's rumored success (the details are not public) in redirecting some of the nation's multibillion dollar spy-satellite programs. A Director of Central Intelligence could have done this but was unlikely to because of the difficulty of attending to his coordination responsibilities while burdened with managing the CIA.

Another fruit of the reorganization has been the creation of the National Clandestine Service within the CIA. This has given that beleaguered agency a needed shot in the arm. Designating the CIA as the lead agency for open source intelligence was a smaller shot in the arm because collection of intelligence data from open sources is less prestigious than human or signals intelligence. This may change, especially once it is realized how challenging a task it is to find the gold in the many billions of web pages.

Some critics of intelligence reform fear that in practice the National Clandestine Service will prove to be little more than a renaming of the CIA's Directorate of Operations. They reason that the head of the service occupies too low a rung on the national security ladder to exert much control over the human intelligence programs of other intelligence agencies, such as the Defense Intelligence Agency and the Federal Bureau of Investigation. General Hayden has reclaimed the title of "national HUMINT manager"[13] and means to make it an accurate description of the position. But how much he will be able to accomplish, given everything else on his platter and the resistance he's bound to encounter from the agencies (apart from his own) that conduct human intelligence, remains to be seen. It is difficult to exaggerate the intensity of turf warfare in the federal government. Hayden has his hands full without fighting battles with the Defense Department and the FBI that he is likely to lose. For in national

13. "HUMINT" means human intelligence.

security as in other areas of government, agencies fight fiercely and usually successfully to repel competitors.[14]

The creation of the National Clandestine Service, like the other reforms that I have mentioned, did not require a statutory reorganization of the intelligence community but merely an order by the President. But this does not make these reforms any less products of the reorganization. For as a practical matter the recommendation for, say, establishing a National Clandestine Service had to come from someone who could speak for the entire intelligence community. Had it come from the Central Intelligence Agency, it would almost certainly have been defeated by the opposition of the other agencies. (It may still be defeated at the implementation stage.) The designation of a particular agency to take the lead in some field of intelligence is the kind of coordination initiative for which stronger overall system management was required than the Director of Central Intelligence could provide. In contrast, the fact that the CIA has been adding operations officers, which it's been doing since before 9/11,[15] is not a development that can be attributed to the reorganization, because its effects are largely confined to a single agency. Similarly, another apparent success—the National Counterterrorism Center—would probably be as great a one, or even greater, had the center been retained in the CIA.

Also to be commended are the efforts of the very able associate DNI for science and technology, Eric Haseltine, to achieve better coordination of intelligence R & D. This is a further illustration that the most promising avenue of achievement for the Office of the Director of National Intelligence is that of systemic coordination, such as designating a lead agency for a particular intelligence function,

14. Amy B. Zegart, *Flawed by Design: The Evolution of the CIA, JCS, and NSC* (1999).
15. Mark Mazzetti, "C.I.A. Making Rapid Strides for Regrowth: Its Overseas Network Swells, Officials Say," *New York Times*, May 17, 2006, p. A1.

resolving a stubborn interagency conflict, and coordinating overlapping functions such as R & D.

I have been discussing the successes of the reorganized system but I must make clear that I am using the word "success" to denote effort rather than accomplishment. Real success is achieved when practices change. What I have been calling a "success" of the reorganized intelligence system is a good idea plus initial steps toward implementation. As opposition within the bureaucracy gathers and hardens, the steps may be halted before the goal is reached, and improvement may turn out to be slight. After all, the best idea in the Intelligence Reform Act was splitting responsibility for the overall management of the intelligence community from responsibility for running the CIA, yet in implementation the idea may amount to little if the Director of National Intelligence continues to find himself so immersed in substantive intelligence issues that he cannot adequately discharge his managerial responsibilities.

Along with the ambiguous successes of the intelligence reorganization have come unequivocal failures. Here are the principal ones known to me:

1. Porter Goss was retained as director of the CIA long after his unsuitability for the position had been demonstrated.

2. *Very* slow progress is being made (outside the analyst subcommunity) in improving information sharing among the intelligence agencies[16] and with other entities, especially local police, that need intelligence-related information.[17]

"Information sharing" may not be the most felicitous term for the

16. An elaborate plan has been published: Program Manager, Information Sharing Environment, Office of the Director of National Intelligence, *Information Sharing Environment Implementation Plan* (Nov. 2006). But in government, plans and fulfillment are entirely different things; the more elaborate the plan (this one runs to 186 pages), the less likely it is to be fulfilled.

17. See, for example, Elizabeth Williamson, "Group Attempting to Simplify Byzantine Terror-Alert System," *Washington Post*, Jan. 24, 2007, p. A21.

goal of enabling intelligence officers to gain access to information that they need in order to do their job but that may reside in the database of another agency. "Sharing" has a connotation of ownership: "I know it's your candy but you must learn to share it with your little brother." A better term would be "information pooling," although it is too late to substitute it; "information sharing" has achieved canonical status in intelligence discussions.

Nirvana would be for all intelligence data to be stored in a single database, or more realistically a series of connected databases, constituting a huge digital library freely searchable by all U.S. intelligence officers and many local and foreign ones as well. Nirvana is unattainable because of security concerns—concerns not only about the trustworthiness of persons who have access to the database but also about the security of the database itself against penetration by hackers, whether wise guys or enemy agents. Such a database would be like a ship without bulkheads. Yet much can be done to alleviate these concerns by the kind of data mining that credit-card and telephone companies do in order to protect their customers by detecting anomalous behavior in the customer's account. My cellphone service was once suspended by the phone company when it discovered that numerous calls to Egypt were being made from my phone number. From my previous pattern of usage, the company correctly inferred that I was not the person making those calls. If an intelligence analyst were discovered by use of techniques similar to those used by phone companies to be accessing databases that contained no data related to his work, this would be a signal to investigate the possibility of espionage before much damage was done.

Turf warfare looms as a stubborn obstacle to the pooling of intelligence data because information is treasure that is squandered by indiscriminate dissemination, which enables competitors to reap the benefit of it. Originators of intelligence data are therefore highly reluctant to share "their" data with others without obtaining compensation in some form, as by swapping for data held by others; such swaps are difficult to arrange. Classification, and the "need to know" principle that enables the originating agency to withhold classified information even from persons who have the requisite security clearances, establish a form of property rights in intelligence data. Property rights have salutary incentive effects, but the clumsy methods by which intelligence agencies enforce their informal property rights are counterproductive. So not only are the incentives to minimize classification weak; the incentives to maximize it are strong even when it is not being used to conceal embarrassing mistakes and feed the self-importance of government officials.

The information-sharing or information-pooling issue is actually a teeming nest of issues: criteria and standards for security clearances and security protocols (protections against penetration of databases and interception of communications), classification standards, encryption technology, security data mining (my Egypt example), software acquisition and maintenance, incentives to create and exchange intelligence information, and open source capability. To resolve these issues in a coherent way is an enormous challenge that underscores the mistake of having loaded the Director of National Intelligence and his staff with short-term crisis-response duties. It is not that these officials fail to appreciate the importance of creating the conditions of improved information sharing; it is that they're unable to give the task the attention it demands.

The departure of John Russack from his post as Program Manager for the Information Sharing Environment after one year was an embarrassing acknowledgment that indeed no progress had been made in the first year of the intelligence reorganization toward solving the problem of intelligence agencies' reluctance to share information with each other fully, expeditiously, and in readable digital form.[18] After a

18. Markle Foundation Task Force, *Mobilizing Information to Prevent Terrorism: Accelerating Development of a Trusted Information Sharing Environment: Third Report of the Markle Foundation Task Force* (July 2006); Karen DeYoung, "GAO Faults Agencies' Sharing of Terror Data," *Washington Post*, Apr. 19, 2006, p. A3. However,

year of treading water, the Information Sharing Environment project, rightly envisaged by Congress as essential to improving the performance of the intelligence community, had to start over from scratch.[19] An entire year was lost because the DNI's attention was elsewhere.

One must not underestimate the difficulty of the information-sharing project, however, including the difficulty of balancing the need for sharing with the need for security. It would not do to give the literally hundreds of thousands of persons who have top-secret clearances access to all classified databases. Security may require that classified databases be "unconnected" with each other and that mutual access be authorized by sharing agreements among the agencies that control the databases. Such agreements should be encouraged.

3. There has been essentially no progress in standardizing security clearances[20]—a project so fundamental to the sharing of intelli-

---

"the [Markle Foundation Task Force] report neglects a few recent innovations that are at least modestly consistent with its recommendations, such as [an executive order] that permits emergency disclosure of classified information to non-cleared persons, and [a DNI directive] that delegates disclosure authority for intelligence information beyond the originator." "Improved Info Sharing: The Path Forward," *Secrecy News*, July 14, 2006, www.fas.org/blog/secrecy/2006/07/.

19. The plan cited in note 16 above is the first major product of Russack's successor, Thomas McNamara. On the inadequacy of the intelligence community's computer technology, see my book *Uncertain Shield: The U.S. Intelligence System in the Throes of Reform*, ch. 6 (2006). On how that inadequacy interacts with our intelligence officers' insufficient linguistic competence to thwart our efforts to prevent terrorists from using the Internet for planning and propaganda, see Evan F. Kohlmann, "The Real Online Terrorist Threat," *Foreign Affairs*, Sept./Oct. 2006, p. 115.

20. "The government recognizes the problem and plans to harmonize the process [of obtaining security clearances] across the intelligence community, but Director of National Intelligence John D. Negroponte cannot say when that will happen, said spokesman John Callahan." Shankar Vedantam, "Polygraph Test Results Vary among Agencies: Discrepancies Affect Security Clearances," *Washington Post*, June 20, 2006, p. A1. The specific problem to which the spokesman was referring is the refusal of agencies to accept the results of polygraph ("lie detector") tests given by other agencies. There is no uniform protocol for administering such tests or interpreting the results, and they are rife with both false positives and false negatives. As a result of the lack of uniformity, a person can pass the polygraph test given by one

gence information that the same official should be in charge of both. The failure to share timely and comprehensive terrorism-related information with state and local authorities, particularly police, which I discuss in Chapter 6, is another casualty of the lack of standardization of security clearances and the related problem of overclassification.[21] Fear of penetration of the agencies by al Qaeda operatives, though it is a much smaller risk than the risk and indeed actuality of Soviet penetration of our government before and during the Cold War, retards progress toward flexible standards for classification and clearances.[22]

4. A related disappointment has been the lack of significant progress in hiring the needed number of intelligence officers with Middle Eastern and Central and South Asian linguistic capabilities. It is related because security concerns inhibit the hiring of many of the people who have those capabilities. Perhaps, then, rather than insist that all analysts know the language of the nation or ethnic community that they analyze—an impractical requirement in the monolingual American culture—our monolingual analysts should be paired with translators. Research on improving translation software should also be a priority, as progress to date has been frustratingly slow. Granted, translation whether human or machine is a distinctly second-best solution to the problem of Americans' lack of intimacy with the languages and cultures of the foreign societies that spawn and nurture

agency and receive a security clearance from that agency yet flunk the test given by another agency and so be refused a security clearance by that agency, thus blocking his access to information classified by it.

21. See U.S. House Committee on Homeland Security Democratic Staff, "Beyond Connecting the Dots: A VITAL Framework for Sharing Law Enforcement Intelligence Information" (Investigative Report Prepared for Congressman Bennie G. Thompson, 2005), www.fas.org/irp/congress/2005_rpt/vital.pdf.

22. See the acute analysis of this risk in Nigel West, "Challenges to the UK's Intelligence Services," *Journal of Homeland Security*, June 2006, pp. 4–5, www.homelandsecurity.org/newjournal/Articles/displayArticle2.asp?article=144. There is also a risk of penetration of our intelligence agencies by foreign nations, such as China.

(that in some cases are) enemies and potential enemies of the United States; nuance, which may be essential to interpretation, is often lost in translation. But best may be unattainable.

5. Little progress has been made in other areas in which greater standardization of the practices of different intelligence agencies, such as training and pay, may be needed. Military intelligence officers, for example, have a different pay scale from civilian ones. The issue is related to that of the optimal use of detailees, discussed below.

6. The public relations of the intelligence community remain abysmal. The Director of National Intelligence and his staff (except General Hayden, a gifted expositor, but now no longer in the Office of the DNI) have been ineffectual in explaining the needs, problems, and importance of national security intelligence and in allaying the fears of civil libertarians.

7. The intelligence community's relations with Congress have deteriorated. The community has lagged in proposing sensible amendments to the Foreign Intelligence Surveillance Act that would regularize the National Security Agency's programs of domestic electronic surveillance. It has either failed to assert itself in this regard or been rebuffed by the White House and the Justice Department. But failure with regard to Congress is a two-way street. Constructive congressional oversight of intelligence since 9/11 has been slight, though I cite several useful congressional studies at various points in this book.

8. Modernization of the intelligence community's computer software (including search and database software), which is greatly inferior to what is available in the private sector, and standardization of security protocols for classified databases (both closely related to point 2 above), are progressing very slowly.

9. Domestic intelligence remains deficient and uncoordinated—an area of grave weakness. The Director of National Intelligence has failed to exert effective control over the domestic intelligence activities of the Federal Bureau of Investigation, the Defense Department,

the Department of Homeland Security, and the other federal agencies engaged in domestic intelligence. He has also failed (see point 3 above) to achieve effective coordination of federal, state, local, and private intelligence and intelligence-related services. With respect to coordination with the nonfederal services (of which local police are the most important because of their vast number and their immense knowledge of the people and activities in local communities throughout the nation), the FBI and the Department of Homeland Security are at each other's throats and the Director of National Intelligence is a bystander.

All these failures are either due to or made worse by the basic design flaw that I identified in Chapter 3: the burdening of the Director of National Intelligence with substantive responsibilities that distract him, as they distracted his predecessors the Directors of Central Intelligence, from what should be his sole responsibility—the overall supervision of the intelligence community.

I want to elaborate on the topic of security, as it is central to several important issues: sharing intelligence data within and across intelligence agencies and with state and local authorities; obtaining language-qualified intelligence officers; and overclassification. Because different intelligence agencies have different criteria for granting security clearances, they are reluctant to share data even with cleared officers of other agencies that do not have (or are contended not to have) equally exacting requirements for a clearance.[23] This reluctance is a particular source of friction with local police, who encounter long delays in obtaining clearances without which they cannot conduct effective intelligence or counterterrorism because they are barred from access to critical information possessed by the FBI and other federal agencies.

Even if an agency accepts the security bona fides of an officer

23. See note 20 above.

from another agency, it is much more likely to provide specific material to him in answer to specific questions than to let him search the agency's database. Apart from the tendency of such a practice to inhibit effective search, which I discussed earlier in this chapter in connection with open source, it slows down the transfer of information. The ideal, as I have said, would be for all intelligence data to be digitized and placed in a single massive database accessible to all intelligence analysts on their computer terminals. The ideal is unattainable at the moment for technical, financial, and security reasons, but reform should be measured by the speed at which the distance is reduced between the ideal and the present, unsatisfactory reality.

The impediments to the granting of security clearances and of access to databases of other intelligence agencies would be an annoyance rather than a serious problem if only the most sensitive data were classified—mainly codes and other highly sensitive technical data, the names and other personal identifying information of spies, plans for specific intelligence operations, and information about our terrorist enemies that we have reason to believe they don't know we have. But because of rampant overclassification, useful data often are not shared even when it is technically feasible to do so and revealing the data to the public would do no harm. Until recently, for example, both the number of persons employed by the intelligence community and the community's total budget were classified. (The budget may still be classified, though it was inadvertently disclosed publicly by one of the deputy DNIs. But continued classification of information known to the public is a peculiarly futile bureaucratic tic.) Although an argument can be made that an enemy could reason from these data to an assessment of our intelligence capabilities and take measures to neutralize them, it would be an ingenious argument rather than a persuasive one. Our current enemies do not have the intelligence collection and analysis capabilities of our former main adversary, the Soviet Union, though we still have to worry about the purloining of our intelligence secrets by nations like China and Russia that though not enemies of the United States are rivals of us on the world stage. Classified information often turns out when declassified or leaked to have been a matter of common knowledge for years; the budget and the number of employees of the intelligence community were known with tolerable accuracy by the public long before they were disclosed by officials.

Overclassification tends to make intelligence officers and other public officials careless and cynical about classification. This is a chicken and egg problem. Because too much is classified, there are many leaks. The leaks create pressure for higher levels of classification, spawning a myriad of separate secret compartments of information to which few people have access.

The more classified knowledge an officer possesses, moreover, the harder it is for him to remember which things he knows that are classified and which that are not, and so he may leak properly classified knowledge inadvertently or conceal unclassified information unnecessarily; for much information that is unclassified is nevertheless unknown to the people who need it. Also, the more secrets one attempts to guard, the more difficult it is to protect all of them. The smaller the basket, the easier it is to watch over all the eggs in it.

The Bush Administration's ambitious program of reclassifying materials that had been declassified has largely been abandoned—indeed there has recently been a mass declassification of materials 25 years old or older.[24] But the problem of overclassification remains. It is further illustrated by the failure to place expiration dates on classifications. Classified materials are sensitive only for a finite time, usually *much* shorter than 25 years. Their classified status should therefore sunset automatically, or at least be reduced—for example from top secret to confidential, or to such subclassifications as "for official use only"—at a specified early date, to avoid clogging government records

24. See Scott Shane, "Secrets to Be Declassified under New Rule at Age 25," *New York Times*, Dec. 21, 2006, p. A36.

with needless amounts of classified material, unless a responsible official certifies the need for continued secrecy. Classification should require approval by senior officials, who should also have authority to declassify, while low-level officers should have authority to classify only in special circumstances.

Overclassification, I emphasize, is a problem not just of either-or (either classified or available to the public), but also of higher and lower. The higher the level of classification, the fewer people will have access, and so the government should be, but is not, scrupulous in reserving the higher levels for secrets whose revelation would do real harm to the country, rather than just cause transient embarrassment.

The role of the Soviet Union in our "classification creep" cannot be overstated. It was an avid and successful practitioner of large-scale espionage against the United States and our allies (notably Britain and West Germany), in part because it could recruit communists in the United States and other Western countries to spy for it. The Soviets penetrated the U.S. and West German governments to a quite high level and stole U.S. atomic secrets. A degree of security-mindedness bordering on paranoia was a natural response by our national security agencies.

The end of the Cold War did not end spying on the United States by foreign nations and so the need for vigorous counterintelligence. But our actual current enemies, as distinct from the merely potential ones, above all the Islamist terrorist groups, have a far more limited ability to penetrate our government than foreign governments do. Our security precautions should discriminate among our enemies, not assume that all are as formidable at espionage as the Soviet Union was. Overclassification, which reduces the effective conduct of intelligence, is less excusable in the current setting than it was during the Cold War.

A culture of overclassification inhibits dissent, because the dissenter doesn't know whether he has access to all the information he needs to make an informed judgment. A military officer engaged in planning the Iraq invasion who was skeptical that Iraq had weapons of mass destruction swallowed his doubts after hearing Colin Powell's United Nations speech; "I figured that people above me had information I didn't have access to."[25] By inhibiting dissent, moreover, overclassification feeds the delusions of omniscience that come naturally to senior officials of the world's greatest power since the Roman Empire reached its zenith. A related effect of overclassification is to enable officials to wave off criticism from outside government on the ground that the outsiders, not being privy to state secrets, cannot possibly be informed critics. Yet in retrospect we know, for example, that outsider critics of the Vietnam War had a better grasp of the essential facts than the insiders, who had truckloads of secret information.

Overclassification enables agencies to bury their mistakes, feeds mistrust and suspicion of government, exacerbates turf warfare by enabling agencies to conceal their encroachments and hog-tie their bureaucratic adversaries, limits the number of informed participants (even informed insiders, such as the military officer whom I quoted) in debates over national security, encumbers the transmission of information within the national security community, as by requiring intelligence officers to work in "SCIFs" (Sensitive Compartmented Information Facilities) when handling highly classified data (mainly from electronic interceptions), encourages leaks that precipitate distracting hunts for the leaker that often just draw attention to the leaked material, gives insiders an illusion of superior insight, keeps "first responders" in the dark,[26] and can deprive the nation as a whole of information that it needs for its protection.

25. Quoted in Thomas E. Ricks, *Fiasco: The American Military Adventure in Iraq* 92 (2006).
26. A factor in the failure to anticipate the Pearl Harbor attack. See Richard A. Posner, *Preventing Surprise Attacks: Intelligence Reform in the Wake of 9/11* 76 (2005).

This last point is illustrated by a National Intelligence Estimate issued in 1995 and classified "Secret" that presciently described the "new terrorist phenomenon" of Islamic extremists bent on attacking the United States and noted that "several targets are especially at risk: national symbols such as the White House and the Capitol, and symbols of U.S. capitalism such as Wall Street." "We assess," the NIE stated, "that civil aviation will figure prominently among possible terrorist targets in the United States" and that terrorists are likely to "identify serious vulnerabilities in the security system for domestic flights."[27] This was not a prediction of the 9/11 attacks, but had it been publicly released it might have stimulated a fruitful national conversation on the need for better airport and airline security. The estimate may have contained some genuine secrets that should have been classified, but there was no reason to classify the portions that I have quoted.

Another harmful consequence of overclassification in the struggle against Islamist terrorism arises from the fact that journalists, academics, and businessmen have in the aggregate greater knowledge of the Arab and Muslim world than intelligence officers do. Often they have better access to it as well because they are *not* intelligence officers—that is, not U.S. government employees and not part of the U.S. national security apparatus. They may be able to work and travel in the Arab and Muslim world with greater ease and even greater safety than most of our national security professionals can. But for the intelligence agencies to be able to exploit their knowledge and access—to be able to brief and debrief them effectively and include them in brainstorming sessions with intelligence officers, in accordance with the analytic-outreach program—the agencies have to be able to share information with them; and that may be difficult to do because so much that intelligence officers know is classified. Security

27. Quoted in Steve Coll, *Ghost Wars: The Secret History of the CIA, Afghanistan, and bin Laden, from the Soviet Invasion to September 10, 2001* 279 (2d ed. 2005).

clearances for these travelers are not the answer. These people don't want to be burdened with national security secrets or identified too closely with the intelligence community. Yet without access to classified information they may not know what to look for on their trips.

This impediment to making some of our most knowledgeable citizens fully a part of our intelligence network is a neglected aspect of the general problem of inadequate pooling of information of intelligence value, a problem that overclassification aggravates. We might even consider outsourcing some intelligence functions. But intelligence officers' lack of needed language skills and cultural sensitivity cannot be fully offset by using private individuals as the intelligence agencies' eyes and ears any more than it can be fully offset by hiring translators. The intelligence community needs many more officers than it has who are fully acculturated to the foreign countries, and domestic ethnic and religious communities, that are its priority concerns. It cannot obtain such officers without relaxing the standards for granting security clearances and—a separate but possibly an equally serious problem—without reducing the rate at which officers are rotated among different foreign assignments and FBI special agents are rotated between intelligence and criminal investigation. The less material that is classified, and hence the less access to classified material intelligence officers require (the fewer compartments of secret information they need to be able to enter), the more the standards for granting security clearances can be relaxed without compromising security unduly.

But this will not happen as long as security officers are allowed to exercise a practical veto over the hiring of intelligence officers.[28] Since such officers are less likely to get credit for taking a chance on a risky applicant who proves to be an excellent intelligence officer than to be blamed if he turns out to be disloyal or indiscreet, the

28. Joshua Rovner and Austin Long, "The Perils of Shallow Theory: Intelligence Reform and the 9/11 Commission," 18 *International Journal of Intelligence and CounterIntelligence* 609, 628–629 (2005).

standards for hiring and clearing applicants are set too high (though in part this is simply the inertial force of practices adopted in the Cold War). As a result, it is very difficult for anyone who maintains contact with relatives in a country that harbors terrorists to become an intelligence officer, even though the people with such contacts are apt to have the linguistic capabilities and cultural insights that the intelligence community desperately needs.[29] There is no out-and-out rule against hiring such people. But the reluctance to do so, as expressed for example in stretching out the clearance process beyond its already protracted normal limits, discourages most applicants.

Another way to state this concern is that the security process is excessively front-loaded. Enormous efforts are made to avoid hiring someone who might turn traitor. But rare indeed is the applicant for employment in an intelligence agency who is *planning* to become a traitor. He becomes a traitor later because of disappointments, resentments, temptations, money problems, and so forth that could not have been foreseen when he was hired. It is important to keep a close watch on people entrusted with the nation's secrets. But it is fanciful for security officers to think they can screen out at the initial hiring stage anyone who might need watching after he has been on the job for five or ten or twenty years and has perhaps become a very different person from the fledgling he was when hired.

My earlier suggestion for using data mining to monitor intelligence officers' searches of classified databases illustrates the possibility of shifting the emphasis in security from initial screening and access control to closer monitoring of intelligence officers' behavior. That would enable the agencies to hire more people who have the linguistic and cultural knowledge that the agencies need.

It might be better if security officers made no decisions or even recommendations about the hiring of applicants but merely forwarded

29. Arthur S. Hulnick, "U.S. Intelligence Reform: Problems and Prospects," 19 *International Journal of Intelligence and CounterIntelligence* 302, 310 (2006).

the applicant's investigative file to the chief of the unit to which he had applied, who would decide whether to hire him, trading off the risk against possible gains.

Just as "information sharing" would benefit from a name change to "information pooling," so "security officer" would benefit from a name change to "risk manager." My objection to the word "security" is its connotation of either-or. You are either secure or insecure, and you certainly don't want to be the latter. Unlike "security," "risk" is a matter of more or less, because it is understood that some risk is bearable and that to try to reduce it to zero would often impose costs that exceeded the benefits. No sane person refuses to leave his house for fear of being run down on the sidewalk by a careening taxicab. But security officers are ingenious in thinking up improbable risk scenarios and devising costly means of eliminating them.

The risk of unauthorized disclosure of a government secret is analytically no different from that of losing a job that you took because it paid more than the alternatives, even though you knew that the higher pay was compensation for the risk that you'd lose the job. The goal should be not that secrets are never revealed but that protecting secrecy is carried just to the point at which the cost of protection equals the benefits, and no further. Not that moles, such as Aldrich Ames and Robert Hanssen, haven't done great harm. Nor is it a good argument against security measures that Ames and Hanssen passed their lie-detector tests: if they had not, they wouldn't have been employed (by the CIA and the FBI respectively) and so could not have become moles. (This is an example of the invisibility of intelligence—in this case counterintelligence—successes: we do not know how many security breaches there would be without careful prehire screening for security risks.) The proper question to ask is whether a small reduction in the probability of security breaches is worth the direct and indirect costs incurred to obtain such a reduction.

Other important personnel issues are not receiving the attention they deserve either. One is the heavy use of contractors in place of employees. Intelligence officers leave the intelligence community at a high rate, as I have noted, because of lucrative opportunities in the private sector. But later some of them are hired on short-term contracts to work for their former (or some other) intelligence agency in order to fill the gap in senior officers left by the rapid expansion of the intelligence community. These contractors are not only expensive; they are birds of passage and sometimes have subtle or not so subtle conflicts of interest. The Office of the Director of National Intelligence is aware of the problem,[30] but is not addressing it with any sense of urgency.

A related personnel issue is the overuse of detailees. Early in his short tenure as Program Manager of the Information Sharing Environment, Captain Russack testified before the Senate Judiciary Committee that his staff would be composed mainly of detailees from other agencies rather than permanent employees of the DNI.[31] I was surprised, thinking detailees a temporary expedient. It would be a mistake for the DNI to make them a major part of his staff after it reaches its equilibrium size, though that appears to have been Negroponte's intention. This is an area (there are others) in which the seductive analogy of the Goldwater-Nichols reorganization of the

30. See Karen DeYoung and Walter Pincus, "Intelligence Plan Targets Training, Keeping Personnel," *Washington Post*, Oct. 19, 2006, p. A18. The intelligence plan to which the authors refer is Office of the Director of National Intelligence, "The US Intelligence Community's Five Year Strategic Human Capital Plan: An Annex to the US National Intelligence Strategy" (June 22, 2006). This glossy pamphlet sets forth laudable goals for better management of the intelligence community's human resources but is vague and aspirational and sets no deadlines for achieving its goals. On the general problem of excessive use of contractors by the Bush Administration, see Scott Shane and Ron Nixon, "In Washington, Contractors Take on Biggest Role Ever: Questions of Propriety and Accountability as Outside Workers Flood Agencies," *New York Times*, Feb. 4, 2007, § 1, p. 1.

31. "Panel II of a Hearing of the Senate Judiciary Committee: Oversight of the Federal Bureau of Investigation," *Federal News Service*, July 27, 2005.

armed forces should be resisted. Officers detailed to the staff of the Joint Chiefs of Staff are moving *within* the Defense Department and thus within the chain of command, and if they do not do their joint work well it will hurt their careers. The parallel in the private sector is the rotation of executives among the different divisions of a corporation. But when the Central Intelligence Agency details an officer to the Office of the Director of National Intelligence, his performance there will not affect his career at the CIA directly, because the Director of National Intelligence is not the ultimate employer of CIA officers; the CIA is. And knowing this, the DNI and his permanent staff may be reluctant to repose full confidence in their detailees, other than senior officers handpicked by the DNI.

What's more, agencies tend to detail their losers—unless they want to make a good impression on the agency to which the detailees are being lent, notably the White House—because of the mysterious reluctance of government agencies to fire underperforming employees even when the employees have no legal or contractual job security. It is not *so* mysterious, however, given the environment that politics and the media create for government personnel actions. The fired employee is likely to turn on his former agency, and his beefs will be propagated by the media and by the agency's political enemies. Even the discredited Michael Brown scored points off the White House and the Department of Homeland Security after he was fired as head of the Federal Emergency Management Agency in the wake of the Katrina debacle and sought to shift the blame to others' shoulders. Hell hath no fury like an official scorned. Prudence suggests that rather than fire an underperforming employee, the agency detail him elsewhere, or find, as they say in government, a "parking space" for him—a job in which, like a parked car, he can do no harm.

Mention of the Cold War and of Goldwater-Nichols is a reminder of the baleful effects of institutional inertia—a form of what economists call "path dependence"—in government. Where you start is likely to determine where you end up even if you would have ended up in a better place had you started somewhere else. A near-paranoid security system made sense in the Cold War but has persisted into an era in which it no longer does, while the successful reorganization of the armed forces provides an irresistible template for reorganizing what is in fact a radically different component of national security. And because ours is a legalistic culture that disvalues spying, we persist in assigning intelligence functions to a law enforcement agency (the FBI) that is not competent to perform them. Nations such as the United Kingdom that have a long history of coping with serious terrorist threats have evolved institutions better suited to dealing with them than ours are, but we have great difficulty moving laterally, as it were, from the path we are on to a better path. The analogy to evolution is precise: evolution will not replace a fish's eye with a bird's eye even if the bird's eye would give the fish better vision, because fish and birds are on different evolutionary paths, which do not intersect.

The bumps on the road toward a better intelligence system would be tolerable if we had a good handle on the terrorist menace, but we don't. We still have no good idea of the capabilities or plans of our terrorist enemies.[32] We may even be victims of our successes. Before being hit hard by the United States after 9/11, al Qaeda was more or less a single entity, though a loose-knit one. Now, as we have learned from the London transit bombings of July 2005, the Toronto bomb plot foiled in June 2006, and the Heathrow plot foiled in August 2006, Islamist terrorism has metastasized at the same time that al Qaeda itself, the original malignancy, retains some unknown fraction of its original lethality. As it fissions, the terrorist challenge ac-

32. "As was the unhappy case before September 11, the FBI still does not understand the scope of al-Qaeda's presence within the United States, does not know whether there really are 'sleeper cells' at large in the land or what terrorist groups really intend to accomplish in the United States." John MacGaffin, "Clandestine Human Intelligence: Spies, Counterspies, and Covert Action," in *Transforming U.S. Intelligence* 79, 91–92 (Jennifer E. Sims and Burton Gerber eds. 2005).

tually becomes more difficult to defeat. And this at a time when a steady drain of experienced intelligence officers to the private sector may, along with the turmoil created by the reorganization, have weakened the intelligence community. The effect of the talent drain may be temporary, however. The expectation of great private-sector jobs for intelligence officers should attract more applicants for the public-sector jobs that provide training and other preparation for the private-sector ones. But it will be many years before this effect fully offsets the talent drain.

Am I being too impatient in expecting more in the way of measurable progress so soon after a reorganization? Is it not naïve to complain that relatively little has been accomplished when the reorganization has been up and running for less than two years? We impatient ones are reminded from time to time that the reorganization of the armed forces inaugurated by the National Security Act of 1947 was not complete until 1986, with the passage of the Goldwater-Nichols Act—in fact, not until years later, for there were serious interservice coordination problems as late as the 1991 war with Iraq. But can we really wait 38 or 44 years to achieve an optimal organization of intelligence? Can we wait even four years (the age of the still-struggling Department of Homeland Security)? And if our government is so constipated that it takes decades to carry out an ambitious government reorganization, isn't that a compelling argument against attempting such reorganizations?

The continuing struggles of the Department of Homeland Security, still floundering despite the determined efforts of its able chief (though like Negroponte, Secretary of Homeland Security Michael Chertoff had no previous experience managing a large enterprise, so that of both these excellent men it is possible to ask whether they met the "right person for the right job" benchmark in Chapter 2) and some excellent deputies, reinforce my doubts about ambitious reorganizations.[33] That Congress has not yet tried to consolidate the intelligence agencies into a single department, on the model of the Department of Homeland Security, is only a small comfort. The principal result thus far of the creation of the Department of Homeland Security has been the layering of a new bureaucracy over 22 agencies with a total of 184,000 employees. Will the main result of the intelligence reorganization turn out to be the layering of a new bureaucracy over 16 or more agencies with a total of 100,000 employees? But this is to exaggerate, since the Director of National Intelligence has very limited control over the intelligence agencies in the Defense Department, which overshadow the rest of the intelligence community. Moreover, one of the problems with the Department of Homeland Security is that its central command staff is *too* thin.[34]

Some central control is needed in intelligence just as it is in border control and infrastructure protection. But increasing the number of levels in a hierarchy can have serious untoward consequences. These include delay, loss, and distortion of the information that travels, as most information does, from the bottom of the hierarchy to the top management level, as well as delay in the transmission of commands, and misunderstanding of them, as they are relayed from the top down after management has made decisions based on the information it received. In other words, there is "control loss."[35] Other bad consequences of a taller governmental hierarchy are internal fights for the attention of senior management (rival agencies now report to the same boss, and they fight each other for his favor); demoralization of the personnel of agencies demoted as a result of

33. See Clark Kent Ervin, *Open Target: Where America Is Vulnerable to Attack* (2006).

34. Stephen E. Flynn, "The Department of Homeland Security: The Way Ahead after a Rocky Start" (atatement before U.S. Senate Comm. on Homeland Security and Governmental Affairs, Jan. 26, 2005), www.cfr.org/publication/7643/department_of_homeland_security.html.

35. Albert Breton, "Bureaucracy," in *The New Palgrave Dictionary of Economics and the Law* 185, 186 (Peter Newman ed. 1998).

the insertion of a new layer of command between them and the President; and underspecialization because the new top echelon can't be expected to be expert in all the diverse missions of the agencies under its command. The last point is one of the lessons of the Hurricane Katrina fiasco. Folding the Federal Emergency Management Agency into the Department of Homeland Security caused to be inserted between the head of the agency and the White House a new official (the Secretary of Homeland Security) who, because of the breadth of his responsibilities, naturally was not an expert in emergency management. The result was avoidable delay and confusion in responding to the New Orleans emergency. Similar dangers loom for a top-heavy intelligence system. The first Director of National Intelligence happened not to be an intelligence professional, but he was cast in that role.

A sunnier view of the performance of the Office of the Director of National Intelligence than I have presented in this chapter emerges from a long article in U.S. News & World Report[36]—until one reads between the lines. The authors explain that they were "granted extraordinary access to nearly two dozen of the most senior intelligence officials in the government, including Negroponte and the chiefs of the CIA, military intelligence, and the National Counterterrorism Center."[37] Officials grant "extraordinary" access to journalists when they want to get their story across to the public (which senior intelligence officials are belatedly trying to do because there has been so much criticism of the intelligence reorganization and its implementation) in more credible form than their own press releases; and journalists have a natural reluctance to bite too hard the hand that feeds them. The successes of the Director of National Intelligence that the authors trumpet are for the most part modest or, in their own word,

36. David E. Kaplan and Kevin Whitelaw, "Playing Defense," *U.S. News & World Report*, Nov. 13, 2006, p. 44.
37. Id. at 46.

"nascent,"[38] and some are nonexistent. For example, the "first-ever communitywide security badge,"[39] an innovation that the authors attribute to the DNI, in fact predates the Intelligence Reform Act and gives the holder access only to buildings, not to the databases in them.[40] The creation of the National Counterterrorism Center, which the authors also attribute to the DNI, likewise predated the act. Other heralded successes unconnected to the reorganization, though they occurred after it, are the replacement of Porter Goss by Michael Hayden and decisions made by Hayden since taking over the CIA.

The authors acknowledge that "the DNI's effort to transform the nation's sprawling intelligence community is still in its early days"[41] and indeed that "to date, most of the nascent reform efforts don't seem to have penetrated deeply into the intelligence agencies' rank and file, where many remain skeptical about the DNI's chances for success."[42] They note that "because it's tough to do background checks on people who have family in Damascus or Tehran, security officers have found it easier to just screen them out."[43]

To summarize, progress to date in implementing the intelligence reorganization decreed by Congress has been modest, though conceivably the replacing of Negroponte may herald a new dawn. Regarding the weakest link in our intelligence system—domestic intelligence, and in particular the FBI's performance of the domestic intelligence function—progress has been glacial. To that issue I turn next.

---

38. Id. at 47.
39. Id. at 46.
40. Later in the article they acknowledge that "security clearances . . . are regulated by individual [intelligence agencies]." Id. at 52.
41. Id. at 46.
42. Id. at 47.
43. Id. at 50.

5

The Three-Cultures Problem

The word "culture" as I use it in this book refers to the behaviors, beliefs, conventions, habits, membership criteria, and tacit understandings that create homogeneity in a social group and set it apart from other social groups. So *organizational* cultures are the behaviors, etc., that set organizations apart from one another—that in the business world, for example, impart a very different "feel" to different firms even when they're in the same industry. Cultures are the uncodified rules of a group and are thus much like customs. And being, like customs, not only uncodified but also decentralized, embedded, and habitual, they resist change. Business mergers often founder on the incompatible organizational cultures of the merged and merging firms, and mergers of government agencies can founder for the same reason. The Department of Homeland Security is the prime current example. But the Office of the Director of National Intelligence may go the same way. Each agency in the intelligence "community" (a word aspirational rather than descriptive) is a little world unto itself. Coordinating, let alone directing, the aggregation of these agencies is made especially difficult by the collision of three distinct, stubborn, and incompatible organizational cultures that are poorly balanced against one another. They are the military culture, the culture of civilian intelligence (mainly the Central Intelligence Agency), and the culture of criminal investigation (mainly the Federal Bureau of Investigation). I discuss their distinctness first, their stubbornness second, and their imbalance third.

No one will deny that the military has a distinctive culture. That distinctiveness is attributable to an up-or-out promotion system that generates intense internal competition, to the emphasis placed on discipline, rank, physical fitness, meticulous attention to detail, and the giving and taking of crisp orders that are expected to be obeyed, and to a strong mission orientation to which intelligence is subordinated. The military views a competing civilian agency such as the CIA, which has none of these attributes, with a degree of hostility and disdain that the agency reciprocates. Aggravating factors are that the military and the CIA are competitors in strategic intelligence and in paramilitary operations (as in Afghanistan, Iraq, and Somalia), and that being at once the customer and the owner of the national intelligence agencies the military has no great wish to share with the agency its spy satellites and other surveillance facilities.

The FBI has a distinctive culture too—unfortunately, one inimical to the conduct of national security intelligence. (This is true to a lesser degree of the military as well—lesser because the national intelligence agencies, although owned by the Defense Department, have a technical rather than a conventional military culture.) The bureau's traditional and still dominant conception of intelligence is of information that can be used to obtain a criminal conviction. A crime is committed, having a definite time and place and usually witnesses and often physical evidence and even suspects, and the crime can usually be placed in a pigeonhole familiar to criminal investigators (it's a bank robbery, a Ponzi scheme, a food-stamp fraud, etc.). These circumstances enable a criminal investigation to be tightly focused and create a high probability that the information gathered in the investigation will lead to an arrest and a successful prosecution. They thus give the FBI a well-defined, readily achievable mission.

National security intelligence, especially counterterrorist intelligence, is different. The aim is to *prevent* the crime, not wait for it to occur and use it as the jumping-off point for an investigation. The key to prevention is detection in advance. That requires casting a very wide investigative net, chasing down ambiguous clues, assembling tiny bits of information—and often failing to detect the impending attack because there is as yet no crime, no definite time and place from which to start the investigation, no witnesses, no physical evidence.[1]

And when a terrorist plot *is* discovered, prosecution is not necessarily the best response. (This is a major theme of Chapter 7.) "In intelligence work, a trial is often a symptom of failure—failure to turn the uncovering of an agent against the enemy or to manipulate the

1. The contrast between criminal law enforcement and national security intelligence has been well explained by a former director of Canada's domestic intelligence service, the Canadian Security Intelligence Service: "Law enforcement is generally reactive; it essentially takes place after the commission of a distinct criminal offence. Police officers are results-oriented, in the sense that they seek prosecution of wrongdoers. They work on a 'closed' system of limits defined by the Criminal Code, other statutes and the courts. Within that framework, they often tend to operate in a highly decentralized mode. Police construct a chain of evidence that is gathered and used to support criminal convictions in trials where witnesses are legally obligated to testify. Trials are public events that receive considerable publicity. Security intelligence work is, by contrast, preventive and information-oriented. At its best, it occurs before violent events occur, in order to equip police and other authorities to deal with them. Information is gathered from people who are not compelled by law to divulge it. Intelligence officers have a much less clearly defined role, which works best in a highly centralized management structure. They are interested in the linkages and associations of people who may never commit a criminal act—people who consort with others who may be a direct threat to the interests of the state." Ward Elcock, "John Tait Memorial Lecture," CASIS [Canadian Association for Security and Intelligence Studies] Conference, Oct. 16–18, 2003, www.csis.scrs.gc.ca/en/newsroom/speeches/speech17102003.asp.

information going to a hostile group."[2] From an intelligence stand-point, arrest and prosecution should be postponed until the terrorist network has been fully traced and its methods, affiliates, financiers, suppliers, and camp followers identified. Even then it may be more effective, because more discreet, to disable the network by sowing suspicion among its members, as by revealing to them who has been talking to the government, than to risk revealing in a public trial the intelligence techniques used to detect the terrorist ring and the knowledge gained through their use.

When a preventive strategy is employed, moreover, much of what is prevented is possible or incipient or intended criminal activity, rather than a prosecutable crime. This deprives the FBI agent, ori-ented toward arresting and prosecuting criminals, of a satisfactory sense of closure to an investigation.

Intelligence officers manipulate the nation's enemies; criminal in-vestigators lock them up. These are different animals. FBI agents are like dogs and CIA officers like cats. The pointer, the retriever, the hound has a definite target and goes for it in a disciplined fashion, loyally obeying its master's directions. The cat is furtive, independent, slinks about in the dark, waits patiently, pounces unexpectedly, and often toys with its victim (plays "cat and mouse") before killing it.[3] "The FBI is a law enforcement organization, the critics said: cops who are good at capturing suspects *after* a crime has been committed,

2. K. G. Robertson, "Intelligence, Terrorism and Civil Liberties," in *Contem-porary Research on Terrorism* 549, 557 (Paul Wilkinson and Alasdair M. Stewart eds. 1987).

3. After writing the above, I discovered the following passage in Ron Suskind, *The One Percent Doctrine: Deep inside America's Pursuit of Its Enemies since 9/11* 92 (2006): "The animosity and distrust between FBI and CIA has a long and impressive history—bespeaking differences, members of both agencies often quip, as great as between cats and dogs. Even in this analogy, both see what they want or need to see. FBI's riff: we're tough and earnest, loyal and true to task, while the CIA is fussy and feline, double-dealing and unreliable. Then there's CIA's counter: we're shrewd, intuitive, and sharp-clawed—moving alone, often quietly, but getting the job done—while the FBI is filled with dumb animals, built to fetch."

but with little aptitude for the tedious work of intelligence gathering and *preventing* a crime by a highly sophisticated foreign terrorist group. Agents were in love with their guns and badges and racking up arrests—which, since the FBI's beginning in 1908, was the way they got ahead in the organization. 'Door kickers,' as one 40-year CIA officer put it when asked what major attribute FBI agents brought to the job."[4]

The CIA is at a disadvantage in this competition. Americans think more highly of dogs than of cats, worship guns (the cult of the gun is big at the FBI), and—to sound the theme of Chapter 7—turn instinctively to law to protect their rights, including the communal rights enforced by the criminal justice system.

The FBI does have a long history of national security intelligence, notably directed against German spies and saboteurs in World War II and Soviet spies and other communist agents afterwards. But hunting down the agents of foreign powers known to be hostile to the United States (classic counterintelligence) is a more focused endeavor—more like criminal investigation—than hunting for the elusive members and supporters of an amorphous terrorist network, or hunting for unknown lunatics with apocalyptic goals and access to weapons of mass destruction (imagine a biological or radiological Unabomber[5]) but who, like terrorists in sleeper cells, haven't struck yet

---

4. Jeff Stein, "FBI under the Gun," *CQ Weekly*, May 1, 2006, p. 1152 (emphasis in original). Because of the rivalry between the CIA and the FBI, the criticisms of the latter by CIA officers must be taken with a grain of salt. But the criticisms have been corroborated by neutral observers. For a case study of the FBI's ineptitude in recruiting agents in the U.S. Muslim community, see Peter Waldman, "Hard Sell— A Muslim's Choice: Turn U.S. Informant or Risk Losing Visa: Moroccan Immigrant Lands in Trouble at the Border: A Walk with Agent Fliflet," *Wall Street Journal*, July 11, 2006, p. A1. The FBI agent seems not to have realized that recruiting an undercover agent from the ethnic community in which the undercover agent will be working is a delicate courtship rather than a one-night stand.

5. A biological Unabomber may well be a greater danger than a biological attack by a terrorist group. See Christian Enemark, "Biological Attacks and the Non-State Actor: A Threat Assessment," 21 *Intelligence and National Security* 911, 926–927 (2006).

and must be stopped before they do. Classic counterintelligence, though it involves most of the same tactics used in counterterrorist intelligence, is somewhat more focused, more manageable, than attempting to detect terrorist plots by forging cooperative relationships with leaders of U.S. Muslim communities, by conducting protracted surveillance, by chasing down rumors and leads that usually lead nowhere, and if necessary by disrupting nascent plots by such constitutional—if sometimes unsavory, because "manipulative"—means as bribery, blackmail, provocation, and disinformation: means that are clandestine and so provide no occasions for public commendation of the government officers who employ them.

Because it engages in disruption as well as detection, a domestic intelligence agency[6] such as the Canadian Security Intelligence Service or MI5 is better called a security service—in fact, MI5's official title is the "Security Service"—than just an intelligence agency. It not only collects and analyzes intelligence data; it attempts to eliminate, though by methods other than those of criminal investigation and prosecution—instead, by methods traditionally associated with intelligence agencies—the terrorist dangers it uncovers. That is not congenial work for most FBI special agents, even, or perhaps especially, when it takes rather gentle forms, suggestive of "community policing."[7] Even traditional counterintelligence is less attractive to most special agents than conventional criminal investigations (most consider it a backwater) because it rarely results in an arrest. In fairness, however, most is not all; the bureau is trying to recruit from among applicants who would derive greater career satisfaction from pursuing

6. Recall from the Introduction the defining characteristics of such an agency. (1) It is an intelligence agency; it has no arrest or other law enforcement powers. (2) Its sole concern is with threats to national security. And (3) to be within the agency's jurisdiction the threatening activity must occur in the homeland rather than overseas.

7. See, for example, Christopher Mason, "World Briefing Americas: Canada: Agents Asked Terror Suspects' Parents for Help," *New York Times*, June 16, 2006, p. A12. Compare Karen DeYoung, "Distrust Hinders FBI in Outreach to Muslims: Effort Aimed at Homegrown Terrorism," *Washington Post*, Feb. 8, 2007, p. A1.

spies and terrorists, however frustrating the pursuit, than investigating ordinary federal crimes.

The highly publicized arrests and indictments in June 2006 of seven Muslims (most of them Americans) in Miami on suspicion of plotting to blow up buildings there along with the Sears Tower in Chicago illustrate the tenacity of the FBI's culture of criminal investigation.[8] The bureau was able to plant an informant in the group, and the members asked him to supply them with money, uniforms, machine guns, explosives, and other materials. He gave them a video camera to case possible targets, and some boots; but "by May [2006], the indictment suggests, the plan had largely petered out because of organizational problems."[9] The FBI appears to have pounced as soon as it had enough evidence of the defendants' involvement in a criminal conspiracy to be able to prosecute them. This was premature from an intelligence standpoint, possibly even from a prosecutorial one.[10] Because the group had no money or backers (except the FBI's informant!), no skills or experience, had organizational problems, and had been penetrated, it was not an imminent threat; so there was no urgency about arresting its members. The group had wanted to get in touch with foreign terrorists but had been unable to do so. The informant might have helped them do so—might even have helped them become part of a serious terrorist network, enabling the bureau

8. Peter Whoriskey and Dan Eggen, "Terror Suspects Had No Explosives and Few Contacts: Sears Tower Plan Never Finished, Authorities Say," *Washington Post*, June 24, 2006, p. A3.

9. Id.

10. See Walter Pincus, "FBI Role in Terror Probe Questioned: Lawyers Point to Fine Line between Sting and Entrapment," *Washington Post*, Sept. 2, 2006, p. A1. Yet the FBI's public affairs officer describes the plot of the Miami 7 as one of five principal terrorist plots thwarted by the bureau in the year ending in September 2006. John Miller, "Law Enforcement, American Style: Remodeling the F.B.I. on Britain's MI5 Won't Work," *New York Times*, Sept. 14, 2006, p. A27. Although Miller says that the FBI is "transforming itself into an intelligence-driven organization," the title of his piece—"Law Enforcement, American Style"—conveys a more accurate sense of the bureau's approach to counterterrorism.

to ascertain the network's scope and membership, methods and tradecraft, even goals and specific plans. The opportunity to exploit the penetration in this fashion was lost by the arrests—about which the Attorney General boasted to an extent that, given the ineptness of the defendants, evoked ridicule.[11]

A senior Justice Department official said: "We can't afford to wait . . . [The suspects in Miami] were of significant concern, and we're not going to allow them to run into somebody who has the means to carry out what they were talking about."[12] That is the wrong attitude, quite apart from the exaggeration in saying that the suspects were "of significant concern"; they were evil-intentioned, but, for the time being anyway, harmless. Finding a "somebody who has the means" to carry out a terrorist attack, as the Miami 7 did not, is more important than prosecuting, as soon as enough evidence to sustain a prosecution has been obtained, plotters who pose no immediate threat to the nation's security. The undiscovered "somebody" is the real threat.

11. Richard Cohen, "Terror Alert: Severe Risk of Hype," *Washington Post*, June 27, 2005, p. A21. An earlier example of premature arrest and prosecution was that of the "Lackawanna 6," who had attended al Qaeda training camps in Afghanistan before 9/11 (thus providing material support for terrorism) but apparently had decided not to join the jihad. Marc Sageman, *Understanding Terror Networks* 68, 152 (2004). See also Richard A. Posner, *Uncertain Shield: The U.S. Intelligence System in the Throes of Reform* 97 (2006). But it seems the Justice Department and FBI were not responsible for the decision to arrest the suspects so soon. Responsibility rested rather with the CIA, which hyped the threat posed by the suspects, and with the Bush Administration's "one percent doctrine." See Matthew Purdy and Lowell Bergman, "Where the Trial Led: Between Evidence and Suspicion; Unclear Danger: Inside the Lackawanna Terror Case," *New York Times*, Oct. 12, 2003, § 1, p. 1; and text at note 27 in Chapter 1 of this book. What was particularly unfortunate about the premature arrest of the Lackawanna 6 was that because "recruitment of agents in place is a difficult task because of the strong emotional bonds among members of the jihad, making them reluctant to betray their friends and their faith . . . , the best avenue for penetration lies in recruitment from the pool of those who went through the training but decided not to join the jihad." Sageman, above, at 180. "The aggressive policy of prosecuting [the Lackawanna 6] without exploring ways to use them to penetrate the jihad was a mishandled opportunity." Id. at 181.

12. Christopher Drew and Eric Lichtblau, "Two Views of Terror Suspects: Die-Hards or Dupes," *New York Times*, July 1, 2006, pp. A1, A10.

Having penetrated the group, the FBI was in a position to manipulate it to the end of discovering, or even creating, links to persons capable of mounting terrorist attacks without the bureau's assistance. Now the group may have been in such disarray that it was not worth cultivation, but if so what did the Justice Department mean by saying that its members were of "significant concern"?

Small fry are easily caught, but upon their arrest any big shots who might have a connection with them scatter. The arrests and prosecutions serve mainly to alert terrorists to the bureau's methods and targets, as well as to bolster its arrest statistics and provide fodder for its public affairs office.

Risk aversion, an abiding characteristic of bureaucracy,[13] plays a big role in the FBI's early-arrest policy. Early arrests assure that members of the group won't escape the bureau's grasp and commit terrorist attacks. Minuscule as that risk may be in a case such as that of the Miami 7, should it materialize—delay in making arrests enabling an attack to succeed—the bureau would find itself unable as a practical matter to defend itself in the court of public opinion. A refusal to take a small risk may create a much greater one—the proper approach is to compare the expected benefits of pouncing with the expected benefits of waiting. But try explaining that to a public distrustful of government and incapable of thinking in probabilities.[14]

The FBI's risk aversion is likely to result in even earlier termination of terrorist stings than of organized-crime stings. When the bureau penetrates a drug gang, it has no compunctions about allowing the gang members to continue selling drugs while agents gather evidence against as many members as possible. No one seems to worry

13. See, for example, Murray J. Horn, *The Political Economy of Public Administration: Institutional Choice in the Public Sector* 122 (1995).

14. See Chapter 1. But in fairness to the bureau, the refusal to take such risks in conducting domestic intelligence operations emanates from the highest level of the Bush Administration level, Suskind, note 3 above, at 158–159; Purdy and Bergman, note 11 above, though being congenial to the bureau's culture it is not resisted.

that by doing this the bureau is allowing illegal activity to continue during a protracted investigation. But if a terrorist act, however minor, were committed because the FBI had failed to pounce at the first opportunity—it had a suspect on a long tether, and the tether broke— there would be an avalanche of adverse publicity that the bureau is not prepared to face.

In my quarter century as a judge, I have been struck by the fact that the drug dealers convicted as a result of stings conducted by the FBI or the Drug Enforcement Administration invariably are clumsy amateurs who failed to take sophisticated precautions against being caught and were in fact caught by unsophisticated means. Meanwhile the drug trade flourishes. The pattern may be repeating itself in counterterrorism—the bureau is able to apprehend only the inept plotters, leaving the others to do their mischief. Not that the inept cannot do great damage. But as they are less likely to do so than sophisticated plotters are, it is an urgent question whether the FBI is up to thwarting sophisticated terrorists. It is unclear whether the bureau has since 9/11 apprehended any terrorist plotter who was capable of bringing off a successful attack. The clearest example of such a terrorist, the "shoe bomber" Richard Reid, was apprehended by the passengers and crew of the airliner that he tried to blow up, not by the FBI. The bureau may lack the patience, the skills, and the orientation that it would need to catch the most dangerous terrorists, although an alternative hypothesis is that there haven't been any such terrorists in the United States since 9/11.

A further illustration of the premature-arrest syndrome is the apprehension in the summer of 2006 of suspects in a plot to attack tunnels in New York City.[15] Secretary of Homeland Security Chertoff, a former chief of the Justice Department's criminal division who accepts the Justice Department-FBI approach to fighting terrorism,

15. Al Baker and William K. Rashbaum, "3 Held Overseas in Plan to Bomb Hudson Tunnels," *New York Times*, July 8, 2006, pp. A1, A23.

was quoted as saying that "we do not wait until the fuse is lit; we swoop in as early as possible," even though "there was never a concern that this [plot] would actually be executed," and even though five of the plotters were still at large and knew they were being pursued. Another official described the plot as "still in the speculative stage." The next stage would have been an effort by the plotters to acquire explosives and visas and to reconnoiter the target. Had the bureau not jumped the gun but instead permitted the plotters to get to that next stage (of course under surveillance), it might have learned more about terrorist methods and American vulnerabilities. In particular it might have learned the identity of persons from whom terrorists can obtain explosives and other weaponry. Since "there was never a concern that this [plot] would actually be executed," the arrests were unquestionably premature.

A foreigner sometimes can see things more clearly than a native because he brings a fresh perspective. That is my reaction to the following passage in the book by Efraim Halevy (the former director of Mossad) from which I quoted in Chapter 3. About the 9/11 attacks he says:

> The principal failure that allowed such a terrible event to occur was the absence of a security service whose prime and only mission should be the prevention of terrorist or other subversive activities inside the United States. Law enforcement, which has been the prime task of the FBI since its inception, does not go hand in hand with security. Quite the contrary. Whereas the FBI agent is trained from the very outset to believe that the end product of his activities is the amassing of sufficient admissible evidence in court to secure an indictment and a guilty verdict, the security agent is first and foremost trained to prevent an act from being committed, to reveal the environment and support systems that make an act possible or probable, and to gather sufficient evidence—sufficient intelligence—to enable the political level to obtain a clear picture of the menaces and what they entail for the individual. Nowhere in the world, except in the United States, are the two functions com-

bined—as long as there is no security service in the United States, there shall remain a yawning gap in the defense of that great nation. There can be no substitute for a security service, entirely independent and separate from the FBI. That could well be one of the reasons for the success of any future attack on American territory.[16]

Will we finally heed this warning, in the wake of the thwarting of the 2006 Heathrow plot? For that plot underscored the *indispensability* of good counterterrorist intelligence. A defense against terrorists as against other enemies of the nation must be multilayered to have a reasonable chance of being effective. One of the outer defenses is intelligence, designed to detect plots in advance of an attack so that they can be broken up before any harm to the nation is done. One of the inner defenses is preventing an attack at the last minute, as by airport screening for weapons. It would have failed in the Heathrow episode because the equipment for scanning carry-on luggage cannot detect liquid explosives. The liquid-bomb threat had been recognized since 1995, when a similar al Qaeda plot, that one against American airliners flying over the Pacific Ocean, was serendipitously foiled.[17] But nothing had been done to counter the threat. Fortunately, the outer defense succeeded in the Heathrow case, as it had in 1995. It succeeded mainly because of MI5[18]— so now at last there is dawning recognition that our own intelligence system, despite its multiplicity of agencies, may indeed have a gap.[19] Had the British authorities proceeded in the manner of the FBI, they would not have continued their investigation for as long as they did, and so might not have been able to roll up 25 plotters. Most of them might still be at large and the exact nature of and danger posed by the plot might not

16. Efraim Halevy, *Man in the Shadows: Inside the Middle East Crisis with a Man Who Led the Mossad* 260–261 (2006).

17. The "Bojinka plot." See Sageman, note 11 above, at 164.

18. "Salute the Spooks," *Economist*, Aug. 19, 2006, p. 23.

19. Philip Shenon and Neil A. Lewis, "Tracing Terror Plots, British Watch, Then Pounce: Experts See Different Tactics in U.S., Which Moves in Quickly," *New York Times*, Aug. 13, 2006, § 1, p. 1.

have been discovered. In fact the British wanted to wait even longer to pounce but were pressured by U.S. and Pakistani authorities to move when they did.[20]

A neglected point is that the FBI's early-arrest policy is unlikely even to produce satisfactory *prosecutions* of terrorists. For the earlier they are arrested, the less convincing will be the evidence that their plotting was more than wild talk, and so the more likely will their ethnic or religious community be to credit their claims of innocence, as happened after the Heathrow plot was exposed. The early-arrest policy, a policy facilitated by the criminalization of the earliest stages in terrorist plotting, under such rubrics as "material support" for terrorism, also fosters complacency about the gravity of the terrorist threat to the nation. When the bureau brags about having caught the Miami 7—terrorists apprehended in the larval stage—the public's reaction is that if those bunglers are the worst we have to fear, we're safe. Yet they may be, to change the metaphor, just the tip of the iceberg. In fairness to the bureau, it is pushed by Congress and the media to show results from its efforts to transform itself into an effective intelligence agency. It is difficult for it to show results other than by pointing to arrests, because other intelligence successes are either classified or simply not demonstrable.

It has been said that the British could wait until the last minute because they can detain suspects for up to 28 days and we can do so for only 48 hours.[21] That is not a correct statement of U.S. law.

---

20. Ismail Khan and Carlotta Gall, "Pakistani Official Says al Qaeda Leader Was Plot's Mastermind," *New York Times*, Aug. 16, 2006, p. A11; Salman Masood, "Judge in Pakistan Dismisses Charges in Reported Plane-Bomb Plot," *New York Times*, Dec. 14, 2005, p. A13. The latter article notes "powerful strains between American and British investigators over the timing of a crackdown on suspects in which British authorities rounded up 25 people."

21. See, for example, Shenon and Lewis, note 19 above, at 4. Why that should affect the timing of an arrest is a little obscure. But if more information can be obtained by a longer detention, a more exact assessment of the risk posed by allowing the plotting to continue may be possible.

Normally, it is true, an arrested person is entitled to a probable-cause hearing within 48 hours. But the rule can be waived in extraordinary circumstances.[22] The government may have a compelling justification, entitling it to invoke the exception, for holding a terrorist suspect incommunicado for longer than 48 hours. That may be the only way to avoid tipping off his accomplices that the government has him and is extracting from him information that it can use to foil the plot and round up the other plotters before their suspicions are aroused. It may also offer the only chance for "turning" him, so that he becomes a double agent, spying on his erstwhile accomplices. Recruiting a double agent tends to be a protracted affair and one that for obvious reasons must be conducted in secret. Holding a terrorist suspect incommunicado also facilitates interrogation without crossing the line that separates lawful interrogation tactics from unlawful ones. A detainee who is isolated, with no access to a lawyer, can more easily be persuaded to disclose information sought by the government than if he is jailed in the usual way.

An incident shortly after the warrantless electronic surveillance program conducted by the National Security Agency was revealed in December 2005 casts further light on the FBI's culture problem. I am referring to leaks by FBI agents expressing skepticism about the program's value.[23] They complained to reporters that the clues that the National Security Agency had given the bureau to follow up had led nowhere. The complaints are symptomatic of the bureau's continued domination by the culture of criminal investigation, despite Robert Mueller's and Philip Mudd's efforts to change that culture.[24]

22. "Where an arrested individual does not receive a probable cause determination within 48 hours . . . the burden shifts to the government to demonstrate the existence of a bona fide emergency or other extraordinary circumstance." County of Riverside v. McLaughlin, 500 U.S. 44, 57 (1991).

23. Lowell Bergman et al., "Spy Agency Data after Sept. 11 Led F.B.I. to Dead Ends," *New York Times*, Jan. 17, 2006, p. A1.

24. Mueller is of course the Director of the FBI. Mudd is an exceptionally able CIA officer—a veteran analyst and former deputy director of the Agency's Counter-

The laser-beam-focused investigation with a high expectation of success that is possible when a crime has been committed is impossible in intelligence activities aimed at preventing surprise attacks because, by definition of "prevention," no attack has occurred and often no plans have been uncovered or plotters identified. Warning intelligence is searching for a needle in a haystack. FBI agents don't like being asked to follow up clues gleaned from the National Security Agency's interceptions because the vast majority of them turn out to lead nowhere, at least so far as opportunities for making arrests are concerned. The FBI participates in about 13,000 prosecutions a year; the average number of terrorist prosecutions (not all of which the FBI participates in) has been only 85 a year since 9/11.[25]

That the opportunities for prosecuting terrorist suspects are meager would not matter from the standpoint of the individual FBI agent if only a few of the agents were assigned to terrorist investigations, but instead many are (though the number is classified). Yet despite that, all the Bureau's intelligence operations officers are trained as conventional FBI special agents and thus imbued with the culture of criminal investigation. If then assigned to intelligence duties, they are asked to adopt a new and incompatible culture. Most of their training, oriented as it is to criminal investigation, will have been wasted. Of the 701.5 hours of instruction that special-agent recruits undergo at the FBI Academy in Quantico, Virginia, 114.5 are devoted to firearms

---

terrorism Center—hired by Mueller in August 2005 to be the deputy chief of the National Security Branch. However, there are three levels of command above Mudd (see Chapter 6), and he lacks direct command authority over FBI special agents assigned to intelligence work. On resistance to Mudd within the bureau, see Scott Shane and Lowell Bergman, "F.B.I. Struggling to Reinvent Itself to Fight Terror," *New York Times*, Oct. 10, 2006, p. A1. The article reports that Mudd is "mocked privately [by some FBI officers] as Rasputin."

25. See Eric Lichtblau, "Study Finds Sharp Drop in the Number of Terrorism Cases Prosecuted," *New York Times*, Sept. 4, 2006, p. A9. On the meager yields from the use of criminal law in counterterrorism, see the further discussion in Chapter 7.

training,[26] 78 to arrest techniques and self-defense, 36 to forensics (scientific evidence, such as fingerprint and DNA evidence), and, until recently, only 37 (but that has now been doubled) to counter-terrorism training, including a few hours of lectures on Islam. Great emphasis is placed in the training program not only on skill in the use of guns but also on achieving and maintaining a high level of physical fitness.[27]

What could be more perverse than training new employees for one kind of work and then assigning them to another for which they have not been trained? The fact that a few special agents are now taking the CIA's training course for operations officers underscores the bureau's inability or unwillingness to tailor its training to the distinctive character of domestic intelligence.

A further impediment to making a career in intelligence attractive to FBI agents is that in the bureau culture the brass ring is being made a special agent in charge of a field office. An agent who specialized in intelligence would be unlikely to obtain the breadth of experience in criminal investigations that is a prerequisite to such an appointment. It is true that no longer will an agent be promoted into a management-level position without having served a tour or tours in the National Security Branch. But that is both a recipe for under-specialization and a denial that intelligence is a full-time career rather than an extension of police work.

Perhaps then it might help if the National Security Branch were physically removed from the field offices and the FBI's Washington

26. The usual number of hours of firearms training in a police academy is 50.

27. Sari Horwitz, "Old-School Academy in Post-9/11 World: New Focus Is on Terrorism, But Training Is Struggling to Keep Up," *Washington Post*, Aug. 17, 2006, p. A1. One official was quoted as calling antiterrorism and intelligence training at Quantico "a work in progress." Five years after 9/11! Horwitz's article describes the computer system on which recruits train at Quantico as "obsolete" but says that the bureau plans "to build a multimillion-dollar state-of-the-art intelligence center at Quantico equipped with secure classrooms and classified computers. But it won't be ready for eight years."

headquarters and given its own set of offices. That would create the impression and maybe the reality of a separate career path, one that does not culminate in becoming a special agent in charge of an FBI field office.

A telling deficiency in the bureau's skill set for national security intelligence is the absence of Arabic speakers. "Five years after Arab terrorists attacked the United States, only 33 FBI agents have even a limited proficiency in Arabic, and none of them work in the sections of the bureau that coordinate investigations of international terrorism, according to new FBI statistics."[28] The bureau has hired translators; but communicating with native Arabic speakers through a translator is an unsatisfactory alternative to being able to talk to them in their own language; and without competence in the language it is difficult to understand the culture. It is true that the vast majority of Arab-Americans are fluent in English, but some are more comfortable speaking Arabic and more approachable by an Arab speaker; some are visitors or other recent arrivals who may speak little or no English; and some may use Arabic to avoid detection or receive instructions from terrorist leaders abroad.

In defense of its refusal to create a separate training and career track for intelligence operations officers, the Bureau argues that such officers must be able to communicate with criminal investigators and that real (that is, CIA-like) operational officers are too rough to conduct intelligence operations in the United States. These arguments share a common assumption: that domestically, as distinct from overseas, the only counterterrorist tool the government has at its disposal is arrest followed by prosecution (or sometimes by deportation proceedings); so domestic intelligence has to be ancillary to criminal investigation. That is a comfortable assumption for an agency dominated by criminal investigators to make and it chimes in with Amer-

28. Dan Eggen, "FBI Agents Still Lacking Arabic Skills: 33 of 12,000 Have Some Proficiency," *Washington Post*, Oct. 11, 2006, p. A1.

icans' legalistic attitudes, but it is false. (Another mistaken belief is that only a criminal investigator can communicate with another criminal investigator.) Almost the only method of disrupting a terrorist organization that is foreclosed to a domestic intelligence agency is the use of physical force. Threats, blackmail, bribes, disinformation, and, of course, surveillance—the rest of the bag of CIA tricks—remain available to intelligence officers operating domestically.

The reason "covert action" has a bad name in some quarters is less because of the tactics sometimes employed than because the goal in some instances is to subvert governments with which we are not at war. In fact, such tactics are used extensively by FBI agents in conducting stings against organized crime. But there the goal is eventual arrests, something it should not be in many, maybe most, terrorist investigations.

All this is not to deny that a keen sense of relevance and probative value—a sense honed by the collection of evidence for use in a criminal prosecution—is important to intelligence work, and intelligence officers can learn in this respect from the FBI.[29] But that doesn't mean they have to *be* FBI special agents. Moreover, there is a general tendency to exaggerate the significance of complementarities as a factor favoring a merger or other combination of different agencies or firms. A cautionary example is the Department of Homeland Security. It's easy to tell a story about how its agencies are engaged in complementary tasks—the Border Patrol, the Coast Guard, the customs and immigration agencies are all, for example, concerned with keeping out unwanted visitors to the United States, and it "makes sense" that if they are under one organizational roof this will enable gaps and overlaps to be eliminated. But in practice things usually don't

---

29. I must correct an erroneous statement in Posner, note 11 above, at 129. I said that Judge Silberman (cochairman of the Commission on the Intelligence Capabilities of the United States Regarding Weapons of Mass Destruction) believes that intelligence officers need to know the legal rules of evidence. That is not his view; his view is the same as I have indicated in the text.

work that way, because the agencies perceive their relation to each other as competitive, and only grudgingly cooperative, and because organizational cultures are stubbornly resistant to change. This is true even in business, where competitive pressures are acute, but it is truer still in nonbusiness sectors, such as government, where there is no financial bottom line to provide a crisp performance measure. No one wants to be pried out of his accustomed groove, and the powers of passive resistance of middle management in government are formidable.[30]

Changing the FBI's culture from one of criminal investigation to one of criminal investigation plus national security intelligence is an especially frustrating endeavor for a reason illuminated by the government's inability to alter the organizational culture of the armed forces during the Vietnam War. Many people inside as well as outside government knew that the culture was poorly suited to the conditions of that war.[31] But our military was optimized to meet a concurrent threat rightly considered more grave, that of a conventional war in Europe. It did not want to compromise its ability to meet that threat by making changes designed to enable it to fight better on a secondary front.

The FBI faces a similar dilemma. Its primary focus is and will remain the investigation of nonterrorist federal crimes, a vital national

---

30. For an excellent discussion of civil servants' passive resistance to their nominal masters, see Ronald N. Johnson and Gary D. Libecap, *The Federal Civil Service System and the Problem of Bureaucracy: The Economics and Politics of Institutional Change* 166–169 (1994). The authors point out that people hold "intense preferences" concerning the role of government in controversial areas and that "professionals seeking employment with the government are often attracted to a particular agency because of its stated mission," and that once ensconced in the agency they may become powerful defenders against efforts to change the mission. Id. at 167–168. These observations are applicable to the FBI.

31. R. W. Komer, *Bureaucracy Does Its Thing: Institutional Constraints on U.S.-GVN Performance in Vietnam* (R-967-ARPA, Aug. 1972); John A. Nagl, *Learning to Eat Soup with a Knife: Counterinsurgency Lessons from Malaya and Vietnam* (paperback ed. 2005).

need that has shaped its organization, incentive structure, and culture. It resists blurring that focus by transforming itself into an intelligence agency. Just as crime-fighters do not make the best intelligence officers, intelligence officers don't make the best crime-fighters. The bureau doesn't want to compromise its main mission by switching emphasis to one that it regards as secondary—understandably, since we know there's a great deal of ordinary federal crime but do not know the magnitude of the terrorist threat inside the United States—and, to a degree, incompatible with the effective performance of the main mission. Already there is concern that the reallocation of resources from conventional crime to terrorism is impairing the bureau's ability to solve bank robberies and other staple offenses within its jurisdiction.[32]

The cultural difference between criminal investigation and national security intelligence is related to the difficulty of developing good performance measures for intelligence work. In the simplest economic model of labor, a model approximated in many business firms, the contribution an employee makes to the employer's bottom line is calculated and the employee paid accordingly; he works hard to maximize his contribution and thus his wage. Some government employers are able to use objective measures of employee performance despite the absence of a profit bottom line. The FBI, when it is conducting criminal investigations rather than intelligence operations, provides a good example: arrests weighted by convictions weighted by the severity of the sentence imposed are an objective measure of the performance of an FBI special agent. Military performance also lends itself to objective or at least quasi-objective verification measures. Intelligence work that cannot be directly related to a mission, whether the mission culminates in an arrest or in a military operation, is much more difficult to evaluate.

32. See Dan Eggen, "Violent Crime Is Up for 2nd Straight Year: Big Cities Showed Largest Increase," *Washington Post*, Dec. 19, 2006, p. A1.

Organizations with well-defined missions tend to be hierarchically organized. They have "tell" rather than "sell" cultures: superiors, thoroughly versed in the mission, tell their subordinates what to do rather than engaging in give-and-take with them as to what should be done. The FBI is a tell culture, the CIA a sell culture. Hierarchical organization works well when objectives and means are well understood, as in the production and distribution of a commodity product. It works badly when the "product" is knowledge acquired under conditions of uncertainty; only by setting out on multiple paths can there be a reasonable hope of finding the one that leads to discovery. That is true of foreign intelligence, the domain of the CIA, but it is equally true of domestic intelligence.

An urgent intelligence project to which the FBI is poorly adapted because of its emphasis on arrests and prosecutions is to determine whether there are any Islamist terrorist cells in the United States (nobody knows), and, if there are, to penetrate them. The urgency is underscored by the terrorist plot in Toronto that was broken up in June 2006, a plot hatched by citizens and other legal residents of Canada. We already knew from the London transit bombings of July 2005, and earlier from Richard Reid's unsuccessful attempt to blow up an airliner, that a Western nation's citizens could be recruited for terrorism, including suicide attacks. But we were reassured by the fact that England, like other European countries, has a large, poorly integrated, partly radicalized Muslim minority, surely unlike the Muslim minorities in Canada or the United States. We have to rethink this comfortable assumption, as our intelligence officials are at last beginning to do.[33] Canada has 600,000 Muslims, most of whom, like

33. See, for example, DeYoung, note 7 above; Lara Jakes Jordan, "New Mission for Law Enforcement Groups: Looking Homeward for Terrorists," *Chicago Daily Law Bulletin*, Aug. 30, 2006, p. 1. "El Fadl, a professor of Islamic law at the University of California, Los Angeles, and an outspoken Muslim moderate, has noted 'a sense of increased alienation and sadness,' among Muslim Americans he knows. The war in Iraq, the heightened scrutiny from domestic law enforcement and intelligence officials, most recently the Bush administration's staunch support for Israel during

most other Canadians, live close to Canada's largely unguarded 4,000-mile border with the United States. Even before the Toronto plot, there had been a serious attempt to mount a terrorist attack on the United States from Canada—Ahmed Ressam's millennium plot to blow up the Los Angeles Airport, a plot foiled by an alert U.S. customs agent at the U.S. border.[34] Britain has some 1.6 million Muslims, and in the wake of the Heathrow plot we now realize that the extremists among them want to attack the United States as well as their own country. The United States has two to three million Muslims. Almost all are loyal, and even among those who hate our government and way of life only a tiny minority would ever turn terrorist. (Some Muslim Americans *have* become terrorists, but they have not mounted attacks inside the United States—yet.[35]) But that tiny minority of a minority could do immense damage—against which our best protection is domestic intelligence.

The danger to America from homegrown Islamist terrorism is given stylized expression in the adjacent diagram. Two distributions of Muslim attitudes are shown. The smaller one, at the bottom, represents Canadian Muslims; the larger one, American Muslims. The area under each curve indicates the size of each group. The left-hand tail of each distribution is occupied by the most moderate members of the group, the right-hand tail by the most extreme. Notice that the

---

the fighting in Lebanon, all have put a strain on their sense that they can be both Muslims and patriotic Americans . . . El Fadl says he hears from imams and the directors of Islamic centers that young Muslim men, in small but significant numbers, have started meeting in secret outside of mosques (places the FBI and police departments have started paying closer attention to) to discuss religion and politics. It's a 'marginal trend,' he says, but a real one nonetheless. A few groups, he says, even go to remote campsites to participate in military training regimens that they've devised." Drake Bennett, "Hearts and Minds," *Boston Globe*, Aug. 20, 2006, www.boston.com/news/globe/ideas/articles/2006/08/20/hearts_and_minds/.

34. See Sageman, note 11 above, at 99–103. The hub of the millennium plot, moreover, was a Canadian citizen, Fateh Kamel. Id. at 139.

35. See, for example, Raffi Khatchadourian, "Azzam the American: The Making of an Al Qaeda Homegrown," *New Yorker*, Jan. 22, 2007, p. 50.

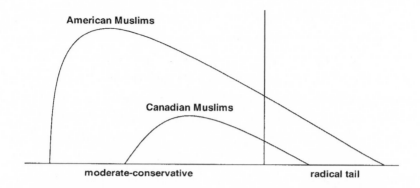

typical member of each group, represented by the highest point on each curve, is more moderate (farther to the left in the diagram) in the case of American Muslims than in the case of Canadian Muslims. But because there are many more American Muslims, their extremist tail (the area under the higher curve to the right of the vertical line) is larger than the Canadian Muslim extremist tail even though the American Muslim community as a whole is more moderate.

And we must not ignore the possibility of future radicalization. "Given the impressive cyber-infrastructure in Europe and in the United States, it is not hard to imagine that al-Qaeda—which is no longer a coherent organization but more of a movement—could radicalize large numbers of disaffected and socially alienated young Muslims and then mobilize them to support suicide terrorism by disseminating its ideas over the Internet to target groups living on either side of the Atlantic."[36] We cannot assume that American Muslim youth is wholly immune from what the Australian counterterrorist expert David Kilcullen believes drives Islamist terrorists—"a sense of adven-

36. Anne Speckhard, "Understanding Suicide Terrorism: Countering Human Bombs and Their Senders," in *Fighting Terrorism in the Liberal State: An Integrated Model of Research, Intelligence and International Law* 158, 171 (Samuel Peleg and Wilhelm Kempf eds. 2006). She may not be correct, however, that al Qaeda is no longer a coherent organization. See Peter Bergen's article, cited in Chapter 1, note 22.

ture, wanting to be part of the moment, wanting to be in the big movement of history that's happening now."[37] The fact that American Muslims tend to be prosperous and well educated is no inoculation against terrorism. For just as there is no psychological profile of an Islamist terrorist, so there is no negative correlation between being a terrorist and being middle or upper class and well educated.[38]

Suppose the FBI could be induced to assign hundreds of its agents to search for domestic terrorist cells, and two years later the agents reported back that they'd searched and found none. How would their contribution to national security be measured? How would their supervisors know whether two years were too many or too few? Maybe the agents had been premature in reporting that there were no terrorist cells; maybe their search hadn't been thorough enough. These uncertainties have disturbing implications for the question who will seek an intelligence career inside the FBI rather than a career as an FBI criminal investigator. An employee who has a choice between a job in which performance is evaluated by objective measures and one that cannot be, and who knows he's a good worker, will prefer the former because a good worker will do well on objective performance measures but may not do well on subjective ones, where favoritism and other factors unrelated to quality of performance will have more room to operate. So the best FBI agents are likely to shun the intelligence track within the bureau. This is a separate problem from that of suboptimization—the impossibility of finding people who are the best at two very different kinds of job—and from the inefficiency of training a new employee for one job and then assigning him to another, for which he has not been trained.

Performance measures for intelligence officers can be made more objective. Gross quantitative measures, such as the number of reports written by an analyst or the number of agents recruited by an oper-

37. Quoted in George Packer, "Knowing the Enemy: Can Social Scientists Redefine the 'War on Terror'?" New Yorker, Dec. 18, 2006, pp. 60, 62.
38. On both points, see Sageman, note 11 above, at 69–98.

ations officer, can be refined by tracing the use made by analysts (other analysts, in the case of analytic reports) and policymakers of the information contained in the reports or supplied by the agents. Here the academic research model may be useful; influence, as proxied for example by number of citations in reputable journals, is a standard method of evaluating academic research[39] and could be adapted to the evaluation of intelligence analysts. Thomas Fingar, the deputy DNI for analysis whom we met in previous chapters, is a former professor well qualified to engineer such an adaptation.

Organizational changes can be evaluated by comparing the number of accurate predictions before and after the change. And remember the discussion of blogs in Chapter 4? Suppose intelligence analysts adopted a blog model rather than an academic model of analysis, and every analyst had his own blog, accessible by all the other analysts. Then analysts could be evaluated by the number of hits to, and comments posted on, their blogs and by the number of other analyst blogs that linked to them. That would be an objective measure of influence within the analyst community, comparable to evaluating competing firms by counting their customers.

But quantitative measures for evaluating the performance of intelligence officers are bound to be highly imperfect. Alternative methods of motivating intelligence personnel are needed. One is the creation of a "high-commitment environment," in which people work hard because they identify with their employer's goals and methods. Another is the creation of a culture of professionalism, in which people work hard because they want to comply with professional norms that they've internalized. Improving all three incentive systems—objective performance measures, commitment, professional norms— should be a priority of the Director of National Intelligence. But no improvements are likely to induce gun-toting FBI special agents to

39. See, for example, J. E. Hirsch, "An Index to Quantify an Individual's Scientific Research Output," Sept. 29, 2005, http://arxiv.org/abs/physics/0508025.

want to hunt for terrorist cells that may not exist, or make the bureau's intelligence analysts—who unlike special agents have their own career track—more than second-class citizens of the bureau. There is a saying in the bureau that there are just two kinds of employee: special agents and clerks. The FBI's intelligence analysts, not being special agents, feel like clerks.

The emergent threat of homegrown terrorism has another and very ominous significance for domestic intelligence. We can prevent foreign terrorists from attacking inside the United States by intercepting them overseas or as they try to enter this country, as well as after they are here. This gives us three bites at the apple (overseas, border, interior). Abroad we can use our armed forces and a wide array of intelligence agencies, including the Central Intelligence Agency and the National Security Agency, and we can also call on the "liaison" services (the intelligence services of friendly countries) for help. With homegrown terrorism we have only one bite, and that a weak one because of the limitations on domestic use of the military, the CIA, the National Security Agency, and even the National Counterterrorism Center, which is not authorized to analyze data on terrorism that has no foreign links. So our limited domestic intelligence capabilities had better be good. But they will not be as good as they can be as long as domestic intelligence is dominated—indeed virtually monopolized—by the FBI.

I have been emphasizing the bureau's distinctive culture but I don't want to lose sight of the equally distinctive military, and non-FBI civilian, intelligence cultures. The coordination of agencies dominated by such different cultures would be difficult at best. But it is more difficult than it should be, because of a profound *political* imbalance among them. The military is at present greatly admired by the public, is immensely powerful politically (in part because of its popularity, in part because of its support by defense contractors), accounts for the lion's share of the intelligence budget, is ambitious to expand its intelligence activities (though this will change with Robert Gates having replaced Donald Rumsfeld as Secretary of Defense), and for these reasons is largely outside the control of the Director of National Intelligence. An organizational change that would reduce the imbalance, recommended by a commission headed by Brent Scowcroft, but rejected by the Bush Administration, is to spin off the national intelligence agencies from the Defense Department, make them their own agency or agencies, and by doing so place them under more effective control by the Director of National Intelligence.[40] That would ameliorate the "twin stars" problem (Secretary of Defense and Director of National Intelligence circling each other warily) that is created by the Defense Department's disproportionate weight in the overall intelligence budget. As for the National Reconnaissance Office and the National Geospatial-Intelligence Agency, divesting them from the Defense Department would restore them to approximately their original status, though they should not be returned to the CIA, where they originated; they have become too large and too specialized.

The imbalance of the intelligence system in favor of the military is unfortunate because, just as with the FBI, the military commitment to intelligence is blunted by competing priorities that often bias its intelligence estimates. During the Cold War, military intelligence exaggerated Soviet military prowess, thereby supporting claims for increased U.S. military expenditures; and during the Vietnam War it underestimated enemy strength, thereby dampening calls for a potentially humiliating withdrawal. In neither instance did the CIA have a stake in the policies that intelligence might influence, and so it is no

---

40. See Bruce Berkowitz, "Intelligence Reform: Less is More," *Hoover Digest*, Spring 2004, p. 49; Walter Pincus, "Intelligence Shakeup Would Boost CIA; Panel Urges Transfer of NSA, Satellites, Imagery from Pentagon," *Washington Post*, Nov. 8, 2001, p. A1. Another former military official, John Hamre, Deputy Secretary of Defense in the Clinton Administration, has expressed support for the spin off. See "Review of the 9/11 Commission's Intelligence Recommendations," Hearings before the Committee on Appropriations, U.S. Senate, 108th Cong., 2d Sess. 52 (2004).

surprise that its strategic intelligence was more accurate than the military's. The pattern has repeated itself in Iraq.

Bias to one side, since the principal mission of the armed forces is to prepare for and fight wars, intelligence is tailored to the support of that mission, in much the same way that FBI intelligence is tailored to the support of criminal investigation. A further problem is that military planning is oriented toward waging conventional warfare, not toward killing and capturing terrorists. That is as it should be, because conventional warfare is what military forces are good at. But the military culture makes it difficult for military intelligence agencies to participate effectively in counterterrorism, even when the Defense Department's civilian leadership (again, much like FBI Director Mueller) wants to push them in that direction. A related point is that, like the FBI, the military must juggle competing priorities; it cannot devote its entire energy to improving intelligence.

The FBI is a popular institution, like the military (though less so[41]), despite its unsatisfactory performance as an intelligence agency—the worst-performing in the run-up to the 9/11 attacks and stumbling repeatedly since. There is also residual distrust of the bureau stemming from the Waco debacle and other pratfalls unrelated to national security. This is not to question that the bureau deserves to be popular. It is a highly competent criminal-investigation agency, with particular distinction in forensic investigation (fingerprints, DNA, tracing explosives, etc.). But that is not the point. The point is that because the bureau is popular, politically influential, and skilled at public relations, and likewise the military, and the CIA is none of those things, the latter is in a vulnerable position, further disadvantaged in the political arena by not having a domestic con-

41. A poll last year revealed a 42 percent approval rating for the FBI. John Harwood, "The Wall Street Journal/NBC News Poll: Washington Wire," *Wall Street Journal,* June 16, 2006, p. A4. The CIA's approval rating was 31 percent. In contrast, a June 2006 Gallup Poll found that 73 percent of respondents had either a great deal or quite a lot of confidence in the military.

stituency, since it neither has a significant domestic presence nor awards fat contracts. It is therefore a natural scapegoat, attacked from both the left (of course) and, surprisingly, the right.[42] Its unpopularity limits the ability of the Director of National Intelligence to protect it against inroads by military and FBI intelligence. For there are cabinet officers (the Secretary of Defense and the Attorney General) between him and both the Defense Department intelligence services and the bureau's intelligence service and they can run interference for their services.

A telling example of the limits of the DNI's powers, and a dramatic example of the FBI's political strength, is that the leaks I mentioned earlier from inside the bureau about the National Security Agency's warrantless surveillance program evoked no public rebuke from the DNI. Or for that matter from Director Mueller or Attorney General Gonzales, even though the FBI is part of the Department of Justice and at the very moment that the bureau leakers were deriding the National Security Agency's program, the Attorney General was defending it before Congress as indispensable to the nation's safety.

---

42. See Spencer Ackerman, "Mole People," *New Republic*, July 31, 2006, p. 10. Not just the paranoid right, but Republicans who believe that the CIA resisted and tried to undermine the Bush Administration's foreign policy.

6

The Continuing
Crisis in Domestic
Intelligence

> We need to end the fiction that the FBI can be trans-
> formed into an effective counter-terrorist outfit. It can't. Its
> culture, traditions, mission and procedures all work against
> such a dramatic transformation. Instead we should let the
> FBI do what it does best—catch criminals—and place
> counter-terrorism responsibilities in a new domestic intel-
> ligence agency.
>
> —Amy Zegart[1]

The FBI's weaknesses as an intelligence agency are documented in
my book *Uncertain Shield*.[2] But the evidence continues to mount up;
the preceding chapter gave only a glimpse of it. One study concludes
that "the FBI has attempted the most ambitious changes" to meet
the terrorist challenge since 9/11, "with perhaps the most disappoint-
ing results."[3] John Lehman, a member of the 9/11 Commission

1. Amy Zegart, "The Sept. 11 Warnings: Spy vs. Spy: Two Agencies, Two Turfs,
and No Communications," *Newsday*, May 26, 2002, p. B4.
2. See also my monograph *Remaking Domestic Intelligence* (2005).
3. Amy B. Zegart, *Failure and Consequence: Understanding U.S. Intelligence and
the Origins of 9/11*, ch. 8 (forthcoming, Princeton University Press, 2007). For other,
especially pungent, criticism, see Jeff Stein, "FBI under the Gun," *CQ Weekly*, May
1, 2006, p. 1152, and, more recently, Scott Shane and Lowell Bergman, "F.B.I.
Struggling to Reinvent Itself to Fight Terror," *New York Times*, Oct. 10, 2006, p. A1.
The latter article is the one that reports that Philip Mudd, the CIA transplant who
is deputy director of the National Security Branch, is mocked by some within the
bureau as "Rasputin" (see note 23 in Chapter 5). It also reports that FBI special
agents are disturbed by what they regard as the "implied ethnic targeting" involved
in counterterrorism; regard Mudd's approach as "vague"; do not want to "neglect

(which had unanimously recommended against creating a domestic intelligence agency separate from the FBI), has now concluded that the bureau's effort "to focus on preventive intelligence rather than forensic evidence—has proved to be a complete failure . . . [T]he bureau will not monitor or surveille any Islamist unless there is a 'criminal predicate.' Thus, the large Islamist support infrastructure . . . here in the United States is free to operate until it actually commits a crime—Our attempt to reform the FBI has failed. What is needed now is a separate domestic intelligence service without police powers such as the British MI-5."[4] The 9/11 Commission's cochairmen have expressed their "deep disappointment in the pace of reform within the FBI."[5]

---

promising cases to, in Mr. Mudd's words, 'search for the unknown'"; and fear that his approach will "take the bureau back to the domestic spying scandals of the 1960's." The "F.B.I. culture still respects door-kicking investigators more than desk-bound analysts sifting through tidbits of data"; turnover in supervisory positions is excessive and few supervisors have relevant expertise; Mudd will leave and the bureau "traditionalists" will "just wait him out"; "the drive to bring criminal charges often eclipses the intelligence imperative"; FBI special agents "still believed that their careers would rise or fall on the cases they brought"; the bureau's terrorism cases appear "to show a gap between public relations and reality"; and "knowledgeable employees say Muslim agents number no more than a dozen of the bureau's 12,664 agents." Id. at A1, A23.

4. John Lehman, "Are We Any Safer?" *Proceedings of the U.S. Naval Institute,* Sept. 2006, pp. 18, 20. Lehman is a Republican, but the proposal to create a U.S. counterpart to MI5 is supported by the influential Democratic Congressman Rahm Emanuel. See Rahm Emanuel and Bruce Reed, *The Plan: Big Ideas for America* 169 (2006). In the wake of the Heathrow plot, there is increased interest, from a variety of directions, in the proposal. See, for example, Morton Kondracke, "Can the Parties Fight Terror Together?" *San Diego Union-Tribune,* Aug. 27, 2006, www.signonsandiego.com/uniontrib/20060827/news_mz1e27kondra.html; Haviland Smith, "In New Terrorism Fight, Britain Shows the Way," *Baltimore Sun,* Aug. 18, 2006, p. 19A.

5. Thomas H. Kean and Lee H. Hamilton, with Benjamin Rhodes, *Without Precedent: The Inside Story of the 9/11 Commission* 334 (2006). "Progress is being made—but it is too slow. The FBI's shift to a counterterrorism posture is far from institutionalized, and significant deficiencies remain. Reforms are at risk from inertia and complacency; they must be accelerated, or they will fail. Unless there is improvement in a reasonable period of time, Congress will have to look at alternatives."

Much evidence supports these concerns. The FBI's computer struggles continue. Their roots are the bureau's weak understanding of the information needs of national security intelligence and the reluctance of a criminal investigation agency to create materials that might be discoverable in litigation and so assist a defendant.[6] One already knew that the bureau had blown more than $100 million on Virtual Case File, a computer system designed to enable FBI special agents to share information among the field offices and with head-quarters. The program was abandoned in 2005 in favor of an even more ambitious program, called "Sentinel," which however "is still not fully staffed," and "it is not clear that the bureau has a management system in place to prevent the huge cost overruns that plagued previous incarnations of the project"—that is, Virtual Case File. Although it is estimated that Sentinel will cost $500 million or more (surely more), the Justice Department's "inspector general's office said it was not yet satisfied that the overhaul [i.e., Sentinel], even if successful, would allow the bureau to share information adequately with other intelligence and law enforcement agencies." So almost five and a half years after 9/11, the FBI is still years away from having computer capabilities adequate to its intelligence mission. The cause is not technical incompetence; it is project-management incompetence reinforced by cultural resistance rooted in the autonomy of the bureau's field offices, the bureau's lack of understanding of national security intelligence needs, and the reluctance of criminal investigators to leave a documentary trail.[7]

The consolidation of the bureau's intelligence-related units to

---

Id. at 344. See also id. at 338. The critical question, unaddressed by the authors, is how *much* improvement should be required, and by when, before alternatives are examined.

6. Eric Lichtblau, "Cost Concerns for F.B.I. Computer Overhaul," *New York Times*, Mar. 14, 2006, p. A24. The *Brady* doctrine requires the prosecution to furnish the defendant with any exculpatory material in the prosecution's possession.

7. Cf. the aptly titled article by Adam Liptak, "Relying on the Notepad in the Electronic Age," *New York Times*, Feb. 12, 2007, p. A14.

form the National Security Branch has produced, as the choice of the word "branch" implies, a counterpart to the London Metropolitan Police (i.e., Scotland Yard) Special Branch, which fuses intelligence with criminal investigation of terrorism, espionage, and other crimes that endanger national security. The FBI fought the creation of the National Security Branch. "A senior FBI official, after spending hours enthusing to a reporter about the 'new FBI,' was caught short when asked whether agents really wanted to work in the bureau's new National Security Branch . . . 'Not really,' he acknowledged, smiling. 'They say to me, "Hey, I joined up to arrest people."'"[8]

But the National Security Branch *does* arrest people; that is the basic problem. Rather than being a pure domestic intelligence agency, the National Security Branch, like Scotland Yard's Special Branch,[9] investigates crimes relating to national security, using intelligence mainly as a tool of criminal investigation. The National Security Branch is trying to be both Special Branch and MI5. Foreign experience, as well as experience with the FBI since it first bestirred itself about rising Islamic terrorism more than a decade ago, warrants skepticism about the viability of such a hybrid. "Special Branch's original nineteenth century role of gathering intelligence on Irish Republican activity in mainland Britain was taken away from it in 1992 and handed to MI5 (it retained a secondary role in support of MI5 on this issue and international terrorism in general)."[10]

A clue to the status of the National Security Branch is that its director reports not to the bureau's director but to its deputy director. And Philip Mudd, the bureau's chief intelligence officer, is not the National Security Branch's director but that director's deputy and

8. Stein, note 3 above.
9. And the Special Branches in the other British police departments; but they are supervised by Scotland Yard's Special Branch. See "Special Branch More Than Doubles in Size: Analysis of the Special Branch's Role in Conducting Surveillance for MI5 and on Public Order," *Statewatch*, Sept. 2003, www.statewatch.org/new/2003/sep/SB.pdf.
10. Id.

thus several rungs from the top of the bureau's command ladder. That is significant in so hierarchical—indeed paramilitary—organization as the FBI. (And hierarchical it is: a second-level manager of special agents reports to a section chief, who reports to a deputy assistant director, who reports to an assistant director, who reports to an executive assistant director, who reports to the bureau's deputy director, who reports to the director.)

Consider the difference, in distance from the top, between the head of the CIA's intelligence analysts (called the Director of Intelligence) and the head of the FBI's analysts. The only officials above the Director of Intelligence are the CIA's director and his principal deputy (the CIA's Executive Director is the number three official but is concerned with administrative rather than substantive matters). The corresponding official in the bureau—the head of the Directorate of Intelligence in the National Security Branch—reports to the head of the branch, who in turn reports to the bureau's deputy director, who reports to the director. Intelligence analysts in the FBI peep up at the bureau's director from the bottom of a deep well. And above the director looms the Attorney General, whose background and perspective are those of a lawyer rather than an intelligence officer.

Mudd's duties, moreover, are not limited to national security intelligence; they include intelligence in support of the bureau's ordinary crime-fighting activities. Though this may cause him to dissipate his energies, it plays into the hands of the bureau's traditionalists, who are happy to have the help of intelligence specialists to solve the crimes that are the bureau's meat and potatoes. The contrast with MI5 is striking. At one time it had intelligence responsibilities with regard to organized crime. No more. As the terrorist menace grew, this part of the agency's portfolio was withdrawn so that it could focus exclusively on threats to national security.

The breadth of the FBI's responsibilities has given rise to problems that are more serious than blurred focus. The pace and perceived urgency of crimes exceed those of shadowy terrorist threats.

One way the FBI surges to meet an unexpected demand on its resources, spawned by some notorious crime or by a crime wave that has local officials squawking for help, is by pulling special agents off terrorism investigations and throwing them at the developing crisis. Special agents learn from this experience where the bureau's real priorities lie.

Notice the parallel between this problem and that of the Office of the Director of National Intelligence being torn between short-term (operational) and long-term (systemic) coordination of the intelligence community. If the same staff is responsible for both immediate response and long-range planning, the former will take precedence and the latter will constantly be interrupted. The problem would be less acute if the bureau did not insist that all its intelligence operations officers be trained as special agents. That makes all of them available to be shifted to criminal investigation if demand surges.

The FBI's efforts at reform are further impeded by high turnover. The first director of the National Security Branch, Gary Bald, announced his resignation only eight months after his appointment. When appointed, Bald was a career FBI agent with limited experience in intelligence. (Negroponte could have vetoed his appointment—was urged to do so—but refused.) Willie Hulon, Bald's successor, has a similar profile. Director Mueller could have appointed Mudd to succeed Bald but probably (I am speculating) felt that an outsider would not command the respect of the FBI special agents employed in the National Security Branch. If this speculation is correct, it is a further testament to the stubbornness of organizational cultures. So maybe the bureau's resistance to fundamental change can be overcome only by appointing to head the branch an insider with an outsider's perspective—someone who would be to the FBI as Gorbachev was to the Soviet Union. (A somewhat ominous precedent, however, considering what happened to the Soviet Union.) Time will tell whether Hulon is such a person. Nothing in his official FBI biography suggests that he is, but the same was true of Gorbachev. But do we have time? Recent events, as I noted in Chapter 1, suggest not.

Bald's abrupt departure from the National Security Branch should not have come as a surprise. There has been extraordinary turnover in the bureau's senior ranks since 9/11, notably in the intelligence-related divisions that were combined to create the National Security Branch; the average tenure of the head of the Counterterrorism Division since 9/11 has been less than a year.[11] One factor in the high turnover is the attractive early-retirement options of FBI agents, though a bigger one is the private sector's greatly increased demand for experienced government security personnel in the wake of the 9/11 attacks. The incentives are mutually reinforcing. An FBI special agent can retire on one-third of his salary after 20 years of service at age 50, while he is still young enough to land a good private-sector job. Bald retired to become the security director of a cruise-ship line at a salary that is a multiple of his salary as an FBI agent, to add to his $50,000+ government pension.

It is common to encourage early retirement from police forces because the work is considered strenuous and dangerous. Most domestic intelligence work is neither. Domestic intelligence officers are not trying to arrest people and, unlike CIA operations officers, are not working in foreign, sometimes hostile or anarchic, countries. There is no reason to expect retirement packages designed for police officers, including FBI agents, to be equally suitable for domestic intelligence officers. But because the bureau's culture is a police culture, no effort has been made to design a separate retirement track for intelligence officers.

That culture's steel grip is further illustrated by the resistance of FBI agents to being transferred from field offices to the bureau's

11. See Shane and Bergman, note 3 above, at A23; Andrew Zajac, "Private Sector Drains FBI Talent," *Chicago Tribune*, May 3, 2006, p. 1.

headquarters.[12] National security threats—in contrast to most ordinary federal crimes, which are prosecuted by the local U.S. Attorney with the aid of the nearest FBI field office—are nationwide and even worldwide in scope. But FBI special agents assigned to field offices (as most of them are) consider that they are working for the U.S. Attorney, whose concerns are parochial. So Mueller wants more agents at headquarters. But agents don't want to move to Washington and lose the rich opportunities that the field offices provide for making arrests. Assignment to headquarters is viewed as a "sell out"; "real agents" are on the street. Cost of living is a factor too; housing costs are astronomical in the Washington area.

Because of resistance to being reassigned to headquarters, there are many vacancies there as agents choose to retire early rather than to be transferred. Not that this is entirely a bad thing; early retirements eliminate agents who are set in their ways by virtue of their long careers with the bureau and so are prone to resist a change in its traditional culture. But the vacancies are one more obstacle to Mueller's endeavor to transform the bureau. And one doubts that many younger special agents will want to be transferred to headquarters either. Suppose a special agent assigned to intelligence wants to conduct long-term surveillance of terrorist suspects in San Francisco, and the U.S. Attorney in San Francisco and the bureau's field office want to arrest the suspects and put them on trial. Will the Justice Department, desperate as it is for statistical evidence of the success of its counterterrorism efforts (which are eating up a large fraction of its budget), side with the intelligence officer?

Mueller is not an intelligence professional, and as a career prosecutor is more comfortable with the FBI's predisposition to fuse intelligence with criminal investigations—"intelligence-led policing"—than, in my opinion, he ought to be. But he is a dedicated, intelligent,

---

12. Richard B. Schmitt, "FBI Agents Rebel over Mandatory Transfers," *Los Angeles Times*, May 22, 2006, p. A1.

and energetic public servant, ably assisted by Philip Mudd. If the two of them cannot transform the bureau in a reasonable time (and Mueller's term as director will expire in 2011), it is unlikely that any other team could—though ironically the turmoil caused by Mueller's strenuous efforts may, as I suggested in Chapter 5, be doing what old-line FBI staff fear: undermining the bureau's ability to fight ordinary federal crimes.

All this said, the efforts of Mueller and Mudd are beginning to have positive effects on the bureau's ability to conduct national security intelligence. If for five years the FBI has been driving with the clutch pressed to the floor, one senses that now the clutch is rising ever so slightly and that forward movement, though slow, is at last beginning. But it hasn't really been five years of wheel spinning—it's been ten. For by the middle 1990s the bureau's then director, Louis Freeh, was aware that the nation faced a serious terrorist threat, and he resolved, like Mueller, though less determinedly (not having the example of 9/11 to spur him), to change the bureau's culture. Freeh's efforts met with no success.[13] And for at least three and a half years after the 9/11 attacks, the bureau insisted that intelligence was merely an adjunct to criminal investigations, drawing a sharp rebuke from the Silberman-Robb Commission.[14] That may still be the dominant view within the bureau.

A decade of successful passive resistance by career officials casts a long shadow over the prospects for durable reform. Additional resources and inspired senior executive leadership will not so far overcome the obstacles that I have described as to obviate the need for a stand-alone domestic intelligence agency. Had we such an agency, no one would suggest merging it with the FBI, just as no one suggests merging MI5 into Scotland Yard or the Canadian Security Intelli-

13. Zegart, note 3 above, chs. 6, 8.
14. Letter to the President from the Commission on the Intelligence Capabilities of the United States Regarding Weapons of Mass Destruction, Mar. 29, 2005, pp. 1–2.

gence Service back into the Royal Canadian Mounted Police, Canada's FBI.[15]

A U.S. counterpart to MI5 or CSIS would make compelling sense, especially if one starts small, as one should.[16] Yet it was not recommended by the 9/11 or Silberman-Robb commissions and it was omitted from the Intelligence Reform Act. The 9/11 Commission's mistake was to confuse a design problem with a performance problem. Not realizing that the FBI's failures in the run-up to 9/11 were inherent in its structure, the commission thought they could be rectified by the bureau's new director, though like his predecessor he had only promises to offer. The Silberman-Robb Commission recognized that there was a structural problem but proposed an inadequate solution, the formation of the National Security Branch. All that did

---

15. CSIS was originally the RCMP's Security Service. On CSIS and Canadian domestic security in general, including oversight, see CSIS Office Consolidation: Canadian Security Intelligence Service Act (July 1984), R.S. 1985, c. C-23 (Feb. 2000); Security Intelligence Review Committee, *SIRC Annual Report 2005–2006: An Operational Review of the Canadian Security Intelligence Service* (2006); CSIS, "Backgrounder No. 2: Accountability and Review," Nov. 2004, www.csis-scrs.gc.ca/en/newsroom/backgrounders/backgrounder02.asp; CSIS, "Backgrounder No. 3: CSIS and the Security Intelligence Cycle," revised Feb. 2004, www.csis-scrs.gc.ca/en/newsroom/backgrounders/backgrounder03.asp; CSIS, "Backgrounder No. 4: Human Resources," Feb. 2004, www.csis-scrs.gc.ca/en/newsroom/backgrounders/backgrounder04.asp; Jacques J. M. Shore, "Intelligence Review and Oversight in Post–9/11 Canada," 19 *International Journal of Intelligence and CounterIntelligence* 456 (2006).

16. A domestic intelligence agency that had a staff of 3,000 would be only 10 percent as big as the FBI. Would that be large enough to do the job, considering that MI5 has a staff of 3,400 and the Canadian Security Intelligence Service a staff of 2,500, though the combined population of Britain and Canada is less than a third that of the United States? I think so. The fact that Canada's service is almost the size of Britain's even though Canada has only half the population suggests that there are significant fixed costs of a security service. And the enormous number of public and private police in the United States, as well as the huge size of the U.S. intelligence community as a whole relative to Britain's and Canada's (Britain has only three nonmilitary intelligence services, and Canada—which has no foreign intelligence service—only two), should enable a domestic intelligence agency to economize on its own personnel.

was change the FBI's table of organization; and such changes are more likely to impede than promote reform. Both commissions exaggerated the power of a committed agency director to alter the agency's culture, given structural impediments to federal-government reform. The Silberman-Robb Commission may have known better, given the sharpness of its criticisms of the bureau, but may have believed that a proposal to create a U.S. MI5 would be too controversial and undermine the acceptability of its other recommendations.

Most students of the 9/11 intelligence failure believe that its proximate cause was the failure of the FBI and the CIA to share terrorist information with each other. They did fail, and it is natural to ascribe the failure to the cultural tensions that I emphasized in Chapter 5. But the root was structural. The different missions of the two agencies would have gravely inhibited sharing even if the agencies had had interchangeable personnel and an inoculation against turf warfare and had not exaggerated the height of the legal "wall" between them. Committed to criminal investigation, the FBI worries that giving information about a terrorist suspect to the CIA could contaminate a criminal investigation because the agency might decide to recruit or deceive the suspect, nudge him to flee abroad, or, by means of the "heavy tap on the shoulder" (see Chapter 7), alert him that he was under investigation. The bureau also worries about receiving information about a suspect from the CIA that the agency might have obtained by methods of interrogation that would render the confession inadmissible in a criminal proceeding and taint any evidence the bureau had gotten from leads supplied by the confession. There would be no such reluctance to share information between two intelligence agencies, one dealing with foreign intelligence (the CIA) and the other with domestic intelligence.

The solution is not, however, to break up the FBI.[17] The bureau

---

17. John Miller, "Law Enforcement, American Style: Remodeling the F.B.I. on Britain's MI5 Won't Work," *New York Times*, Sept. 14, 2006, p. A27, intimates,

should retain the National Security Branch, which like Scotland Yard's Special Branch would conduct intelligence as an adjunct to criminal investigation—this is anyway the bureau's conception of how national security intelligence should be conducted. Criminal investigation *is* an important counterterrorist and counterespionage tool, though one that is being overused, and arrests are an important adjunct to intelligence operations even when prosecutions do not result and may not have been intended. (More on these points in Chapter 7.) No doubt as the new agency grew the National Security Branch would shrink, as it is trying to perform both tasks—intelligence in support of criminal investigation, and pure intelligence—and if the second were taken over by another agency the branch could get by with a smaller staff. But this assumes that the new agency would be effective. If not—if it turned out to be a failed experiment—little harm would have been done because the National Security Branch would wane only as the new agency waxed.

If the terrorist threat is indeed growing, incremental improvements in the FBI's conduct of domestic intelligence are unlikely to yield a net advantage in our struggle with our terrorist foes. If two runners increase their speed by the same amount, the gap between them does not shrink. We should especially ponder the risk of homegrown terrorism (discussed briefly in Chapter 5), as underscored by "second generation" warning of Richard Falkenrath, the head of the New York City Police Department's counterterrorism bureau:

> Despite the success of U.S. overseas efforts in degrading al-Qaeda as an organization, its powerful radical influence on the City's younger generation—especially among its sizeable Muslim community—continues to pose a serious threat from within.
>
> We consider the fuel that ignites this inside threat—extremist militant ideology and influences—as the most critical challenge in addressing this inside threat in New York City. We are especially

without quite saying, that I favor breaking up the FBI. I explicitly rejected any such notion in chapter 5 of *Uncertain Shield*.

concerned with the radicalizing influence of the Internet, coupled with the potential role of its 2nd and 3rd generation citizens as the receptors of these influences and as the future radicalizing agents.

In addition, Islamic conversion and radicalization among the population in the prison system is a trend that may contribute to new threat emergence among the indigenous Muslim population. Within the prison system, inmates, seeking protection or prayer privileges, "convert" to Islam. Though most prisoners revert back to their original religion following their release from prison, a segment of the convert population continues their conversion process outside the prison. This process is aided and abetted by an imam/mosque network that guides recent parolees to particular mosques for employment, temporary housing and for some—international travel to the Middle East or South Asia for further indoctrination.

There is no question that many countries—the United Kingdom, for example—face a threat of "homeland" terrorism that is more acute than that faced by the United States. Again, the NYPD takes no comfort in this conclusion. The possibility of a "homegrown" terrorist attack against New York City or any other American city is real and is worsening with time as the radicalization process unfolds.[18]

The implications for domestic intelligence are stark. As Falkenrath explains,

The rise in the "homegrown" terrorist threat underscores the importance of an effective domestic counterterrorism and intelligence program. It is no secret that the preponderance of the federal government's unilateral intelligence collection and counterterrorism activities, as well as its liaison relationships and joint operations with partners in the war on terror, are directed against terrorist operatives

18. Richard A. Falkenrath, "Prepared Statement of Testimony before the Committee on Homeland Security and Governmental Affairs, United States Senate" 16 (Sept. 12, 2006). One implication is that radical Islamic organizations in colleges and universities should be monitored, discreetly but carefully. Cf. Anthony Glees, "Campus Jihad," *Wall Street Journal*, Oct. 23, 2006, p. A15. Marc Sageman, in his important book *Understanding Terror Networks* 114–115, 143–144 (2004), emphasizes the role of mosques in the creation of the Islamist terrorist movement.

and networks abroad. These intelligence and counterterrorism activities abroad are tremendously useful in combating transnational
terrorist threats: when a terrorist group seeks to deploy into the
United States from abroad, as the 9/11 hijackers did, a lead generated abroad can quickly lead to the individuals already in, or trying
to enter, the homeland.

But "homegrown" terrorists, by definition, have only limited, if
any, linkages across national boundaries. Thus, compared to transnational terrorism, there are relatively fewer benefits to be gained
in combating "homegrown" terrorism from the federal government's
vast intelligence and counterterrorism program abroad. While no
comprehensive accounting of the country's expenditure and investment on domestic as opposed to international counterterrorism has
ever been conducted, it is clear that the domestic element is but a
small faction of the international element.

The implications are obvious: the country is under-investing in
the sort of capabilities most needed to combat the most dynamic
element in the spectrum of terrorist threats—the "homegrown" element—to the homeland. In combating "homegrown" threats, the
burden shifts instead almost entirely to local law enforcement. A
"homegrown" threat—presents few obvious inherent indicators and
the few signatures are subtle and embedded within the daily activities of a vast civilian population. Such threats are most likely to be
detected by dedicated investigators with both intimate knowledge
of the population in question and mastery of human intelligence
tradecraft who are backed by the full power and resources of a
major law enforcement agency.

This is one of the reasons why the NYPD has decided to augment its joint counterterrorism investigative work with the FBI with
an organizationally distinct intelligence program operating under
separate legal authorities. Put differently, in the NYPD's view, a
reformed FBI and an aggressive, genuinely *joint* Joint Terrorism
Task Force are necessary—indeed, are vital—but are not sufficient
to combat the threat we face. So far as I am aware, the only such
domestic intelligence program in the United States today is the
New York Police Department's.

An important question for the Congress and the Administration

is whether some additional domestic intelligence and counterterrorism capacity is required in the rest of the country.[19]

Indeed it is required. And it is a striking vote of no confidence in the
FBI that New York City should decide to establish its own national
security intelligence service.

The reader may wonder how effective that service can be as part
of a police department if I am right that intelligence and policing do
not mix well. But that is not what I said. I said that intelligence and
criminal investigation do not mix well. The FBI is not a full-service
police force; it is a detective bureau. A police force has a preventive
as well as an investigative function. Police walk a beat or cruise in
patrol cars or intervene in domestic disputes or station guards at
schools and public events not mainly to catch criminals but to prevent
crime, which is also the mission of the New York City Police Department's intelligence and counterterrorism bureaus. (Hence the department's emphasis on building bridges to the large Muslim community in New York City.[20]) It is not the FBI's mission. Changes in
crime rates are important measures of police success, but are rarely
mentioned in connection with the FBI. The one recent—and telling—exception is the complaint that crime rates are rising in part
because the bureau's attention and resources are being deflected from
ordinary crimes to the terrorist threat.

If I am right in what I have said so far, the question arises why a
domestic intelligence agency has not been created yet. One reason is
that the creation of the National Security Branch gave the Director
of National Intelligence an excuse for postponing further consideration of the needs of domestic intelligence; the new entity had to be
given a chance to prove itself. Yet it was given no deadline for fur-
nishing the proof; nor has it set one for itself. Success in its trans-

19. Falkenrath, note 18 above, at 18–19.
20. See Robin Shulman, "Liaison Strives to Bridge Police, Muslim Cultures,"
Washington Post, Jan. 24, 2007, p. A2.

formative endeavors is a continuously receding horizon. Since no criteria have been suggested for determining success, there should at least be rigorous annual audits of progress made. At this writing, none is planned.

I mentioned in Chapter 1 another lame excuse for the Bush Administration's unwillingness to consider establishing a domestic intelligence service: that because we are at war there is no time to create a new national security agency. Still another lame excuse is that having created two new security agencies, the Department of Homeland Security and the Office of the Director of National Intelligence, the administration cannot create a third. Why not? Don't good things come in threes any more? And wasn't the administration lukewarm (presciently, I might add) about creating those two agencies, the initiative for both of which came from Congress? But behind the argument may lie a purely political concern that to create a domestic intelligence agency this late in the day would be taken as an embarrassing acknowledgment that, more than five years after 9/11, the administration *still* hasn't gotten the organization of our intelligence system right. Such a criticism could be finessed, however, by pointing out that as our adversaries change, so must we; the increased threat of homegrown terrorism, which only domestic intelligence can thwart, requires the strengthening of our ability to conduct domestic intelligence effectively.

It has been suggested that creating a new agency would take longer than changing the FBI's existing culture.[21] The opposite is more likely. A small new agency would not have to overcome the resistance to change of a large proud old one. Conceivably the National Security Branch will someday attain genuine autonomy within the bureau, much as the Marine Corps has attained genuine autonomy within the Navy, of which nowadays it is only nominally a part.

---

21. See, for example, Henry A. Crumpton, "Intelligence and Homeland Defense," in *Transforming U.S. Intelligence* 198, 210 (Jennifer E. Sims and Burton Gerber eds. 2005).

The parallel transformation of the National Security Branch is likely to take a lot longer than creating a domestic intelligence agency and making it operational and effective. Recruitment should not be difficult. Of course, some potential applicants would be wary of throwing in their lot with a new, untested venture, if the alternative were joining a prestigious agency such as the Federal Bureau of Investigation. But others who wanted to be civilian intelligence operations officers would not be satisfied with a choice between the CIA, which requires extended sojourns abroad, and the FBI, where intelligence officers (especially analysts) continue to be second-class citizens—alien intruders in a criminal investigation agency. They would risk joining the new venture. We need more domestic intelligence officers; creating a domestic intelligence agency is a way to obtain them without having to increase compensation or lower standards.

If I am right that the nation faces a growing terrorist threat, the fact that a new agency cannot be made operational and effective overnight is an argument for creating it now, so that it will be operational and effective in time to augment our defenses against terrorism when the need becomes urgent. It would take time for the National Security Branch and a domestic intelligence service to learn to work together (for there would be the same dog versus cat culture clash that makes it difficult for the FBI and the CIA to work together), overcoming the kind of friction that the Royal Canadian Mounted Police and the Canadian Security Intelligence Service has experienced, especially when CSIS was first created.[22] Friction between Scotland Yard's Special Branch (and the other Special Branches) and MI5 is minimized in part by their long experience of working together and in part because MI5 actually directs Special

22. See Commission of Inquiry into the Actions of Canadian Officials in Relation to Maher Arar, *Report of the Events Relating to Maher Arar*, vol. 3: *Analysis and Recommendations* 318–319 (2006); "Lessons to Be Learned: Report of the Honorable Bob Rae, Independent Advisor to the Minister of Public Safety and Emergency Preparedness, on Outstanding Questions with Respect to the Bombing of Air India Flight 182" (2005).

Branch, which accepts that its function is to provide police support for MI5.[23]

A related concern with creating a separate domestic intelligence agency is coordination and control. Where would such an agency be lodged? And how would disagreements between it and the FBI be resolved? Logically, both a Security Service and the FBI belong in the Department of Homeland Security. That is the set-up in the United Kingdom, where both Scotland Yard and MI5 report to the Home Secretary, and in other countries, including Canada, where both the Royal Canadian Mounted Police and the Canadian Security Intelligence Service are lodged in the Department of Public Safety. It is the set-up in the New York City Police Department as well, where the intelligence and counterterrorism bureaus report to the police commissioner, and in most other cities, where the police report to the mayor, not to the district attorney. District attorneys work with police; they do not own the police, the way the Justice Department owns the FBI.[24] The problem with reconstituting our internal security apparatus in a rational way is that until the Department of Homeland Security gets its act together, nobody is going to want to put another agency under its control. The trend is the opposite; the department's control over the Federal Emergency Management Agency has been loosened.

The fact that the FBI is part of the Department of Justice reinforces the bureau's unsound belief that law enforcement is *the* answer to terrorism. But the bureau is not about to be pried loose from the department. So for the time being at least, a Security Service would have to be a free-standing service, like the CIA, reporting to the Director of National Intelligence. When the bureau and the new service disagreed, as they would be bound to do from time to time over

23. "Special Branch More Than Doubles in Size," note 9 above, at 2; Peter Gill and Mark Phythian, *Intelligence in an Insecure World* 43 (2006).

24. A similar mystery is why the federal Bureau of Prisons is in the Justice Department. Lawyers are no more correctional officers than they are detectives.

such questions as how long to conduct a particular investigation before arresting anyone and whether to limit investigative methods in a particular case in order to be sure of producing evidence admissible in court, the disagreement would be referred to a higher level for resolution, perhaps to the President's assistant for homeland security.

The Bush Administration may be worried that attempting to create a new intelligence agency would open a Pandora's Box, given congressional dissatisfaction, sharpened by Democratic control of Congress, with how the administration is waging the "war on terror." But, if so, a domestic intelligence agency could be a build-out from an existing agency, such as the Office of Intelligence and Analysis in the Department of Homeland Security. Indeed, that department could on its own initiative have fashioned OIA as a Security Service. It could still do so. That it has not done so may be due not only to the department's acute growing pains but also to the fact that Secretary Chertoff, like Robert Mueller a former prosecutor, conceives of intelligence as an adjunct to criminal investigation rather than as its own thing. The department contains several intelligence services, including the Coast Guard's tiny though well respected one. The Office of Information Analysis is its only department-wide intelligence entity, however, and it has limited functions and resources and no operational capabilities. It winnows information gathered by border, customs, and transportation-security officers, looking for information of intelligence value to local police and other personnel who might be able to counter terrorist threats. (So it is a fusion center, like the state fusion centers—see next paragraph.) The information-collection function is worthwhile, as is OIA's commitment to open source intelligence, which can more easily be shared with nonfederal security personnel.

Apart from specific disabilities of the Office of Intelligence and Analysis that stem from its being part of a deeply troubled department,[25] a Security Service would be better placed to orchestrate the

25. See Robert Block, "Homeland Security Attracts More Scrutiny: Veteran Spy

communication of threat information to local police because the service would have the fullest picture of the terrorist menace. The importance of promptly communicating threats to the people who are best placed to neutralize them cannot be exaggerated; a failure in that regard was a factor in the Pearl Harbor disaster.[26] Of almost equal importance is that the threats be filtered to minimize the number of false alarms, with their potentially fatal lulling effects (see Chapter 1). That makes it essential that one agency be responsible for threat communication, and it should be the agency that specializes in collecting and analyzing domestic intelligence.

Another unconvincing justification for not creating a counterpart to MI5 is that the United States has 17,000 police forces and the United Kingdom only about 50. But obviously the FBI, with only 56 field offices, cannot liaise directly with 17,000 police forces. The states know this; at latest count, 46 of them, plus the District of Columbia, had created intelligence fusion centers that consolidate the (very limited) intelligence capabilities of the local police forces in their state.[27] The FBI and the Department of Homeland Security are fighting over which shall liaise with the state fusion centers—a clue that more than five years after the 9/11 attacks little progress has been made in knitting together state and local police, the Department of Homeland Security's border-control units (including the Coast Guard, the Border Patrol, the Transportation Security Administration,

Seeks Bigger Seat at Table for Department's Intelligence Operations," *Wall Street Journal*, Feb. 5, 2007, p. A7.

26. See Richard A. Posner, *Preventing Surprise Attacks: Intelligence Reform in the Wake of 9/11* 76, 78 (2005).

27. Shane Harris, "Fusion Centers Raise a Fuss," *National Journal*, Feb. 10., 2007, p. 50. See also National Criminal Intelligence Resource Center, "State and Regional Intelligence Fusion Center Contact Information," Mar. 8, 2006, www.fas.org/irp/agency/ise/state.pdf. See also U.S. Dept. of Homeland Security, "The DHS, State, and Local Fusion Center Support Implementation Concept" (DHS draft, Jan. 18, 2006); Mary Beth Sheridan and Spencer S. Hsu, "Localities Operate Intelligence Centers to Pool Terror Data: 'Fusion' Facilities Raise Privacy Worries as Wide Range of Information Is Collected," *Washington Post*, Dec. 31, 2006, p. A3.

and Immigration and Customs Enforcement), the FBI, and private security personnel into a coherent network for the collection of intelligence-related data at ground level and the communication of threat information to local agencies well placed to act on such information.[28] The rise of the fusion centers is in part a response to friction between federal and local authorities.[29]

It is not as if MI5's liaison job were a cakewalk because Britain has few policemen. The small number of its police forces is misleading. As of 2003, and excluding Scotland and Northern Ireland, there were 136,000 officers in the 43 police forces in England and Wales.[30] Nevertheless, MI5 has been able to do what the FBI and the Department of Homeland Security have been unable to do—integrate local police into the national domestic intelligence system. It is a vital mission. Local police, border patrol, customs officers, and private security and intelligence personnel gather enormous masses of information at the source, as it were. They are well positioned to notice anomalies that may be clues to terrorist plotting. We need an agency that will integrate local police and other information gatherers into a

28. See U.S. House Committee on Homeland Security Democratic Staff, "Beyond Connecting the Dots: A VITAL Framework for Sharing Law Enforcement Intelligence Information" (Investigative Report Prepared for Congressman Bennie G. Thompson 2005), www.fas.org/irp/congress/2005_rpt/vital.pdf; Bennie G. Thompson, "LEAP: A Law Enforcement Assistance and Partnership Strategy: Improving Information Sharing between the Intelligence Community and State, Local, and Tribal Law Enforcement" (U.S. House of Representatives, Sept. 28, 2006). Not everyone agrees with this gloomy assessment. The police chief of Los Angeles has praised the cooperation he receives from the FBI in terrorist cases. William J. Bratton, "We Don't Need Our Own MI5," *Washington Post*, Oct. 18, 2006, p. A21. The only example he gives, however, is of local police discovering documents indicating an impending attack on Los Angles and obtaining the assistance of the FBI in arresting the plotters. That is not an example of the bureau's excelling at intelligence. The bureau is happy to be handed a terrorism case by local police on a silver platter.

29. See Harris, note 27 above, at 51; Sheridan and Hsu, note 28 above.

30. Olivia Christophersen and Jason Lal, "Police Service Strength England and Wales, 30th September 2003," Home Office Online Report 13/04, www.homeoffice.gov.uk/rds/pdfs2/rdsolr1304.pdf.

comprehensive national intelligence network, as MI5 has done in Britain.[31]

To suggest that the Federal Bureau of Investigation can be that agency overlooks the deeply rooted tensions that have long inhibited cooperation between the bureau and the rest of the law enforcement community and continue to do so.[32] The bureau does not want the local police to steal its cases, and vice versa. Moreover, it is a self-consciously elite institution whose stars—the special agents[33]—look down on local police and are reluctant to share information with them, engendering resentment. Although discovering and thwarting domestic terrorists depend critically on the alertness of local police, they have not been told what to be on the lookout for.[34] Lacking police powers or a law enforcement function, a domestic intelligence agency separate from the FBI could operate as an honest broker among all the institutions that gather information of potential significance for national intelligence. The leads that enabled the Canadian Security Intelligence Service to unravel the Toronto terrorist plot came from local police.

Here is Falkenrath on the federal government's shortcomings in coordinating our vast array of actual and potential intelligence gatherers:

> The federal government, while well-intentioned, has no overarching vision for terrorism-related information sharing with state and local agencies and no clear federal direction or leadership. Part of the

31. See "Special Branch More Than Doubles in Size," note 9 above.

32. See Alasdair Roberts, *Blacked Out: Government Secrecy in the Information Age* 143–146 (2006). An irritant is the FBI's decision to require polygraph tests of state and local police assigned to the bureau's Joint Terrorism Task Forces. See Chapter 3, n. 19; Kevin Johnson, "FBI to Give Police Lie-Detector Tests; Aims to Prevent Espionage and Information Leaks," *USA Today*, June 19, 2006, p. A3.

33. Recall that one reason intelligence analysts have difficulty gaining status and respect in the bureau is that bureau tradition has it that there are only two classes of employees—special agents and clerks.

34. Lara Jakes Jordan, "New Mission for Law Enforcement Groups: Looking Homeward for Terrorists," *Chicago Daily Law Bulletin*, Aug. 30, 2006, pp. 1, 24.

problem was made clear by the Government Accountability Office in its March 2006 report, which identified 56 different sensitive but unclassified designations that federal agencies use "to protect information that they deem critical to their missions." At least three Cabinet-level officers—the Secretary of Homeland Security, the Attorney General, and the Director of National Intelligence—have substantial oversight responsibility for the federal government's information-sharing system; none of them appears truly engaged by the topic. The only established information-sharing mechanism with real coherence and consistent value is the sharing of usually case-specific, classified information with the Joint Terrorism Task Force; this mechanism works reasonably well for what it is, but even it has significant limitations. From the NYPD's perspective, the utility of the Department of Homeland Security's information-sharing initiatives is severely limited by DHS's apparent inability to treat various state and local agencies differently according to their role, their sophistication, their potential contribution to the national mission of combating terrorism, and their size and power. Consequently, NYPD's collaboration with other members of the Intelligence Community and with foreign law enforcement and intelligence agencies is substantially more valuable than is our collaboration with DHS.[35]

The New York City Police Department is one and two-thirds the size of the FBI. Although its counterterrorism and intelligence bureaus are not on the scale of their counterpart units in the bureau (the units that were combined to form the National Security Branch), they provide New York City with more protection against terrorism than the FBI, with its nationwide responsibilities, can do. New York City's police department is the largest in the country, but it should not be the only one that, to my knowledge at least, has committed adequate resources to counterterrorism. Los Angeles, the nation's second-largest city, with half the population of New York City, has assigned only 80 police officers to intelligence and counterterrorism; the corresponding figure for New York City is 1,000.[36] An important

35. Falkenrath, note 18 above, at 20.
36. Nevertheless the Los Angeles department appears to be doing good counter-

role for a federal intelligence agency—a role the FBI is unwilling to play but that a domestic intelligence agency would place at the top of its agenda—is to promote, train, and help finance intelligence units in the nation's major police forces.

It has been argued that often a terrorist suspect must be threatened with arrest and prosecution in order to get his cooperation, and an agency that lacked arrest powers could not do that. But of course it could—it could threaten to turn the suspect over to the FBI or to local police. MI5 and Special Branch work hand in glove. And notice the tension between this argument and the argument one sometimes hears that a domestic intelligence agency would invade privacy and stifle dissent. Not only would such an agency have no powers that the FBI does not have; it would have fewer powers, because it would have no authority to arrest people.

Fewer powers, yes—but in making such a comparison it is important to distinguish the possession from the exercise of legal powers. Although the Attorney General's investigatory guidelines have been loosened since 9/11,[37] they still seem tighter than the Constitution or federal statutes require. I say "seem" rather than "are" because the guidelines (which are multiple and overlapping) contain various escape hatches and because parts of them are classified. But what is undeniable is their complexity, ambiguity, excessively bureaucratic character, and continued heavy emphasis on *criminal* investi-

---

terrorist work. See Chapter 7. Chief Bratton is one of the nation's outstanding police chiefs.

37. See "Attorney General's Guidelines for FBI National Security Investigations and Foreign Intelligence Collection," Dept. of Justice, Oct. 31, 2003, www.fas.org/irp/agency/doj/fbi/nsiguidelines.pdf; "Attorney General's Guidelines on General Crimes, Racketeering Enterprise, and Terrorism Enterprise Investigations," Dept. of Justice, May 30, 2002, www.usdoj.gov/olp/generalcrimes2.pdf; "Attorney General's Guidelines Regarding the Use of Confidential Informants," Dept. of Justice, May 30, 2002, http://149.101.1.32/olp/dojguidelines.pdf; "Attorney General's Guidelines on Federal Bureau of Investigation Undercover Operations," Dept. of Justice, May 30, 2002, www.justice.gov/olp/fbiundercover.pdf.

gation of terrorists. By "excessively bureaucratic character" I have in mind particularly the multiple levels of approval within the bureau and the Department of Justice required for permission to conduct a terrorist investigation.[38] The guidelines are not tailored to the collection of intelligence. They are further evidence that the FBI remains mired in its traditional culture of criminal investigation.

Consider the statement that "these guidelines do not authorize investigating or maintaining information on United States persons solely for the purpose of monitoring activities protected by the First Amendment."[39] Should this be understood literally? Suppose an imam who is an American citizen or permanent resident, and therefore a "United States person," is preaching that it is the duty of every Muslim to oppose Americans with force. This is constitutionally protected speech as long as there is no incitement to violence—no purpose and likely effect of imminently inducing murder or mayhem. It would be simple prudence, however, for the government to make discreet inquiries about the background and acquaintances of the imam, his finances, the reaction of members of his congregation to his preaching, and so forth, and to retain pertinent information collected in the course of the inquiry.

These activities would not violate the First Amendment. But might they not be be forbidden by the guidelines[40] because the sole purpose of the inquiry, and of retaining the information gathered in

38. See, for example, the provisions on "authorization and renewal" of terrorism investigations in "Attorney General's Guidelines on General Crimes, Racketeering Enterprise, and Terrorism Enterprise Investigations," note 37 above, at 17–18.

39. Id. at 7–8.

40. Except that "for the purpose of detecting or preventing terrorist activities, the FBI is authorized to visit any place and attend any event that is open to the public, on the same terms and conditions as members of the public generally." "Attorney General's Guidelines on General Crimes, Racketeering Enterprise, and Terrorism Enterprise Investigations," note 37 above, at 22. But presumably it cannot open an investigation if all it hears in the public place is speech protected by the First Amendment. Nor can it, without opening an investigation, conduct "online searches for information by individuals' names or other individual identifiers." Id.

it, was to monitor speech that happened to be protected by the First Amendment, though not immunized by the amendment from unobtrusive investigation? As important, would FBI special agents and their supervisors interpret the prohibition broadly in order to avoid criticism by civil libertarians and perhaps by liberal judges as well? Would they worry that should the imam ever cross the line into illegal activity, a prosecution of him for that activity would be undermined by evidence that the government had investigated him before he crossed the line? I fear that the answers to these questions are yes.

What is important from the standpoint of protecting civil liberties is not that a domestic intelligence agency comply with guidelines designed for a different type of agency, but that it comply with the law. The tepid public response to the revelation that the National Security Agency has been "spying on Americans" suggests that the public would accept the creation of a domestic intelligence agency if the need for and limited powers of the agency were carefully explained and if it was subjected to the sort of strict administrative oversight to which the Canadian Security Intelligence Service is subject.[41] The main concern of civil libertarians is not with how many agencies engage in domestic intelligence but with the threat to civil liberties that civil libertarians perceive in the collection of such intelligence by *any* agency, including the FBI, a traditional *bête noire* of civil libertarians.[42] It is not who does it, but what it does, that

41. See Security Intelligence Review Committee, note 16 above, and Chapter 7 of this book.

42. Notice the contradiction in the following statement by an opponent of creating a U.S. counterpart to MI5: "The beauty of the FBI is that its focus on violations of criminal laws keeps FBI agents from violating civil liberties. Without that framework, agents might begin to stray into investigating political beliefs or dissent, as they did *when J. Edgar Hoover was FBI director*. In doing so, they would lose their compass, forgetting what their target is and botching investigations because of a lack of proper focus." Ronald Kessler, "An American MI5 Is the Wrong Approach," *NewMax.com's Washington Wire with Ronald Kessler*, Aug. 21, 2006, www.newsmax.com/archives/articles/2006/8/20/210306.shtml (emphasis added). Nothing in the structure of the FBI prevents its violating civil liberties, as it has done in the past. But Kessler is

concerns them. That is why giving the nation's senior intelligence official (the Director of National Intelligence) control for the first time over both domestic and foreign intelligence stirred little controversy.

A domestic intelligence service separate from the FBI would be *more* sensitive to civil liberties than the bureau because maintaining the loyalty of the large U.S. Muslim community would be a priority for such a service, undiluted by the desire to make arrests and assist in prosecutions; whereas from the bureau's standpoint the background from which terrorism emerges is no more interesting than the background from which any other federal crimes emerge. This difference between criminal investigation and domestic intelligence is the difference between counterinsurgency kill tactics and a "hearts and minds" strategy that recognizes that the key to success in counterinsurgency is winning over the population in which the insurgents hide and recruit.

And because a domestic intelligence agency's sole mission would be national security intelligence and it would therefore not hire on the basis of who could do both intelligence and criminal investigation, it would give far more weight than the bureau does to hiring applicants who have needed linguistic and cultural skills. Judging by the trivial number of Arabic-speaking FBI special agents—see Chapter 5—the bureau gives no weight to those factors.[43] The new agency could borrow a leaf from the bureau, however: its director could be given a term of years, like the FBI director, to give him some insulation from political pressures.

It would be important, given the need to conciliate the loyal Muslim community, to avoid giving the impression that the agency had been created just to investigate Muslims. Fortunately, that would not

---

correct to note the FBI's "focus on violations of criminal laws." That focus is unchanged despite the manifest limitations of the criminal process as a counterterrorism tool.

43. See also Jeff Stein, "Can You Tell a Sunni from a Shiite?" *New York Times*, Oct. 17, 2006, p. A21.

be its only mission. Although I have not emphasized the full range of a domestic intelligence agency's functions in this book, they include intelligence directed against espionage in this country by foreign powers, where the FBI's record has been mixed.[44] Nor are all terrorists whose activities endanger national security (for the agency would not concern itself with all political crime or even all terrorism) Muslim. The struggle against Islamist extremism will end one day, just as the Cold War ended; the need for effective domestic intelligence will not.

The case for creating a U.S. domestic intelligence service separate from the Federal Bureau of Investigation is strong, but it is not conclusive. Some of the bureau's problems as an intelligence agency are independent of the drag of its culture and organization. For example, its early-arrest policy, which I criticized in Chapter 5, is due in part to the "one percent doctrine" imposed on it by the Bush Administration; the administration presumably would have imposed the doctrine on a separate domestic intelligence agency, were there one, as well. And such an agency would, like the bureau, struggle to find among

44. See, for example, William E. Odom, *Fixing Intelligence: For a Secure America* 167–172 (2003). Odom summarizes his reasons for thinking that the bureau is not up to performing classic counterespionage: "The two tasks require fundamentally different cultures. Law enforcement agencies thrive on media attention. Counterintelligence agencies perish from it. Criminal catchers are hopeless at catching spies because spies are generally much smarter and more patient than criminals, and they enjoy the support of a foreign government. Counterintelligence agencies need not have arrest authority to uncover spies. They can leave it to law enforcement agencies to make arrests. The technology and sophistication of espionage transcend the characteristics of most criminal activities, allowing spies to overwhelm cops." Id. at xxx. See also id., ch. 8. For other criticisms of the FBI's performance in the counterintelligence role, see discussion and references in Jack Kelly, "More Bumbling by the FBI: Evidence Mounts That the Bureau Can't Handle Counterintelligence," *Pittsburg Post-Gazette*, Jan. 21, 2007, www.post-gazette.com/pg/07021/755301-373.stm. A recent article—Lisa A. Kramer and Richard J. Heuer, Jr., "America's Increased Vulnerability to Espionage," 20 *International Journal of Intelligence* 50 (2007)—argues that a variety of technological and sociological trends are increasing the nation's vulnerability to espionage.

its applicants enough persons with the most urgently needed linguistic skills and cultural sensitivities. But perfection is not an attainable goal of American government—or of any government: MI5 has not kept England free from terrorist attacks.

But considering how strong, even if not airtight, the case for a U.S. domestic intelligence service is, one might have expected the Director of National Intelligence to order a detailed study of the desirability and feasibility of creating such an agency. Such a study could resolve not only the general issues canvassed in this chapter and the preceding one (and in my earlier books), but also specific issues of budget, office space, computer and communications support, recruitment, training, compensation, security, legal authorities, table of organization, relations with other agencies, and a timetable for making such an agency operational. It would be a terrific project for the Office of the Director of National Intelligence because none of the individual intelligence agencies has an interest in doing it. Granted, knowledge that such a study was under way might leak, infuriating the FBI and frightening some civil libertarians. And the study might be taken to acknowledge the administration's continuing failure to solve problems of intelligence that it has been aware of ever since the 9/11 attacks, though I have suggested how such a criticism might be finessed.

Even if the creation of a domestic intelligence agency is considered off the table, a vigorous commitment on the part of the Director of National Intelligence to domestic intelligence reform could yield significant improvements. The National Security Branch could be physically removed from FBI headquarters and given its own quarters, perhaps next to the CIA; physical propinquity can have a significant effect on an organization's outlook. (And instead of being assigned to FBI field offices, NSB personnel could work out of the offices of the CIA's National Resources Division, its domestic branch.) The NSB could be authorized to adopt methods of recruitment, compensation, management, retirement, and so forth modeled on those used by intelligence agencies, rather than on those of the FBI. In other words, the NSB could be given much more autonomy within the bureau than it enjoys at present. Since the bureau isn't about to give it that autonomy, the push must come from the Director of National Intelligence. So far, there has been no push.

More than five years have elapsed since domestic terrorism was recognized as a substantial threat to the nation, yet there is still no architecture of domestic intelligence. It is time that there were at least the architectural drawings. That there are none reflects the lack of any "coordinating entity to ensure that domestic intelligence collection is strategically utilized, both horizontally through the federal government, and vertically among federal, state, and local entities."[45] No single official in the Office of the Director of National Intelligence presides over domestic intelligence as a whole except the DNI himself, who has neither the time nor the inclination to make domestic intelligence a priority (this is likely to be true of Negroponte's successor as well, a military officer). Operations units in the domestic intelligence agencies report to the deputy DNI for collection, analytic units to the deputy for analysis; and both deputies have foreign as well as domestic responsibilities and deem the former paramount. No senior official of the Office of the Director of National Intelligence is assigned full time to domestic intelligence. From the standpoint of FBI rank and file and middle (even senior) management, the Director of National Intelligence is a dwarf star in a distant galaxy.

Plans are no good without implementation, as I emphasized in Chapter 4. But in the case of domestic intelligence, there aren't even the plans.

One reason the disarray in domestic intelligence is being neglected is the pressure of the immediate (see Chapter 3). Another is that the principal officials in the Office of the Director of National

45. Stephen Marrin, "Using Intelligence to Protect Homeland Security," 18 *International Journal of Intelligence and CounterIntelligence* 549, 557 (2005).

Intelligence, including the DNI himself (both Negroponte and his successor), have no background in domestic intelligence. They are foreign-intelligence experts prone to regard domestic intelligence as a briar patch because of the many players (including the Department of Defense), the hot-potato character of "spying on Americans," the FBI's aggressive public relations, the disorganization of the Department of Homeland Security, and the esoteric statutory limitations on the conduct of domestic intelligence (see Chapter 7). Moreover, the executive branch has a freer hand in foreign policy, including foreign intelligence, than in domestic policy. This is due partly to the constitutional design, partly to the urgent need for discretion, expertise, concentration, and speed in the conduct of a nation's foreign relations, partly to Congress's having less interest in foreign than in domestic matters,[46] and partly to the tangle of laws, privacy and civil liberties concerns, and federal-state relations in which domestic intelligence is enmeshed.

The unwillingness or inability of the Director of National Intelligence to take a firm hold of domestic intelligence was conspicuous in the eruption of controversies over the warrantless electronic surveillance conducted by the National Security Agency (see Chapter 7) and over other domestic intelligence activities by agencies in the Department of Defense. The Pentagon agency called "Counterintelligence Field Activity" is conducting domestic intelligence on a large scale.[47] Although its stated mission is to prevent attacks on military

46. A theme of Amy B. Zegart, whose book *Flawed by Design: The Evolution of the CIA, JCS, and NSC* (1999), emphasizes the modest role that Congress has played in the design of the nation's national security agencies.

47. See, for example, Eric Lichtblau and Mark Mazzetti, "Military Expands Intelligence Role in U.S.: Pentagon and C.IA. Defend Requests for Financial Records," *New York Times*, Jan. 14, 2007, § 1, p. 1; Karen DeYoung, "Pentagon Probed Finances: Citizens' Records Culled in Expanded Intelligence Efforts," *Washington Post*, Jan. 14, 2007, p A12; Robert Block and Jay Solomon, "Neighborhood Watch: Pentagon Steps Up Intelligence Efforts inside U.S. Borders: Post–9/11 Campaign Includes Tracking Antiwar Protests, Mining Large Databases: 'Collecting' vs. 'Receiving,'" *Wall Street Journal*, Apr. 27, 2006, p. A1.

installations in the United States, the scale of its activities suggests a broader involvement in domestic security. Another Pentagon agency that has gotten into the domestic intelligence act is the Information Dominance Center, which developed Able Danger, a promising data-mining program derailed by the Bush Administration's failure to explain and defend it in the forum of public opinion. A similar program, Total Information Awareness, was derailed—in another public-relations fiasco, symptomatic of the government's failure to shape domestic intelligence with adequate attention to public sensitivities—by the involvement of Admiral John Poindexter, who after serving as Reagan's National Security Adviser had been convicted of perjury, obstruction of justice, and related offenses arising from his participation in the Iran-Contra affair, though the conviction was reversed on technical grounds. (But apparently the Total Information Awareness program continues under different auspices.[48]) "The military's counterterrorism effort is hampered by bureaucratic duplication, officials said, citing in particular an overlap between new government centers," including the National Counterterrorism Center. "The . . . government-wide national security bureaucracy still does not respond rapidly and effectively to the new requirements of the counterterrorism campaign. The report [prepared by retired General Wayne A. Downing, Jr. at the request of the Pentagon] said more streamlining was necessary across a broad swath of the civilian bureaucracy and military."[49]

All this may change now that Robert Gates is Secretary of Defense, for he is a former CIA director "unhappy about the dominance of the Defense Department in the intelligence arena."[50] But things may look different from his new vantage point; the office shapes the man as much as the man the office.

48. Shane Harris, "Signals and Noise," *National Journal*, June 17, 2006, p. 50.
49. Thom Shanker, "Study Is Said to Find Overlap in U.S. Counterterror Effort," *New York Times*, Mar. 18, 2006, p. A8.
50. Robert M. Gates, "An Intelligent CIA Pick: And, Yes, Hayden Will Stand Up to the Pentagon," *Washington Post*, May 18, 2006, p. A23.

The controversies that have arisen over protecting the United States against attacks from within demonstrate at once the importance and the sensitivity of domestic security, which stirs acute fears both of terrorist attacks (hence the Dubai Ports World controversy) and of civil liberties abuses (hence the controversies over the National Security Agency, Counterintelligence Field Activity, Total Information Awareness, and Able Danger). These fears, though exaggerated, require focused attention by the Office of the Director of National Intelligence on domestic intelligence—and for the further reason that domestic intelligence is a cockpit of conflict among the three separate intelligence cultures that I described in Chapter 5.

Part Two

How Else to Counter Terrorism?

7

The
Judicialization of
Counterterrorism

Elimination of the threat of terrorism should take priority over prosecutions aimed at making examples of past terrorists.[1]

In June 2006, the Supreme Court in the case of *Hamdan v. Rumsfeld*[2] invalidated the military commissions that the President had established to try captured terrorists—commissions that had never conducted any trials. Two months later a federal district judge in Detroit ruled that the National Security Agency's Terrorist Surveillance Program—the controversial program, secret until revealed by the *New York Times* in December 2005 on the basis of a leak, for conducting electronic surveillance without warrants and therefore outside the boundaries of the Foreign Intelligence Surveillance Act—violates both the Act and the Constitution.[3] As a judge I cannot comment

---

1. Marc Sageman, *Understanding Terror Networks* 180 (2004).
2. 126 S. Ct. 2749 (2006).
3. American Civil Liberties Union v. National Security Agency, 438 F. Supp. 2d 754 (E.D. Mich. 2006), at this writing on appeal to the U.S. Court of Appeals for the Sixth Circuit. (Similar cases are pending in other districts.) For a range of views on the legality of the program—whatever exactly it is—see the materials published by the Federalist Society under the title *Terrorist Surveillance and the Constitution* (2006).

publicly on the correctness of her decision, since at this writing the case is pending on appeal. But I can remark the strangeness of confiding so momentous an issue of national security to a randomly selected member of the federal judiciary's corps of almost 700 district judges, subject to review by appellate and Supreme Court judges also not chosen for their knowledge of national security matters. And the further strangeness that the Foreign Intelligence Surveillance Court and the Foreign Intelligence Surveillance Court of Review (which hears appeals from the Foreign Intelligence Surveillance Court, though thus far there has been only one appeal in the 19 years since the Foreign Intelligence Surveillance Act was enacted) have been bypassed, so far as adjudicating the legality of the National Security Agency's program is concerned, in favor of the federal district court in Detroit. The reason is that the jurisdiction of the two foreign intelligence surveillance courts is limited to the grant or denial of foreign intelligence surveillance warrants, and the program under attack involves (or involved—see below) warrantless surveillance.

A Senate bill (S. 2453 in the last Congress) to revise the Foreign Intelligence Surveillance Act contemplated the submission of the Terrorist Surveillance Program and any future such programs to the Foreign Intelligence Surveillance Court for an opinion on its legality—a problematic procedure because federal courts are forbidden to render advisory opinions. A court might even hold that a surveillance "program," as distinct from the surveillance of a specific, named individual, is a "general warrant"; the Fourth Amendment expressly forbids general warrants.

In an abrupt about face, the Bush Administration announced on January 17, 2007, that henceforth it will seek warrants for interceptions of the sort that the National Security Agency has been conducting without warrants under the Terrorist Surveillance Program.[4]

---

4. See Eric Lichtblau and David Johnson, "Court to Oversee U.S. Wiretapping in Terror Cases: Shift by the Government: Justice Dept. Cites Accord Speeding Warrants for Domestic Listening," *New York Times*, Jan. 18, 2007, p. A1.

The reason suggested in media accounts is that negotiations with the Foreign Intelligence Surveillance Court have reassured the administration that the court will issue warrants for such interceptions. There is a whiff of S. 2453, and a hint of a revised understanding by the Foreign Intelligence Surveillance Court of the outer boundaries of the Foreign Intelligence Surveillance Act; for it seems that the program is to continue, only with warrants. General Hayden, the author of the program when he was director of the NSA, had said it involved a "subtly softer trigger" for an interception than the act allowed.[5] This implies, if the program is indeed unchanged, that the Foreign Intelligence Surveillance Court is willing to bend the act to bring the administration back into the fold. But maybe not; other possibilities are that the program has proved unproductive, that the administration is hoping to moot legal challenges to the program that it expects to lose, and that the administration doesn't think it can convince a Democratic Congress to amend the act to the administration's liking. It is too soon to tell. I would have liked to see the act amended, as explained later.

From *Hamdan* and the Detroit case and the interbranch negotiations over the Terrorist Surveillance Program we discover that the nation lacks a coherent judicial dimension to the struggle against terrorism. One reason, discussed in Chapter 8, may be that there is no official with overall responsibility for counterterrorism policy. Another is that very few judges other than the handful assigned to the two foreign intelligence courts have security clearances or, more to the point, know anything about national security, including the scope and gravity of the terrorist threat and the best methods of combating it. It's not as if terrorism were a staple of federal litigation. Still another reason is that the Bush Administration has given a higher priority to pressing its capacious conception of presidential power on the courts

5. Quoted in Shane Harris and Tim Naftali, "Tinker, Tailor, Miner, Spy: Why the NSA's Snooping Is Unprecedented in Scale and Scope," *Slate*, Jan. 3, 2006, www.slate.com/id/2133564.

(with limited success) than to working with Congress to create a statutory framework for using law as a weapon against terrorism.

But the basic problem is simply that the criminal justice system is designed for dealing with ordinary crimes, not with terrorism, especially terrorism of the magnitude that the nation may be facing. Consider the rules of criminal procedure that entitle a person who is arrested to a prompt hearing before a judge to determine whether there is probable cause to believe he's committed a crime, that entitle the defendant to trial by jury, that require that criminal trials be open to the public, that entitle the defendant to confront the witnesses against him and require the government to disclose at trial all its evidence, that limit the use of hearsay evidence, that exclude evidence seized in violation of the Constitution, and that require proof of guilt beyond a reasonable doubt. The requirement of a prompt hearing forces the government to tip its hand and impairs its ability to extract information from a suspect. A public trial gives terrorist defendants a platform for propaganda and recruitment—for broadcasting their grievances and preening themselves as martyrs. A public trial may also yields clues to the government's investigative methods and reveal classified information, and may make the intelligence services of foreign nations, on which we rely heavily for assistance in the struggle against global terrorism, reluctant to share intelligence information with our intelligence agencies, fearing that it will become public in our court proceedings.[6] Public trials create a risk of witness intimidation, and public jury trials invite intimidation of jurors as well.

Requiring proof beyond a reasonable doubt—rather than just requiring, as in civil cases, that the plaintiff show that the defendant is more likely than not to have committed the wrong of which the plaintiff is complaining—weights false positives (convicting innocent persons) much more heavily than false negatives (acquitting guilty

6. Jennifer E. Sims, "Foreign Intelligence Liaison: Devils, Deals, and Details," 19 *International Journal of Intelligence and CounterIntelligence* 195, 211 (2006).

persons). So do other rules of the criminal process, such as the rule excluding evidence designed to establish the defendant's propensity to engage in the conduct of which he has been accused and the rule forbidding the trier of fact to infer guilt from the defendant's refusal to take the stand. The criminal law's systematic weighting of false positives more heavily than false negatives is questionable when the defendant is a terrorist determined to wreak mayhem on a large scale and likely to do so if acquitted.

People have difficulty understanding tradeoffs between false positives and false negatives because they have difficulty thinking in probabilistic terms. The more rights that criminal defendants enjoy, the more guilty people who are exonerated; the fewer rights that criminal defendants enjoy, the more innocent people who are convicted. The choice of the level of rights alters the respective probabilities, and making the correct choice requires weighting those probabilities by the consequences. The probabilities are very difficult to estimate, and so let's assume that they're equal—that for every change in the quantum of criminal defendants' rights, the probability of each type of error (the false positive and the false negative) changes by an equal percentage. So if a small curtailment of defendants' procedural rights would increase the number of false positives by 1 percent, it would reduce the number of false negatives by 1 percent. We know that modern, technologically enhanced, suicidal terrorism can cause enormous damage, so on the assumption of equal and opposite probabilities of error it is arguable that criminal defendants should have fewer rights in terrorism cases than in run-of-the-mill criminal cases.

Against this suggestion, however, it can be argued that the graver the crime, invariably the heavier the punishment and so the greater the injustice if an innocent defendant is convicted. That is indeed a serious objection to relaxing the requirement of proof beyond a reasonable doubt in terrorist cases. While the objection could be met by making the punishments for terrorist crime less severe, this would reduce the efficacy of criminal punishment as a counterterrorist measure. But this point is just a further illustration that the criminal justice system is not well adapted to dealing with terrorism.

Other countries have greater flexibility to tailor their judicial procedures to the special problems posed by terrorism; we are boxed in to an extent by our eighteenth-century Constitution as it has been interpreted by the Supreme Court. But the qualification "to an extent" is vital, and so is "as it has been interpreted." We are less tightly boxed in by the Constitution, even as "amended" by the Supreme Court's countless constitutional decisions, than many civil libertarians believe.[7] One often hears it said, with relief on the part of civil libertarians and anxiety on the part of national security experts, that the Constitution prevents us from emulating the tough measures that England has taken to fight terrorism. If true, this is unfortunate because England has a much longer history of dealing with serious terrorist threats than the United States does. Queen Elizabeth I faced grave danger from religious fanatics, yearning for martyrdom, dispatched to England by foreign powers with which England was at war in the sixteenth century. Germany peppered England with spies during World War II. The provisional wing of the Irish Republican Army waged clandestine war against England for decades. And today England faces a more serious threat of homegrown Islamist terrorism than the United States. We should learn from the experience that England has accrued over the centuries.

Although our political and legal culture derives from England—a British intelligence officer even played a major behind-the-scenes role in the creation of the Office of Strategic Services, the forerunner to the CIA[8]—our Bill of Rights has no direct counterpart in English law. But the difference between the two nations' civil liberties cultures is narrowing as a result of England's having signed the European

7. See Richard A. Posner, *Not a Suicide Pact: The U.S. Constitution in a Time of National Emergency* (2006).

8. See Thomas F. Troy, *Wild Bill and Intrepid: Donovan, Stephenson, and the Origin of CIA* (1996).

Convention on Human Rights. And in considering the effect of our Bill of Rights on measures to combat terrorism we must bear in mind the difference between what the Bill of Rights actually says and how the Supreme Court has interpreted its words; judicial interpretations of the Constitution are mutable, whereas the words themselves can be changed only by the cumbersome procedures for formally amending the Constitution. We should also bear in mind the tradition of flexible interpretation of the Constitution that permits judicial departures from, as well as judicial elaborations of, the actual language of the document, and the balancing of competing interests as a technique of flexible constitutional interpretation. We should remember too that there is nothing novel or illiberal in trading liberty off against safety. We do it all the time, for example in limiting the ownership of guns or requiring seatbelts and infant seats in automobiles.

A further consideration, one of particular importance in national security cases, is that judges in our system are with rare exceptions generalists rather than specialists. Very few of us know much about the menace of terrorism or the efficacy and limitations of alternative measures for countering it. This should make us cautious about setting our judgment against that of the officials and staffs (the staffs more than the political-level officials) of the executive and legislative branches, who have the relevant knowledge. Because the Constitution is so difficult to amend, judges should treat it as a loose garment rather than as a straitjacket—a protection against clear and present dangers to civil liberties rather than the platform of the American Civil Liberties Union.[9] An eighteenth-century document should not be interpreted to bar measures essential to the defense of the nation against twenty-first century threats.

England is a liberal democracy, like the United States, and Americans living in or visiting England, and therefore fully subject to En-

9. These points are argued in Posner, note 7 above. See also Eric A. Posner and Adrian Vermeule, *Terror in the Balance: Security, Liberty, and the Courts* (2007).

glish law while they are there, do not walk in fear that they are at the mercy of a secret police. Like all other nations of the European Union, England has abolished capital punishment. It is in most respects more liberal than the United States. Yet both before and especially after September 11, 2001, England has deployed counterterrorism measures that frighten our civil libertarians, such as[10]

(1) conducting criminal trials without a jury if there is fear of jurors' being intimidated by accomplices of the defendant;

(2) placing persons suspected of terrorism under "control orders" that require them to consent to being questioned or monitored electronically or forbidden to associate with certain persons, and that limit their travel;

(3) detaining terrorist suspects for up to 28 days (with judicial approval) for questioning, without charges being lodged;

(4) conducting deportation proceedings from which the alien and his lawyer may be excluded—the alien is not entitled to be fully informed of the reasons for deporting him; "his" lawyer is appointed by and, more important, is responsible to the government rather

10. The sources for this list are as follows: Antonio Vercher, *Terrorism in Europe: An International Comparative Legal Analysis* (1992); Dana Keith, "In the Name of National Security or Insecurity? The Potential Indefinite Detention of Noncitizen Certified Terrorists in the United States and the United Kingdom in the Aftermath of September 11, 2001," 16 *Florida Journal of International Law* 405 (2004); Helen Fenwick and Gavin Phillipson, "Legislative Over-Breadth, Democratic Failure and the Judicial Response: Fundamental Rights and the UK's Anti-Terrorist Policy," in *Global Anti-Terrorism Law and Policy* 455 (Victor V. Ramraj, Michael Hor, and Kent Roach eds. 2005); Kent Roach, "Must We Trade Rights for Security? The Choice between Smart, Harsh, or Proportionate Security Strategies in Canada and Britain," 27 *Cardozo Law Review* 2151 (2006); Laura K. Donohue, "Anglo-American Privacy and Surveillance," 96 *Journal of Criminal Law and Criminology* 1059 (2006). The British post-9/11 terrorism legislation is, however, strongly criticized in Dirk Haubrich, "September 11, Anti-Terror Laws and Civil Liberties; Britain, France and Germany Compared," 38 *Government and Opposition* 3 (2003), as being insufficiently sensitive to civil liberties.

than to the defendant; and evidence that is classified may be concealed from the defendant;

(5) indefinitely detaining aliens who have been ordered deported but cannot actually be removed from the country (there may be no country willing to take them);[11]

(6) criminalizing persons who encourage terrorism by "glorifying" it in words that imply that the listener should engage in the glorified activity;

(7) authorizing the issuance of search warrants by security officials rather than just by judges;

(8) conducting "traffic analysis" and other data mining of Internet communications without a warrant[12] (Internet service providers are required to install devices to enable Internet communications to be intercepted in transit); a warrant must be obtained to read an intercepted communication, but it may be granted by an executive official rather than a judge;

(9) authorizing judges to issue "Public Interest Immunity Certificates" to intelligence agencies, allowing them to withhold from public judicial proceedings highly sensitive information concerning informants or techniques.[13]

11. The judicial committee of the House of Lords, England's highest court, has invalidated this practice. The situation in England is now similar to that in the United States: a deportee who cannot be removed from the country can be kept in custody indefinitely only if he poses a continuing danger to the country. Zadvydas v. Davis, 533 U.S. 678 (2001).

12. A warrant is not required in order "to monitor patterns, such as web sites visited, to and from whom email is sent, which pages are downloaded, of which discussion groups a user is a member, and which chat rooms an individual visits." Donohue, note 10 above, at 1179–1180.

13. Britain is not the only country that has a political and legal culture similar to ours and from which we might want to borrow ideas for combating terrorism more effectively. Canada—the foreign nation that is most like the United States—is another. See Kent Roach, "Canada's Response to Terrorism," in *Global Anti-Terrorism Law and Policy*, note 10 above, at 511; Richard G. Mosley, "Preventing Terrorism, Bill C-36: The Anti-Terrorism Act 2001," in *Terrorism, Law and Democracy, How Is Canada Changing Following September 11?* 147 (2002).

Contrary to the widespread belief that England, unconstrained by a legally enforceable bill of rights, has gone much further in curtailing the legal rights of terrorist suspects than our Bill of Rights would permit, most of the measures I've listed would not violate the Bill of Rights. The Bill of Rights gives illegal aliens many fewer rights in deportation proceedings than enjoyed by defendants in criminal proceedings; allows criminal suspects to negotiate for "control" orders in lieu of incarceration; and does not require that searches be conducted by warrants, whether issued by judges or by other officials, but only that they not be "unreasonable." Nor does the Constitution require a criminal suspect *always* to be brought before a magistrate for a probable-cause hearing within 48 hours of his arrest. Not only is there no such requirement in the constitutional text; we saw in Chapter 6 that while the Supreme Court has imposed such a requirement by way of free interpretation of the Constitution's due process clauses, the Court excepts cases of "bona fide emergency or other extraordinary circumstance."[14]

That exception is important, and codifying it should be a priority in congressional deliberations on strengthening our laws against terrorism. The judicial formulation is too vague to be of much use in terrorist investigations, especially with the FBI gun-shy about testing the outer bounds of its legal authority. Congress needs to decide for

14. In Hamdi v. Rumsfeld, 542 U.S. 507 (2004), the Supreme Court held that an enemy combatant, even if a U.S. citizen, could be detained without criminal process until the conclusion of hostilities, which is a lot longer than 28 days. But Hamdi had been apprehended in Afghanistan, and it is an unsettled question whether the Supreme Court would authorize similar treatment of a U.S. citizen apprehended in the United States on suspicion of being a member of a foreign terrorist organization. (That was Jose Padilla, who has since been transferred to a regular federal court for trial on terrorism-related criminal charges.) There is the further question, which the courts have not yet answered, whether the end of hostilities against al Qaeda (perhaps we will eventually destroy it, or perhaps it will dissolve voluntarily) would terminate Hamdi's status as an unlawful combatant even if some terrorist group derived from or somehow connected to al Qaeda continued fighting us, whether in Afghanistan or elsewhere.

how much longer than 48 hours it should be permissible to detain a terrorist suspect. The fixing of that outer bound should depend on the likelihood that protracted detention would yield important benefits for national security in additional arrests or a fuller detection, penetration, and disruption of terrorist activities or preparations. There must be limits. The longer the period of detention, the greater the hardship to the person detained (who may, after all, be innocent) and the less likely further detention is to yield significant information or the recruitment of a double agent. The benefits diminish with time, and the costs increase; when the curves cross, the detainee should be brought before a judicial officer to decide whether further detention is necessary. There should be a fixed outer limit—to start with, perhaps 28 days, with the government required (as under English law) to seek periodic reauthorizations from a judge during the 28 days.

The English measures that would present the most difficult constitutional issues if adopted in this country are conducting criminal trials without a jury and forbidding the "glorifying" of terrorism, unless the glorification amounts to an incitement to imminent terrorist activity. Yet, taking the second point first, my "unless" qualification is critical because "glorifying" that came within it would be punishable under U.S. law as well, so that the objection to punishing the glorifying of terrorism is less to the principle of the English law than to the vagueness of the word "glorifying." As for criminal trials without a jury, this provision of the Bill of Rights can probably be bypassed by trying suspected terrorists (at least if they are foreigners apprehended abroad, or, if American, apprehended in a combat setting) before military commissions, where there is no right to a jury. Just how far such commissions can go to relax the other procedural safeguards that the Constitution imposes on orthodox criminal trials is an unsettled question. It will not be answered until the Supreme Court decides the constitutionality of the Military Commissions Act of 2006—the law reauthorizing the commissions (in somewhat altered form) in order to comply with the *Hamdan* decision, which had ruled that the President lacked authority to create them on his own; congressional action was necessary to authorize their creation.

And why *military* commissions? Some of our Islamist enemies, such as the Taliban when they ruled Afghanistan, are military, and if they violate the laws of war, trial before a military commission is appropriate. But most terrorists are not soldiers. Homegrown terrorism may become a major threat in the United States, as it has become in England, but it would be odd to describe it as a *military* threat unless it attained a scale that would justify calling it a rebellion. Yet the prosecution of homegrown terrorists might be as problematic for the conventional court system as the prosecution of international terrorists is, while a special terrorist court might be as appropriate for the former as for the latter. Many special courts, or court-like administrative tribunals, have been established under Article I of the Constitution. They do not exercise the "judicial Power of the United States" in the sense that this phrase bears in Article III, and so they are not cabined by conventional features of federal adjudication, such as that criminal cases be tried by life-tenured judges (and often by jurors as well), appointed by the President and confirmed by the Senate. There are abundant foreign precedents for specialized tribunals, and specialized procedures, for terrorist trials. And there is a U.S. precedent in our two foreign intelligence surveillance courts, though they are Article III rather than Article I courts. A special terrorist court composed of Article III judges, like the two FISA courts, would be less likely to roil constitutional waters than an Article I court would be.

The choice of military commissions reflects both America's legalistic tradition and American provincialism. Legalistic thinking tends to be dichotomous, classificatory—a squeezing of novel problems into old categories by main force. We have a bin called criminal law enforcement and a bin called waging war, and we think that any counterterrorist measure has to be squeezed into one or the other. We have a history of using military commissions (how lawyers love precedents!); and so to escape some of the constraints of criminal law enforcement we declare "war" on terrorism and convene military commissions to try terrorists. This sterile dichotomizing may even be a factor in the reluctance to consider creating a domestic intelligence agency. The Federal Bureau of Investigation is part of the Justice Department and does criminal investigation. The Defense Department fights terrorism by means that include military commissions and electronic surveillance. A domestic intelligence agency would fit neither box comfortably. So instead of creating such an agency we have tried to alter our legal procedures to enable the use in law enforcement of the methods that such an agency would use, such as permitting hearsay and other forms of information that do not fit the rules of evidence, to nail terrorists.

Our cultural provincialism—the instinctive American sense that we have nothing to learn from foreign countries—is reinforced by the inherent provincialism of law. Legal systems differ a great deal across countries, even countries that belong to the same legal phylum, as do the English-speaking nations. Much of the difference is superficial. But it is nonetheless daunting. Learning a foreign legal system is like learning a foreign language—indeed, it may well require learning the country's language. That is not a problem for us in learning the law of an English-speaking nation, but law is not just a rhetorical artifact; it is also an artifact of a country's political, social, and economic culture and institutions, and they have to be understood for a legal transplant to avoid being rejected. Yet we should be able to learn, and benefit from learning, how other democratic countries, especially those with more experience than we have with terrorism, tailor their counterterrorist measures. The literature is extensive and much of it in English.[15] Without violating the letter or even the spirit of our

15. See, besides the references in note 10 above, *Europe Confronts Terrorism* (Karin von Hippel ed. 2005); *Legal Instruments in the Fight against International Terrorism: A Transatlantic Dialogue* (C. Fijnaut, J. Wouters, and F. Naert eds. 2004); *European Counterterrorist Efforts: Political Will and Diverse Responses* (Paul Gallis,

Constitution we could experiment with trying terrorists in specialized courts[16] or with using investigatory magistrates empowered to compel testimony from suspected terrorists under pain of holding them in contempt of court if they refused to testify.

So we could go quite a distance in the direction of English counter-terrorist law. One question is why we haven't, since 9/11; the answer may be that the Bush Administration overestimated what it could do on its own (more precisely, what the courts would permit it to do on its own), without bringing Congress more into the picture. But the question that interests me is how far we should *want* to go in that direction. The answer depends importantly on how salient a role the formal legal system, and in particular the criminal justice system, should play in the struggle against terrorism. As I indicated in Chapter 5, I believe that we are overinvested in criminal law as a response to terrorism, and this regardless of specific constraints that the courts and Congress have placed on criminal law enforcement and might be persuaded to relax. That is, this overinvestment is not, at least not primarily, a result of the courts' or Congress's having made investing in criminal law enforcement unprofitable by giving criminal defendants too many rights. Rather it is a symptom of an overlegalized political culture, in which litigation is seen as the answer to every problem. Conservatives rail against trial lawyers, activist judges, vague laws, and the proliferation of tort and other civil suits. What they miss is that our profligate recourse to the criminal process, and our prison population hugely swollen by draconian drug laws, are symptoms of the same underlying problem—an unconscious and often foolish faith in the legal system to alleviate our social and political

---

coordinator, 2004); *Confronting Terrorism: European Experiences, Threat Perceptions and Policies* (Marianne van Leeuwen ed. 2003); Human Rights Watch, "Setting an Example? Counter-Terrorism Measures in Spain" (Report No. D1701, Jan. 2005).

16. See, for example, Vercher, note 10 above, at 303–322; Nathalie Cettina, "The French Approach: Vigour and Vigilance, in *Confronting Terrorism*, note 15 above, at 71, 82–83.

woes. Democrats and Republicans play leapfrog in advocating new legal remedies for perceived social ills.

Criminal law enforcement is no more likely to win the "war on terrorism" than it is to win the "war on drugs." It is maladapted to both struggles. We should be deemphasizing the effort to prevent terrorism by means of criminal prosecutions, especially but not only in the regular courts, which are not designed for the trial of people who pose a serious threat to national security. Our counterterrorism efforts would be more effective, and at the same time the dilemma of defeating terrorism while respecting essential civil liberties minimized, if we downplayed the judicial role in counterterrorism.

This would mean less striving to prevent terrorism by criminal prosecutions, whether in courts or in military tribunals; a diminished use of devices, such as the warrant, that are used mainly in criminal law enforcement; and an expanded recourse to executive and legislative rather than judicial oversight to curb abuses to which counterterrorism undoubtedly is prone. It is prone to abuse because of the fear that terrorism engenders and terrorism's political nature, which makes political opinions and advocacy a concern of national security.

It is telling that no one was actually tried by the military commissions established in the wake of 9/11 before they were held unconstitutional by the Supreme Court almost five years later[17] and that criminal prosecutions of terrorists have been few and often trivial. One study states:

- Only four individuals have been convicted of federal crimes of terrorism, per se.

- Nobody affiliated with a radical Islamic group has been convicted

---

17. On the difficulties involved in prosecuting cases before a military commission, see Jess Bravin, "At Guantánamo, Even 'Easy' Cases Have Lingered: Balky Intelligence Agencies, War-Torn Crime Scene Hinder Legal Process," *Wall Street Journal*, Dec. 18, 2006, p. A1.

of crimes related to chemical, biological, radiological, or nuclear weapons.

- No sleeper cell with logistical or tactical links to al Qaeda has been convicted.

- The vast majority of cases turn out to include no link to terrorism once the case goes to court.

- No consistent definition of terrorism or of a terrorist emerges from the data [in the study] . . .

- Conviction, no matter how short the period of time or how minor the charge, is the primary goal.

- The DOJ's [Department of Justice's] pattern of pursuit is focused on early detection rather than conviction on federal terrorism charges.

- The DOJ often announces potential terrorism cases as such before the evidence is in place that will enable prosecution for a federal crime of terrorism.[18]

According to another study, "the median sentence for those convicted [since the 9/11 attacks] in what were categorized as 'international terrorism' cases—often involving lesser charges like immigration violations or fraud—was 20 to 28 days, and many received no jail time at all."[19] In fact terrorist prosecutions seem to be petering out,[20] to the embarrassment of the Justice Department and the FBI.

18. New York University Center for Law and Security, "Terrorist Trial Report Card: U.S. Edition: Executive Summary" (New York University School of Law, Nov. 2006).

19. Eric Lichtblau, "Study Finds Sharp Drop in the Number of Terrorism Cases Prosecuted," *New York Times*, Sept. 4, 2006, p. A9.

20. Id.; Dan Eggen, "Terrorism Prosecutions Drop: Analysis Shows a Spike after 9/11, Then a Steady Decline," *Washington Post*, Sept. 4, 2006, p. A6. Eggen's article summarizes Transactional Records Access Clearinghouse (TRAC), "Criminal Terrorism Enforcement in the United States during the Five Years since the 9/11/01 Attacks" (TRAC Report, Sept. 3, 2006), http://trac.syr.edu/tracreports/terrorism/169/. For striking examples of hyped FBI terrorist investigations and prosecutions, see Scott

A notable example is the case of Jose Padilla, arrested four and a half years ago on suspicion of planning a "dirty bomb" attack and later accused of planning to blow up apartment buildings and commit other mayhem:

> A Republican-appointed federal judge in Miami has already dumped the most serious conspiracy count against Padilla, removing for now the possibility of a life sentence. The same judge has also disparaged the government's case as "light on facts," while defense lawyers have made detailed allegations that Padilla was illegally tortured, threatened and perhaps even drugged during his detention at a Navy brig in South Carolina . . . The difficulties [that the government is having with the case] have reignited a debate in legal circles over whether terrorism suspects such as Padilla can be effectively prosecuted in regular criminal courts.[21]

The government's failure (or perhaps inability) to bring anyone to trial before a military commission may have contributed to its losing the *Hamdan* case. Had the Court been reviewing a judgment rendered after a trial conducted by such a commission, it might have been persuaded that the procedures were adequate to prevent miscarriages of justice. The Court can also be criticized, however, for its impatience in refusing to hold its fire until a trial had been held that would have lent concreteness to judicial consideration of the legal issues. It is true that the Court's ruling was based on a lack of legislative authority for the commissions, and such a ruling is, in principle, unrelated to the adequacy of their procedures. But in practice, judges' sense of the "fairness" or "justice" of a proceeding is likely to influence their decision on whether the proceeding is authorized, at least in a close case, which *Hamdan* was.

Shane and Lowell Bergman, "F.B.I. Struggling to Reinvent Itself to Fight Terror," *New York Times*, Oct. 10, 2006, pp. A1, A23.

21. Dan Eggen, "Padilla Case's Troubles Raise Questions on Anti-Terror Tactics," *Washington Post*, Nov. 19, 2006, p. A1. The court of appeals, however, has reinstated the dismissed count. See United States v. Hassoun, No. 06–15845, 2007 WL 218762 (11th Cir. Jan. 30, 2007).

Criminal law enforcement discourages crime by a combination of deterrence and incapacitation. Contemporary international terrorists are difficult to deter. Not only are many of them suicide attackers, but as political criminals the others may expect if captured to be released from prison, as part of a swap or a political settlement, before completion of their prison terms. As for incapacitation, locking up terrorists (those who survive the terrorist attack) has only a limited preventive effect because the supply of replacements is so large.[22] Nor is it necessary to put a terrorist on trial in order to be able to imprison him indefinitely. The Constitution does not require a full-scale criminal trial in order to detain a person who is a demonstrable threat to national security.[23]

The Constitution does, of course, require a trial if the government wants to execute a person. But executing terrorists, at least before the political movement to which the terrorists belong has been crushed, is usually a mistake. It creates martyrs, as the English learned to their sorrow when they executed the leaders of the Easter Rebellion in Ireland in 1916. It is one thing to execute an enemy when the alternative is a short prison sentence, or to execute the leaders or for that matter the followers of a defeated movement or regime, as in the case of the Nazi leaders executed after World War II; but Islamist terrorism has not been defeated and it thrives on martyrdom. Obviously the threat of execution does not deter would-be martyrs, as they do not expect to survive their attacks. But neither, in all likelihood, does it deter the leaders of terrorist movements, even though they do not seek martyrdom. To be a terrorist leader is already to accept a high probability of being killed—the *incremental* probability of death by execution will usually be slight.

22. In economic terms, the supply of terrorists is highly elastic, meaning that if one is killed or captured, creating a demand for a replacement, the demand will be quickly filled by someone from the large reserve army of potential terrorists.

23. Posner, note 7 above, at 66–67. But if a terrorist suspect is detained on the ground that he poses a danger to national security, there should be periodic judicial review to determine whether his continued detention is justified.

Granted, there is more to terrorism than leaders and suicide bombers. Peripheral players are deterrable by threat of criminal punishment.[24] An important example is criminals who sell weapons to terrorists.[25] Nor am I advocating that we turn the other cheek. Just and prudent retribution can be ferocious without being channeled through the legal system. Our military and quasi-military efforts against terrorism have inflicted substantial costs on our terrorist enemies. And however the Military Commissions Act of 2006 fares in the courts, the Constitution casts a longer shadow over criminal prosecutions than it does over nonlegal (by which I do not mean illegal) methods, even when lethal, of combating terrorism. (A longer shadow and also a lengthening one.[26]) Most of the rights conferred by the Bill of Rights, as expansively interpreted by the Supreme Court, are rights of criminal defendants. Efforts to curtail those rights, whether through judicial interpretation or by shifting prosecution to non-Article III courts, encounter particularly strident opposition from civil libertarians. We shall see that electronic surveillance is less constrained by the Fourth Amendment when it is not used to generate evidence for criminal prosecutions.

Criminal law enforcement may seem the only *domestic* counterterrorist tool that we have unless martial law is declared and the military turned loose on domestic enemies. But as we saw in Chapters 5 and 6, that is incorrect. Intelligence services disrupt as well as detect, and not only by engaging in forms of covert action that comply with U.S. law only when they are deployed abroad. The term "covert action" requires careful definition. It is too often equated to efforts

---

24. That deterrence retains considerable utility as a method of counterterrorism is strongly argued in Paul K. Davis and Brian Michael Jenkins, *Deterrence and Influence in Counterterrorism: A Component in the War on al Qaeda* (2002).

25. See David P. Auerswald, "Deterring Nonstate WMD Attacks," 121 *Political Science Quarterly* 543 (2006).

26. See Jack Landman Goldsmith and Cass R. Sunstein, "Military Tribunals and Legal Culture: What a Difference Sixty Years Makes," 19 *Constitutional Commentary* 261 (2002).

to subvert foreign governments. That is indeed the activity in which the CIA achieved unwanted notoriety. But all the term means or should mean is clandestine activity in support of national security. It covers a wide range of tactics, some clearly inappropriate for domestic intelligence or security operations but others uncontroversially used in combating ordinary crimes and properly usable for domestic counterterrorism as well. Once detected, therefore, a terrorist plot can often be lawfully neutralized without prosecution of the plotters. Some of them can be deported (deportation is civil rather than criminal and administrative rather than judicial, though there is judicial review); some "turned" to work for us by offers of money or other assistance, by threats, or by promises (turning an enemy into a friend is one way of dealing with some enemies); some discredited in the eyes of their accomplices; some paid off; some frightened into sullen quiescence by a "heavy tap on the shoulder" (a warning to the suspect that his activities and inclinations are known to the authorities and that he is being watched); some sent off on wild-goose chases by carefully planted disinformation; some bought off by amnesties; and some monitored in the hope that they will lead us to their accomplices

And some can be held in administrative detention or otherwise restricted in their movements (if a judge decides they're dangerous[27]) until the terrorist threat abates and then either tried in the regular way or released. For it is not true that preventive detention—detention other than pursuant to a criminal charge or conviction—is alien to the American legal system. An insane person, for example, can be detained indefinitely (though with frequent judicial review) if he is adjudged a serious danger to himself or others. The same thing should be possible if the person is dangerous not because he is insane but because his religion or his politics impels him to mass murder.

The greatest value of allowing detention of terrorist suspects for

27. See note 11 above.

more than 48 hours would lie neither in facilitating prosecution nor in keeping them out of circulation without a prosecution, however, but rather in aiding intelligence by enabling the government to get more complete and timely information about the scope, direction, timing, personnel, and links to other networks of the plot that has been detected.

I am not suggesting that criminal law should be dispensed with in the struggle against modern terrorism, any more than military force should be, though the efficacy of military force as a way of combating terrorism is easily exaggerated as well.[28] If all terrorists were so fanatical as to be undeterrable by threat of criminal punishment, the methods available to intelligence services in the domestic environment would often fall flat. The tap on the shoulder would lack weight if it didn't convey an implicit threat to prosecute a suspect who refused to play ball.[29] And sometimes the heavy tap is inferior to prosecution because it just drives the suspect deeper into a secret terrorist milieu, so that intelligence loses track of him. Moreover, many of the handicaps to using the criminal law against terrorists dissolve when terrorist suspects are prosecuted for violating ordinary crimes—a form of lawful police harassment.[30] That is part of the explanation for those light sentences in the Justice Department's antiterrorist cases; the defendants were suspected terrorists prosecuted for ordinary crimes. In general, however, when the government is not looking to put a terrorist suspect on trial, it has more constitutional and statutory

28. Our successful campaign against Afghanistan in the wake of the 9/11 attacks was mainly a CIA show, as was the Predator strike that killed terrorist leaders in Yemen, while the invasion and occupation of Iraq by our armed forces have not been antiterrorist triumphs.

29. Or to detain him indefinitely, without prosecution, on the ground that he is too dangerous to let loose. But if he is that dangerous, the heavy tap on the shoulder would probably not be an effective method of neutralizing him.

30. See, for example, Robert Block, "An L.A. Police Bust Shows New Tactics for Fighting Terror: Officers Use Local Laws to Arrest Small Offenders with High-Risk Potential," *Wall Street Journal*, Dec. 29, 2006, p. A1.

space in which to seek to neutralize him, using methods that often are more effective than criminal law enforcement.

Marc Sageman, noting that the global jihad is a series of networks of social groups,[31] argues for

> a coordinated attack targeted against [the terrorists who constitute the networks'] social nodes. They are particularly vulnerable because most communications and human contacts go through them. Arresting these individuals would degrade these networks into isolated units, singletons or cliques, who would consequently be incapable of mounting complex large-scale operations owing to lack of expertise and logical and financial support. Small-scale operations would be very hard to eradicate completely, but without spectacular successes to sustain their motivation for terrorism, isolated operators will lose their enthusiasim.[32]

Arresting the "social nodes" is one way of disrupting a terrorist network, but not the only way, since, as we have seen, there are other ways of neutralizing an enemy besides arresting him. Nor, as we have also seen, need arrest connote prosecution. Detention and punishment are not synonyms.

A mischievous example of attempting to judicialize counterterrorism is warrant fetishism. Warrants, which our civil libertarians venerate, are actually constrained rather than required or encouraged by the warrant clause of the Fourth Amendment. All the clause does is impose *limitations* on warrants—that they be supported by oath (or affirmation) and probable cause and describe with particularity the person, house, etc., to be searched and the things to be seized. Surveillance, even when it takes the form of wiretapping or other electronic interception and so is deemed a search under the Fourth Amendment, need not—at least if the actual language of the amendment is deemed authoritative—be conducted on the authority of a

31. Sageman, note 1 above, ch. 5.
32. Id. at 176.

warrant. The Fourth Amendment permits warrantless surveillance provided that it is reasonable.

We should break ourselves of the habit of thinking that legal rules are always the best way of preventing abuses. Congress struggled in the Military Commissions Act to define the legal limits of coercive interrogation. An alternative would have been to require that the interrogation of terrorist suspects that uses methods forbidden in an ordinary criminal investigation be expressly authorized in writing by the Secretary of Defense, the Attorney General, or the President himself. Accountability would be substituted for deniability and legal hairsplitting.

So let me suggest that the best way to end the debate over the propriety of the National Security Agency's Terrorist Surveillance Program—for it seems unlikely that the administration's recent retreat will end it—would be for Congress to amend the Foreign Intelligence Surveillance Act along entirely different lines from those that have been proposed. (Surveillance is, of course, a tool of intelligence; I discuss the National Security Agency's program in this part of the book, which deals with alternative methods of combating terrorism, because FISA regulates electronic surveillance for national security purposes on the analogy of the regulation of electronic surveillance in criminal investigations.)

After the Supreme Court ruled in a conventional criminal case that wiretapping and, by implication, other forms of electronic surveillance were to be deemed "searches" within the meaning of the Fourth Amendment, Congress enacted Title III of the Omnibus Crime Control and Safe Streets Act of 1968. Title III created procedures for obtaining warrants for electronic surveillance that were modeled on the procedures for conventional search warrants. Ten years later—and thus long before the danger of global terrorism was recognized and electronic surveillance transformed by the digital revolution—the Foreign Intelligence Surveillance Act was enacted. It is a complicated statute but basically it provides that interceptions in the United States of the international communications of a U.S. citizen, or permanent resident, or of anyone in the United States if the interception is made here, be conducted pursuant to warrants based on probable cause to believe that one of the parties to the communication is a foreign terrorist.

That is the wrong approach, as 9/11 has taught us. It remains usable for regulating the monitoring of communications of known terrorists, but it is useless for finding out who is a terrorist,[33] even though "the problem of defeating the enemy consists very largely of finding him."[34] Hence the importance of "collateral intercepts"—such as intercepts of communications that seem likely to yield information of intelligence value even if probable cause to believe that a party to the communication is a terrorist is lacking.

It is true that surveillance not cabined by a conventional probable-cause requirement produces many false positives—interceptions that prove upon investigation to have no intelligence value. But that is not a valid criticism. We must not forget the necessity of balancing false positives against false negatives. The failure to detect the 9/11 plot was an exceptionally costly false negative. The intelligence services have no alternative to casting a wide net with a fine mesh if they are to have reasonable prospects of obtaining the clues that will enable the next attack to be prevented.[35]

33. See, for example, K. A. Taipale, "Whispering Wires and Warrantless Wiretaps: Data Mining and Foreign Intelligence Surveillance," *Bulletin on Law and Security*, Spring 2006 (New York University Law School, Center on Law and Security), http://whisperingwires.info/; Taipale, "The Ear of Dionysus: Rethinking Foreign Intelligence Surveillance" (Jan. 26, 2007; forthcoming in *Yale Journal of Law and Technology*). Taipale's Center for Advanced Studies in Science and Technology Policy has published helpful analyses of the use of data mining for national security. See www.advancedstudies.org; also notes 35–36 below.

34. Frank Kitson, quoted in Bradley W. C. Bamford, "The Role and Effectiveness of Intelligence in Northern Ireland," 20 *Intelligence and National Security* 581, 586 (2005).

35. A further drawback of FISA, according to Taipale, "The Ear of Dionysus," note 33 above, at 11 n 42, is that it is now possible to buy a telephone (a "VoIP"

The Terrorist Surveillance Program involves an initial sifting, performed by computer search programs, of electronic communications for clues to terrorist activity. The sifting uses both "content filtering" and "traffic analysis" to pick out a tiny percentage of communications to be read. Content filtering is Google-like searching for words inside the communication. Traffic analysis is examining message length, frequency and time of communication, and other noncontent information that may reveal suspicious patterns; thus traffic analysis can't be foiled by encryption because the information is not content-based.[36] The National Security Agency has obtained call records from telephone companies to aid in its traffic analysis. If the agency has the phone number of a known or suspected terrorist, it can use call records to determine the most frequent numbers called to or from that number and then determine the most frequent numbers called to or from *those* numbers and in this way piece together a possible terrorist network—all without listening to any conversation. That comes later.

So the search sequence is interception, data mining, and finally a human search of those intercepted messages that data mining or other information sources have flagged as suspicious. Computer searches do not invade privacy because search programs are not sentient beings. Only the human search should raise constitutional or other legal issues.

---

phone—short for "Voice over Internet Protocol") to which a local U.S. phone number can be assigned even if the phone is used outside the United States. Two terrorists in Pakistan could be talking to each other by means of such phones yet the National Security Agency would think it a conversation between two U.S. persons in the United States, which the Foreign Intelligence Surveillance Act does not permit the government to intercept. This is an example of how FISA has been rendered obsolete by unanticipated technological advances.

36. See note 12 above; Hazel Muir, "Email Gives the Game Away," *New Scientist*, Mar. 29, 2003, p. 19. Skeptics of the value of data mining for intelligence abound, see, for example, Jeff Jonas and Jim Harper, "Effective Counterterrorism and the Limited Role of Predictive Data Mining" (Cato Institute, Policy Analysis No. 584, Dec. 11, 2006), but are forcefully rebutted in Kim Taipale, "The Privacy Implications of Government Data Mining Programs" 7–14 (Statement before the U.S. Senate Committee on the Judiciary, Jan. 10, 2007).

Communications read by an intelligence officer and thus "searched" in the legal sense could as a technical matter include— what the Foreign Intelligence Surveillance Act forbids unless there is probable cause to believe that a party to the communication is a terrorist or an agent of a foreign power—communications to which a U.S. citizen is a party and communications that are purely domestic rather than international. Although the Bush Administration has denied that it is monitoring purely domestic communications, such monitoring is within the Terrorist Surveillance Program's feasible technical scope.

Instead of requiring probable cause to believe that the target of an interception is a terrorist, the Foreign Intelligence Surveillance Act could be amended to require merely reasonable suspicion. But even that would be too restrictive; effective surveillance can't be confined to suspected terrorists when the object is to discover who may be engaged in terrorism or ancillary activities. Further attenuation of FISA's standard for obtaining a warrant may be possible. Maybe the issuance of a warrant could be authorized on the basis of a showing that while the target was probably not a terrorist, national security required making assurance doubly sure by intercepting some of his electronic communications. A model (and an example of how we can learn from foreign experience) might be the criterion for issuing a search warrant to the Canadian Security Intelligence Service: it can be issued on the basis of a factually supported "belief, on reasonable grounds, that a warrant—is required to enable the Service to investigate a threat to the security of Canada."[37] Such a criterion might pass muster under the Fourth Amendment, which requires probable cause for the issuance of a warrant but does not state what it is that there must be probable cause to believe. The Supreme Court has said that it must be probable cause to believe that the search will

---

37. CSIS Office Consolidation: Canadian Security Intelligence Service Act (July 1984), R.S. 1985, c. C-23, § 21(2)(a) (Feb. 2000).

yield contraband or evidence of crime—when the search is part of a criminal investigation.[38] That is an example of my earlier point that the Constitution binds the government more tightly when it is exerting its powers to convict people of crimes. A search intended not to obtain evidence of crime but to obtain information about terrorism might, as under Canadian law, require only probable cause to believe that the search would yield such information.

The lower the standard for getting a warrant, however, the more porous the filter that the requirement of a warrant creates, bearing in mind the ex parte character of a warrant proceeding. If all the application need state is that an interception might yield data having value as intelligence, a judge would have no basis for refusing to issue the warrant. Alternatively, reliance on warrants could invite legislation to expand the reach of the criminal laws relating to terrorism in order to make it easier to establish probable cause to believe that a search will reveal evidence of crime.

Warrants that satisfy FISA's standard as traditionally understood should continue to be required for all physical searches, because they are far greater intrusions on privacy than an electronic interception is, and for all electronic surveillance for which FISA's existing probable-cause requirement can be satisfied. With these exceptions, civil libertarians' preoccupation with warrants is not only harmful to national security (and possibly to civil liberties, if it induces legislation to expand the reach of the criminal law) but also anachronistic. The government's ready access to the vast databases that private and public entities compile for purposes unrelated to national security has enabled it to circumvent much of the protection of privacy that civil libertarians look to warrant requirements to secure.[39]

The fuss that some Americans make about electronic surveillance

---

38. Zurcher v. Stanford Daily, 436 U.S. 547, 554–555 (1978).

39. See, for example, Arshad Mohammed and Sara Kehaulani Goo, "Government Increasingly Turning to Data Mining: Peek into Private Lives May Help in Hunt for Terrorists," *Washington Post*, June 15, 2006, p. D3; Posner, note 7 above, ch. 6.

is remarkable when one considers how little value we actually place on privacy, as illustrated by the point just noted—the right of the owners of the databases to which we promiscuously convey our private information to share it with the government. Americans give up their political privacy for the convenience of one-click buying of books, even though Amazon.com can create a political profile of everyone who buys its books and share those profiles, either voluntarily or in response to a subpoena, with the government.

Still, unreflective though it may be, the public anxiety about electronic surveillance and data mining is a political fact to which the intelligence system must adjust. There are a number of possible measures, apart from requiring warrants, by which Congress could minimize abuses of domestic surveillance programs. If all were adopted, the risk of such abuses would be slight.

1. Congress could create a steering committee for national security electronic surveillance, composed of the Attorney General, the Director of National Intelligence, the Secretary of Homeland Security, and a retired federal judge or justice appointed by the Chief Justice of the United States. The committee would monitor all such surveillance to assure compliance with the Constitution and laws.

2. The National Security Agency could be required to submit to the steering committee, to departmental inspectors general, to the Privacy and Civil Liberties Oversight Board (a White House agency created by the Intelligence Reform Act), to the congressional intelligence and judiciary committees, and to an independent watchdog agency of Congress modeled on the General Accountability Office, every six months a list of the names and other identifying information of all persons whose communications had been intercepted in the previous six months without a warrant, with a brief statement of why these persons had been targeted.

3. The responsible officials of the National Security Agency could be required to certify annually to the watchdog groups that there had been no violations of the statute during the preceding year.

False certification would be punishable as perjury. But lawsuits challenging the legality of the Terrorist Surveillance Program should be precluded. Such lawsuits distract officials from their important duties, to no purpose if the kind of statute that I am suggesting were enacted. The statute should sunset after five years.

4. The use of intercepted information for any purpose other than investigating threats to national security would be forbidden. Information could not be used as evidence or leads in a prosecution for ordinary crime—this to alleviate concern that wild talk bound to be picked up by electronic surveillance would lead to criminal investigations unrelated to national security.

Violations of this provision would be made felonies punishable by substantial prison sentences and heavy fines. But the punishments must not be made too severe lest they cause intelligence officers to steer so far clear of possible illegality that they fail to conduct effective surveillance. The risk of abuses is not great enough to justify savage penalties in order to deter them, because intelligence officers have no interest in assisting in the enforcement of criminal laws unrelated to national security. A neglected point is that violations of privacy and civil liberties tend to emanate from the White House and the top management level of executive branch agencies rather than from the working or middle-management levels.

5. To limit the scope of surveillance, "threats to national security" should be narrowly defined as threats involving a potential for mass deaths or catastrophic property or other economic damage. That would exclude, for the time being anyway, ecoterrorism, animal-rights terrorism, and other types of political violence that, though criminal, do not threaten catastrophic harm (yet).

Congressional action is also needed to protect the phone companies that cooperated with the National Security Agency's surveillance program from potentially immense liability for allegedly having violated federal law protecting the privacy of telephone records; a number of suits are pending. The intelligence system is enormously dependent on informal assistance from private companies in communications, banking, and other industries. At times such assistance is made a legal duty, as in the federal law requiring banks to report cash transactions of $10,000 or more. Most of the assistance is voluntary. But if voluntary assistance—even when tendered in a national emergency, as in the wake of the 9/11 terrorist attacks—places companies in legal jeopardy, such assistance will dry up. The Foreign Intelligence Surveillance Act needs to be amended not only to authorize more extensive domestic surveillance than its anachronistic terms permit but also to insulate from liability conduct that may have violated the act or some other statute but that would be permitted under the amended regime.

Why are such ideas (except legal immunities for business) for regularizing domestic surveillance getting little attention from Congress and the administration? Why am I a voice crying in the wilderness? One possibility, diminished however by the administration's recent retreat on warrantless electronic surveillance, is that the administration wants to retain a completely free hand and thinks it can fend off the sort of restrictions that I have sketched. (It is remarkable how tepid the public reaction to the Terrorist Surveillance Program has been.) A related possibility is that the administration's aggressive claims of presidential power prevent its acknowledging the legitimacy of congressional controls over intelligence and hence of a legislative solution to the controversy over the program. Still another possibility is that because no one is in charge of domestic intelligence, no one is formulating a comprehensive legislative and public-relations strategy for ending the controversy over the role of electronic surveillance in such intelligence. And another is the grip of our legalistic culture, which makes us think that the regulation of national security *must* be modeled on the regulation of criminal law enforcement. The culture may have the administration by the throat.

We should be playing to our strengths, and one of the greatest of them is technology. We may not be able to prevail against terrorism with one hand tied behind our back. Critics of surveillance argue that since our enemies know that we monitor electronic communications, they will foil us by simply ceasing to use such communications. That is wrong. We know it is wrong because we do intercept terrorist communications.[40] But if it were true that our monitoring caused the terrorists to abandon the telephone and the Internet, that would be an enormous victory for counterterrorism, as it is extremely difficult to coordinate and execute a major terrorist attack if all communications among the plotters must be face to face to avoid detection. The greater danger is that encryption and other relatively cheap and simple countermeasures will defeat our surveillance.

Opponents of efforts to amend the Foreign Intelligence Surveillance Act point out that the Foreign Intelligence Surveillance Court has almost never turned down an application for a warrant. In 2005, for example, although more than 2000 applications were filed, not a single one was denied in whole or in part.[41] The inference the critics wish drawn is that FISA is not inhibiting surveillance. The correct inference is that the Justice Department is too conservative in seeking warrants. The analogy is to a person who has never missed a plane in his life because he contrives always to arrive at the airport eight hours before the scheduled departure time. The effect of the legalistic miasma of which I have been complaining in this chapter is to cause law enforcement agencies, notably the FBI, to avoid not only violating the law but also steering so close to the wind that they might be accused, albeit groundlessly, of violating the law, or of being "insensitive" to values that inform the law, even when those values have not been enacted into law.

An example is the "wall" that before 9/11 inhibited communica-

40. See, for example, James Bamford, "He's in the Backseat!" *Atlantic Monthly*, Apr. 2006, p. 67.
41. Letter of April 28, 2006, to J. Dennis Hastert, Speaker, U.S. House of Representatives, from William E. Moschella, Assistant Attorney General, www.fas.org/irp/agency/doj/fisa/2005rept.html.

tion between intelligence officers and criminal investigators. Quickly dismantled (or so it is claimed—actually, it was merely lowered) after the 9/11 attacks, the wall was a product of the Justice Department's exaggerated fear of jeopardizing criminal prosecutions by using, as leads or evidence in prosecutions, information obtained by intelligence operations, including FISA surveillance:

> The 1995 procedures [that established the wall] dealt only with sharing between agents and criminal prosecutors, not between two kinds of FBI agents, those working on intelligence matters and those working on criminal matters. But pressure from the [Justice Department's] Office of Intelligence Policy Review, FBI leadership, and the FISA Court built barriers between agents—even agents serving on the same squads. FBI Deputy Director Bryant reinforced the Office's caution by informing agents that too much information sharing could be a career stopper. Agents in the field began to believe—incorrectly—that no FISA information could be shared with agents working on criminal investigations.
>
> This perception evolved into the still more exaggerated belief that the FBI could not share any intelligence information with criminal investigators, even if no FISA procedures had been used. Thus, relevant information from the National Security Agency and the CIA often failed to make its way to criminal investigators.[42]

The legalistic atmosphere that envelops the Justice Department, including the FBI (notice that the bureau played a role, though not the dominant one, in building the wall), persists in the Attorney General's guidelines for terrorist investigations, discussed in Chapter 6, even as liberalized after 9/11. So still another reason, besides the reasons discussed in previous chapters, for creating a domestic intelligence agency outside the FBI is to begin clearing away the legalistic underbrush that is impeding the nation's response to the terrorist threat.

---

42. National Commission on Terrorist Attacks upon the United States, *The 9/11 Commission Report* 79 (2004).

8

Counterterrorism Strategy and Structure; An Ounce of Prevention?

Counterterrorist intelligence, both foreign and domestic, and its "action" counterparts, are only one set of tools for countering terrorism. By "action counterparts" to counterterrorist intelligence I mean actions taken by the intelligence community itself to thwart, as distinct from merely discovering, a terrorist plot. This is the domain of covert action abroad, where U.S. laws in general do not apply, and of a milder version of covert action inside the United States, such as the heavy tap on the shoulder. The emphasis to be placed on one set of counterterrorist tools, such as the action side of intelligence, over another requires a strategic judgment. I have argued that we are overemphasizing criminal law enforcement relative to both the information and the action sides of intelligence. This overemphasis is both cause and effect of the FBI's inadequate performance of its domestic intelligence duties.

Another questionable strategic judgment, besides the decision to emphasize criminal law as a counterterrorist tactic, has been to place paramount emphasis on a "forward" counterterrorist strategy. Of course there is much appeal to nabbing foreign terrorists at the source so that the fight is fought far from American shores. Military and CIA operations in Afghanistan, the Philippines, and elsewhere have imposed large costs on our terrorist enemies and should be continued. As usual, however, we are the prisoners of our past. Ever since the Civil War ended—and that was surely a special case—we have fought our wars far from home, usually successfully. But fighting terrorists abroad is not enough. It is true that abroad we can use our armed forces and our foreign-intelligence services and get help from the intelligence services of friendly (even some unfriendly) nations, and all this without being impeded by the limitations that U.S. law imposes on counterterrorist operations within the United States. Killing our enemies in combat has fewer political negatives than executing them, and even just targeting them in their home countries and wherever else they can be found abroad is important to keep them on the run and thus disrupt their planning, training, and traveling. But operations abroad are very costly and can give rise to serious diplomatic problems. And their efficacy is limited by the difficulty of penetrating terrorist groups in the terrorists' home communities, where they blend in and may be protected by their coethnics, and because of the immense catchment area from which terrorist groups can draw in their home countries to replace members killed or captured and because it is easier to replace a fallen terrorist on home ground than in Western countries such as the United States or the United Kingdom, which try to close their borders to terrorists.

Because the forward strategy is insufficient, we must not allow its appeal to distract us from the need for better homeland defenses— better domestic intelligence, better border control, better target protection ("hardening"), better communication among the different levels of government, better preparations for emergency responses to attacks. It should actually be easier to detect a terrorist plot inside the United States than outside, especially if our control over entry into the country ever improves to the point at which we will admit a possible terrorist to the United States only when we want to track or turn him (as the British did to captured German spies in World War II) so that he becomes the means of our discovering other terrorists or of poisoning the terrorist network by enabling us to feed it lies through him. And, though this may change, at present terrorists have difficulty finding neighborhoods or communities in the United States whose residents, even if coethnics, they can trust. By the same token, when a terrorist is captured in the United States his gang will find it difficult to replace him either with a U.S. resident or with a recruit from abroad.

So domestic intelligence must not be regarded as a mere adjunct to the forward strategy. But it is only one of our inner defenses, and it cannot be counted on to prevent all terrorist attacks, especially if we persist in ignoring the dysfunctional aspects of FBI intelligence and the general disarray of our domestic intelligence set-up, including the turf warfare between the bureau and the Department of Homeland Security that has impeded efforts to knit all the intelligence gatherers in the nation into an effective warning network.

Inner and outer defenses, forward and homeland strategies—these are just two ways of partitioning our counterterrorism options. A more systematic taxonomy, borrowed from the British, divides defense options into *prevention, pursuit, protection,* and *response. Prevention* in this schema refers to political, diplomatic, economic, educational, public relations, and other efforts (including limitations on immigration) to remove conditions that foster terrorism and terrorist recruiting. *Pursuit* refers to efforts to detect and disrupt terrorist plots and apprehend and punish the plotters. Both prevention and pursuit are intelligence functions, though not exclusively so. Border control is another important method of prevention and pursuit. Criminal enforcement and military force are both methods of pursuit.

Protection refers mainly to hardening targets (and thus includes airport and airline security, except that terrorist watch lists are an aspect of pursuit) and to counterproliferation efforts, such as trying to find and disarm "loose nukes." Protection is thus an inner defense, as is *response*, which means trying to mitigate the consequences of an attack once it has occurred, as by rescuing trapped persons, evacuating endangered populations, imposing a quarantine, arresting looters, putting out fires, clearing debris, repairing damage to buildings and infrastructure, and administering medical aid. Prevention and pursuit overlap the forward-homeland dichotomy, but protection and response are firmly in the homeland category. They are also examples of inner defense; so is domestic intelligence as distinct from foreign.

The benefits of protection and response, but also, to a degree, of pursuit, are not limited to reducing the threat posed by terrorists and other enemies. This is obvious in the case of response. Casualties resulting from fires, diseases, chemical leaks, collisions, and so forth, whether caused by accidents, nature, or ordinary criminals, require the same emergency response as casualties resulting from similar calamities caused by terrorists or enemy nations. But it is a neglected aspect of protection, as is illustrated by the mishandling of the crisis created by the flooding of New Orleans as a result of Hurricane Katrina. Preoccupied with the threat of terrorism, the Department of Homeland Security allowed its attention to wander from threats of natural disaster. Since the New Orleans levees were equally vulnerable to a natural disaster and to a terrorist attack, the potential benefits from protecting them were greater than if the levees had been vulnerable to either nature or terrorism but not to both. Similarly, detecting an epidemic in its incipience may enable it to be nipped in the bud whether or not its origin is terrorist. Hence the desirability of an "all risks" approach to homeland security[1] and the utility of applying the analysis of catastrophic risks in general to the design of our defenses against terrorism.[2]

1. As emphasized in Kent Roach, "Must We Trade Rights for Security? The Choice between Smart, Harsh, or Proportionate Security Strategies in Canada and Britain," 27 *Cardozo Law Review* 2151, 2157–2167 (2006).
2. See Richard A. Posner, *Catastrophe: Risk and Response* (2004).

The focus of this chapter is on issues of protection.[3] But I want first to discuss the institutional structure of counterterrorism in light of the range of counterterrorist options that I have listed. It is both important and difficult to coordinate our many intelligence agencies, but it is more difficult and as important to coordinate the intelligence system with the other elements of a counterterrorist strategy. A simple structure is illustrated by the New York City Police Department, which has separate bureaus for intelligence and counterterrorism, the latter responsible for protection and response. The intimate relation between the functions can be illustrated with an example from Richard Falkenrath's testimony that illustrates both:

> The Lower Manhattan Security Initiative (LMSI) is an in-depth, intelligence-driven counterterrorism plan designed to improve the security of lower Manhattan, perhaps the single most important center in the global financial system. When fully implemented, Lower Manhattan will be one of the most target-hardened areas in the nation. This initiative will include closed circuit surveillance cameras and License Plate Recognition readers (LPRs) on every bridge and tunnel coming into and leaving lower Manhattan. In addition, steel barriers will be used to block access to sensitive streets and locations. Mobile LPRs will be mounted on helicopters and deployed in nondescript vehicles to aid in the tracking and interdiction of suspect vehicles, and upwards of 1,000 officers will be dispatched from a central coordination center. This will significantly enhance our response capacity to any major incident affecting lower Manhattan.[4]

At the federal level, as we know, the intelligence component of our domestic counterterrorist effort is primarily the FBI's responsibility. The other components are scattered across a number of agen-

---

3. On which see generally Michael d'Arcy et al., *Protecting the Homeland 2006/2007* (2006).
4. Richard A. Falkenrath, "Prepared Statement of Testimony before the Committee on Homeland Security and Governmental Affairs, United States Senate" 7 (Sept. 12, 2006).

cies, many in the Department of Homeland Security. This is a frightening thought because of the disordered state of that department. It is responsible for border control, airline and other transportation security, identification of vulnerable targets, and, both directly and through grants to state and local agencies, target-hardening and disaster response. Its two most respected agencies, however—the Coast Guard and the Secret Service—are by statute guaranteed almost complete autonomy from departmental direction. And after the Katrina debacle Congress gave the Federal Emergency Management Agency substantial autonomy as well—a sign of the low regard in which the department is held.

Since local police play a vital role both in gathering information that may have intelligence value and in combating terrorist attacks directly, both the FBI and the Department of Homeland Security have a claim to responsibility for liaising with local police, and these competing claims have as we know engendered friction and confusion. Information sharing between federal and local counterterrorism authorities should be a two-way street, with the federal agencies conveying to the local authorities information both about specific threats and about what to look for in general, and local police conveying to the federal agencies information about suspicious local activities. But because so much of the threat information that the federal government has and local security personnel need is classified, and the process of obtaining security clearances is slow, the Department of Homeland Security inefficient, and the FBI reluctant to share information with anybody (even internally!), the flow of information from the federal to the local level is inadequate. That in turn inhibits the reverse flow, since local security personnel do not know what information the federal government wants.

The Department of Homeland Security is too large, too poorly organized, and has too many disparate responsibilities to be charged with either threat assessment (determining the likeliest terrorist targets) or threat warning (sharing terrorist information with local police and other nonfederal agencies). These are intelligence functions that should be performed by the domestic intelligence agency that we so sorely need.

Intelligence has to be coordinated with protection and response. The only official charged with that coordination is the President's assistant for homeland security and counterterrorism, Frances Townsend. Though able and energetic, she is stretched too thin because her oversight responsibilities embrace the entire Department of Homeland Security, and many of its activities are only tenuously related to counterterrorism. A Security Service separate from the FBI could not only conduct domestic intelligence but also coordinate federal efforts to counter terrorism directed against the U.S. homeland.

That would not be the complete answer to the question how best to coordinate all aspects of counterterrorism. It is sobering to contrast our ad hoc methods of coordination with the exceptionally comprehensive, highly reticulated French system presided over by what has been described as the "all-powerful" Inter-Ministerial Liaison Committee Against Terrorism.[5] France is not only a smaller country than the United States but is highly centralized, with no trace of the federalism that so complicates American government. We cannot hope to have as effective a coordination of counterterrorism as the French do. But we could do better than we are doing. We should be thinking ahead to a time when the Department of Homeland Security has gelled sufficiently to justify placing both the FBI and a Security Service in the department. That would greatly simplify the coordination of the full range of domestic counterterrorism capabilities.

I want to discuss two critical issues of what I am calling protection: ranking targets and allocating resources for their defense.

The number of potential terrorist targets in the United States is,

5. Kevin A. O'Brien, "France," in *Europe Confronts Terrorism* 19, 26 (Karin von Hippel ed. 2005).

as a practical matter, unlimited, since the primary aim of our terrorist enemies is simply to harm the nation rather than to achieve some tactical objective, such as knocking out a key military facility. But the larger the number of potential targets that the government picks out as candidates for hardening against attack, the more difficult it becomes to compare them for purposes of establishing priorities. Yet without comparisons it is impossible to rank potential attacks by their gravity, which is essential because of the impossibility of protecting every possible target.

We have some rough sense of the highest-value potential targets, and the first step is simply to list them, and the second to compare them. Meaningful comparison requires taking an all-risks approach, since the benefits of protecting a target, as of responding to a disaster, need not be limited to countering terrorism and other intentional threats. Meaningful comparison also requires use of the concept, introduced in Chapter 1, of "expected cost" or (a term that readers may find more intuitive) "expected loss." An expected loss is the loss if some risk materializes discounted (multiplied) by the risk—that is, by the probability of the loss. The concept of expected loss enables threats having very different probabilities and losses, and thus targets of very different value, to be placed on the same scale for purposes of comparison. It also disciplines comparison by forcing the analyst to think separately about risk and loss, or in other words about the probability and the magnitude of a contingent harm, such as the harm that would be inflicted by a terrorist attack.

It might seem that if probabilities cannot be quantified—and most of the probabilities relevant to counterterrorism cannot be—a cost-benefit or risk-assessment approach is futile. Not so.[6] Statisticians distinguish between "risk" and "uncertainty," reserving the first term for probabilities that can be quantified (10 percent, 20 percent, etc.) and the second for probabilities that cannot be. Most of the

6. See Posner, note 2 above, ch. 3, for a fuller discussion.

decisions that people make, in private life as in public life, are decisions under uncertainty in the statisticians' sense. Consider the decision to marry one person or another (or to keep looking, or not to marry at all), or the decision to embark on one career rather than on another. Such decisions are made in a setting of profound uncertainty about the consequences of the alternatives among which the decision maker must choose. But that does not mean that the decision-making process lacks structure. We do not make such decisions by flipping a coin. Similarly, we can structure decisions about counterterrorism even when we cannot conduct rigorous cost-benefit analysis.

Consider the following simple matrix for arraying potential threats:

	High Loss	Low Loss
High Probability		
Low Probability		

Obviously the most serious threats are in the High Loss/High Probability box, and if no greater precision is possible, the analyst might decide to confine analysis to the threats in that box. But it should be possible to do better. On the loss side, a helpful initial distinction is between *primary* and *secondary* losses. Primary losses are deaths, injuries, property damage, short-term economic disruption (such as the grounding of civil aviation for several days after the 9/11 attacks), and psychological harm. If the magnitude of the attack, which will tend to vary with the target's value (the obverse of the potential loss) is specified, the primary losses can be quantified by means of established economic techniques for valuing human life and limb,[7] in-

7. See, for example, W. Kip Viscusi, *Rational Risk Policy: The 1996 Arne Ryde Memorial Lectures*, ch. 4 (1998); Viscusi and Joseph E. Aldy, "The Value of a Sta-

cluding techniques for quantifying emotional harm. (Quantifying property damage and other purely financial losses is straightforward.)

Secondary losses are much more difficult to quantify. They include political, social, economic, and legal costs incurred in the course, or as a consequence, of responding to the primary losses. They can of course be very great; the entire costs of the Iraq war, already in the hundreds of billions of dollars (excluding casualties and the increased risk of terrorism due to the war), may be secondary losses caused by the 9/11 attacks, with few offsetting benefits. The secondary losses, both direct and indirect, resulting from enhanced airline security in response to the 9/11 attacks have been estimated at almost $10 billion a year,[8] not counting increased highway deaths from the substitution of driving for short flights because of the increased inconvenience and fear of flying since 9/11.[9]

The secondary losses caused by a terrorist attack will generally be proportional to the primary losses and so need not be calculated separately in ranking potential attacks, though they must be calculated when one is deciding whether proposed countermeasures are cost-justified. But when an attack creates "dread," the secondary losses may exceed the primary; that would be true of a radiological attack. The 9/11 attacks illustrate the operation of dread; death in an airplane crash (or in a very high building) engenders special fear because of the instinctive human fear of heights.

One method of getting a handle on the total losses likely to be caused by a potential terrorist attack is by comparison with past attacks, such as those of 9/11. After the primary consequences of a potential attack are compared with those of the 9/11 attacks and an

---

tistical Life: A Critical Review of Market Estimates throughout the World," 27 *Journal of Risk and Uncertainty* 5 (2003).

8. Computed from Jerry Ellig, Amos Guiora, and Kyle McKenzie, "A Framework for Evaluating Counterterrorism Regulations" 31–34 (Mercatus Center, George Mason University, Sept. 2006).

9. See id. at 35–36.

estimate of secondary consequences is added (bearing in mind that the more frequent terrorist attacks are, the fewer the secondary consequences will be—people can get accustomed to almost anything, in time), the loss from the attack can be expressed as a fraction or multiple of the loss caused by the 9/11 attacks.

Probability is often and in the present setting positively correlated with the length of time over which the event of interest may occur. The probability of a terrorist attack in the next year is much greater than the probability of such an attack in the next 24 hours. But one must not make the mistake of thinking that if the annual probability of the attack is assumed to be constant, the probability that it will occur sometime in the next 10 years will be 10 times the annual probability. If annual probabilities could simply be summed to determine probabilities over longer intervals, then given an annual probability of, say, 10 percent of some event's occurring, the probability of its occurring within ten years would be 100 percent (that is, it would be certain to happen); obviously it would be less than 100 percent. Recall from Chapter 1 that the formula for computing the probability that an event with an annual probability of p will occur sometime during the next n years is $1 - (1 - p)^n$. So if p is .1 and n is 10, the probability that the event will occur sometime during the period is not 100 percent, but 65 percent.[10] But that is cold comfort, for 65 percent is much higher than 10 percent.

For some terrorist risks the assumption of a constant annual probability is clearly invalid. But that is cold comfort too. The risk of a biological attack is growing because of the continuing rapid advances in bioengineering and the increased number of people trained and experienced in biotechnology. This is probably true of the risk of nuclear and radiological attacks as well. One factor in the growth of these risks is simply the publicity that weapons of mass destruction

10. The lower the annual probability of the event, the closer the cumulative probability will come to the simple multiple of p and n. See Posner, note 2 above, at 119.

are receiving. The publicity is bound to affect the thinking of terrorists.

The probability of an attack is influenced by the intentions and resources of potential attackers, about which little is known in the case of al Qaeda and similar terrorist groups. But it also depends on feasibility conditions that may be easier to determine. Consider two principal ways in which attacks fail: they are detected, or they are attempted but do not succeed because of mistakes or bad luck by the attackers. The likelier that detection or botched implementation is, the lower the probability that an attack will be attempted—also the greater the cost of the attack to the attacker—or if attempted will succeed. Detectability increases with the size of the group plotting the attack because of the greater likelihood of defection and penetration, while the likelihood of a failure in implementation increases with the technical complexity of the attack—more can go wrong, especially if the attackers are deficient in technical skill. Detectability is also a positive function of complexity. The technically complex plot will take longer to organize because costs generally are inverse to the length of time allowed for finishing a project, and the more protracted the plotting the more likely it is to be discovered. The technically complex plot may also require buying suspicious materials or equipment or recruiting experts from outside the organization, which will greatly increase the risk of detection. The 9/11 plotters wisely did not try to hire pilots but instead took flight training themselves.

Realistically, all that intelligence, or any other counterterrorist measure taken in advance of a terrorist attack, can achieve against determined and sophisticated terrorists is to increase the costs to them. The measures can make a complicated plot more so by compelling the plotters to take more elaborate precautions against discovery, and such precautions will increase the length of time that the plot requires to mature (as where electronic surveillance induces terrorist plotters to substitute couriers for the telephone in organizing the plot), and therefore increase the likelihood of detection. This is vital because the most destructive terrorist schemes are likely to be complicated rather than simple, and therefore particularly vulnerable to defensive measures that increase their complexity. The riskier the scheme, moreover, the more likely it is to be abandoned before it is executed.

The conditions that bear on the feasibility of a terrorist scheme have to be matched up with what is known, meager as it may be, about the intentions and resources of potential attackers. Compare al Qaeda with homegrown Muslim terrorists, such as the Heathrow and Toronto plotters, and homegrown "lily white" terrorists, such as the Unabomber. Al Qaeda plots are likely to be complex because al Qaeda seems to want to match or trump the 9/11 attacks and because orchestrating from abroad a terrorist attack within the United States is difficult and time-consuming. Homegrown Muslim terrorists will tend to lack organizational and technical skills. Unabombers may be the most dangerous if they get their hands on weapons of mass destruction because their attacks are one-man affairs and therefore extremely difficult to detect in advance.

Some effort at attaching geographic and time coordinates to potential attacks may be feasible. Al Qaeda is likely to continue to focus on symbolic targets. Homegrown Muslim terrorists are likely to operate in areas of substantial Muslim population, where they would not stand out from their surroundings. (These two points coalesce to make New York City a particularly inviting target, though an offsetting factor is the city's unique commitment of resources to counterterrorism.) A Unabomber could strike anywhere. Biological and cyber attacks are becoming more likely because of the rapid advance of technology in these areas and the increasing number of people who have the skills needed to mount biological or cyber attacks.

Some effort should be made to "size" the pools of potential attackers—for example by estimating the number of radical young Muslim men in the United States and the number of nuclear, chemical, and biological scientists having psychiatric histories.

Just as an attack is less likely the more narrowly it is specified in time, place, ethnicity, skill required, motive, and method, so it is proper to lump together multiple potential attacks that can be thwarted by the same countermeasures. Thus, rather than trying to estimate the probability of each one of a variety of potential biological attacks, the government might try to estimate the probability of all biological attacks—and natural epidemics as well—that might be foiled by means of broad-spectrum vaccines.

Here are two examples of how my analysis might be applied to specific attack scenarios:

1. *Attack by a small homegrown Muslim terrorist group on the New York subway system in rush hour, using homemade bombs made from commodity chemicals.* The probability of such an attack seems high, though remember that all probabilities in the analysis of terrorist attacks are relative—the actual annual probability of such an attack is probably less than 1 in 1000. The feasibility conditions are excellent. They include motivation, technical simplicity, fewness of persons required to devise and carry out the project, precedent—the July 7, 2005, attacks on the London transit system, including its subway—and widespread public discussion of the possibility of such an attack. The primary consequences of the attack if it occurred would be a significant number of deaths (though probably no more than 50). The secondary consequences would be disruption of transportation in New York and massive direct expenditures on securing the subway system by means of surveillance cameras and other sensors, armed guards, and passenger screening as at airports—the last would induce huge delays and inconvenience. This assumes that the American public, unlike the British public, which is more fatalistic, would insist on such security measures. I am not certain that it would, but it might well. If so, and if (at a guess) the annual probability of such an attack is .0002 (1 in 5,000) and the cost to society if the attack occurred would be $100 billion in the year of the attack, then the annual expected loss is .0002 $\times$ $100 billion = $20 million. That is an

underestimate because the protective measures adopted in the wake of the attack would be continued in subsequent years, perhaps indefinitely, and the costs of those measures would be a loss caused by the attack.

2. *Attack by a genetically modified smallpox bioweapon created by a "mad scientist" bent on killing as many people as possible.* The probability may seem slight, but slight or not slight it is growing as the number of people with the requisite technical skills (which are modest) increases. The feasibility conditions are good. Although the perpetrator of such an attack would have to hire a bioengineer to aerosolize the virus, he probably could do so, especially abroad, without tipping his hand. Sprayed in a major U.S. airport and impervious to existing vaccines (a deficiency that would make imposing and enforcing a quarantine very difficult), such a bioterror attack could cause millions of deaths. Assume an annual probability (beginning in 2010) of such an attack of .00001 (1 in 100,000) and a death toll of 1 million Americans. Valuing each death at $7 million—the current consensus "value of [American] life" estimate by economists, based on behavior toward risk—would yield a loss estimate of $7 trillion and an annual expected loss, therefore, of $70 million (actually an underestimate because it excludes secondary consequences). Notice that the estimate of expected loss is higher than in the case of the subway attack, even though the probability assumed is much lower.

The analysis and examples presented here are crude and incomplete. But they could be refined. And once a range of potential attacks was constructed with their associated estimates of expected loss, the focus would shift to the cost and efficacy of countermeasures for each of the attacks that had a sufficiently large expected loss to warrant further consideration.[11] The countermeasures can be analogized to investment opportunities. In the first example (the subway attack),

11. For a sense of the complexity of the required analysis, see Lawrence M. Wein et al., "Preventing the Importation of Illicit Nuclear Materials in Shipping Containers," 26 *Risk Analysis* 1377 (2006).

there is a potential $20 million "profit" from investing in a counter-measure; in the second example the potential profit is $70 million. These are maximum value estimates, as no feasible countermeasure is likely to eliminate all risk of an attack. Suppose the second risk, the one valued at $70 million a year, could be reduced by 10 percent by an annual expenditure of $5 million; then the expenditure would yield a $2 million profit (10 percent of $70 million = $7 million − $5 million = $2 million). Whether to incur the expense would depend on a comparison of alternative uses of the money, either in counterterrorism or in other social or private projects. Quantification will always be incomplete and sometimes arbitrary, but thinking in quantitative terms disciplines thought and discourages lazy reliance on intuitions.

The second issue of protection (but it is also one of response) that I want to take up is how best to allocate resources to protect against terrorist attacks. To focus the analysis, consider the controversy over the allocation by the Department of Homeland Security in 2006 of some $700 million to American cities for counterterrorism. The amounts allocated to New York and Washington, perhaps the prime U.S. targets for the most damaging kinds of terrorist attack, were about 40 percent lower than the 2005 allocations. Officials of those cities were indignant.[12] Other large cities saw their allocations cut sharply as well. In part the cuts were due to Congress's having reduced the appropriation for this program. But in larger part they were due to a decision to shift money to smaller cities. The Department of Homeland Security defended the shift on two grounds: (1) federal money should be used to build physical capacity to respond to terrorism rather than to fund recurring expenses such as salaries of emergency-response personnel; (2) New York, Washington, and a few other major cities had received the lion's share of the allocations since

12. Dan Eggen and Mary Beth Sheridan, "Anti-Terror Funding Cut in D.C. and New York," *Washington Post*, June 1, 2006, p. A1.

the beginning of the program because they are indeed the prime terrorist targets but their urgent needs had been taken care of and it was time to attend to the lesser targets.

Now obviously the federal government and not just states and their political subdivisions should spend money to protect the nation from terrorist attacks. As we learned from the 9/11 attacks, a successful attack on a city or on any other major target is bound to have consequences far beyond the state in which the city is located. But should the federal government make grants to cities (or to states, in the case of likely terrorist targets that are not cities or in cities) for counterterrorism, or should all federal counterterrorist money be spent on federal projects? The argument usually heard for the grant approach is that the locals know better their vulnerabilities and how best to reduce them. They do know which targets are valuable and least well protected and they know a great deal about the competence of their response personnel. But most of them know little about terrorist threats—terrorist plans, methods, preferred targets, and so forth. (New York City is the principal exception.) Many of those threats, moreover, emanate from groups that are not local, and the pooling of threat information across thousands of cities and other communities would be extremely difficult without some central hub. So protection against terrorism is a shared federal-state-local responsibility.

Response is also a shared responsibility. An effective system of counterterrorism, like one of domestic intelligence, must rely heavily on local facilities and personnel. This is implicit in the all-risks approach, since terrorist attacks would have effects similar to those that local responders are trained and equipped to counter. But the federal government should pick up part of the tab. Left to themselves, cities will tend to underspend on counterterrorism because the benefits of their expenditures will accrue in part, maybe in major part, to other, perhaps far distant, cities. The terrorist caught in city X may have been planning an attack in city Y.

But when a pot of federal money is available to be divided up among local governments, pork-barrel politics is bound to distort the allocation. Concern with this problem led the Department of Homeland Security to use anonymous committees of local security and emergency-response officials to vet the grants. But partly because of their anonymity and partly because many of these officials are only quasi-professional, this version of peer review was not credible and yielded some ridiculous results, such as the designation of Old MacDonald's Petting Zoo as a part of the nation's vulnerable critical infrastructure. (The official in charge of the grants program was later fired.)

Nevertheless, some criticisms of the allocation are naïve, such as that higher per capita grants to small states than to large ones are a sign that resources are being misallocated. The criticism ignores fixed costs. Suppose it costs $1,000 to establish a minimum counterterrorist program for a state and $10 per capita on top of that to provide the same level of protection across states, regardless of population. Then if the population of State A is 10, the cost per capita will be $110 ([$1,000 + ($10 × 10)] = $1,100 ÷ 10 = $110), while if the population of State B is 100—ten times as great as A's—the cost per capita of protecting its residents will be only $20 ($1,000 + ($10 − 100) = $2,000 ÷ 100 = $20). Yet there is no discrimination in favor of the less populous state if each is given $1,000 plus $10 per resident, despite the discrepancy in the per capita grant (the total grant divided by population) that will result ($110 versus $20), and despite the fact that the less populous state will receive 55 percent of what the 10 times more populous state will receive ($1,100 versus $2,000).

There is, however, a danger that local governments will use the federal money simply to replace the expenditures they would otherwise have made on counterterrorism. A city that wants to spend $10 million on such measures, and would spend it out of its own funds if it had to, but gets a grant of $10 million from the Department of Homeland Security, may reallocate the $10 million of its own funds to some unrelated program. To the extent that such reallocations occur, the department's $700 million program, with all the paperwork, peer reviews, and political controversy that are entailed, is not a security measure at all but just a general federal subsidy of local government. Or almost just that, for to get the $10 million the city will have to accept the department's conditions on how the money may be used; and the substitution effect could be further reduced if the federal grant were made conditional on a matching expenditure by the city. But notice that the less of its own money the city spends on counterterrorism, the less secure it will be against terrorist attacks, and it can use the lack of security to argue for an increased federal grant next year!

The Department of Homeland Security is probably correct, though it has backed down under political pressure,[13] that its grants should favor communications equipment, computers, emergency vehicles, pathogen detectors, containment shields, and other capital goods over salaries. For while effective counterterrorism measures tend to be labor-intensive, a city is likely to overinvest in labor-intensive measures because most of the labor hired for them will be local while the equipment will probably be manufactured elsewhere.

The most serious problem that afflicts local counterterrorist efforts is poor interagency coordination,[14] as we learned from the Hurricane Katrina debacle. The further down the governmental ladder one moves, the more acute the coordination problem becomes, because more agencies have a role in protection and response. At the local level one finds city, county, state, and federal agencies involved

13. Eric Lipton, "Federal Antiterror Funds May Now Be Used for Police Salaries: A Rule Change Allows Grants to Pay Officers Assigned to Counterterrorism Tasks," *New York Times*, Jan. 6, 2007, p. B11.

14. See, for example, Amy B. Zegart, Matthew C. Hipp, and Seth K. Jacobsen, "Governance Challenges in Port Security: A Case Study of Emergency Response Capabilities at the Ports of Los Angeles and Long Beach," in *Protecting the Nation's Seaports: Balancing Security and Costs* 155 (Jon D. Haveman and Howard J. Shatz eds. 2006).

in public safety and in ancillary activities such as transportation, communications, medicine and public health, infrastructure protection, and emergency food supplies. The sheer number of these agencies would make effective coordination extremely difficult at best—transaction costs rise with the square of the number of transactors[15]—but the difficulty is compounded by rivalries among the different levels of government. A city does not want to cede control of its agencies to the county, the county to the state, or the state to the federal government.

Problems of coordination are particularly acute at the response stage because unified command is essential to an effective response to an emergency; that is one of the lessons of the Katrina disaster. Counterterrorism grants to local governments should be conditioned on the agreement of all relevant levels of government to the designation of a single official (not necessarily federal) to command all agencies in an emergency. A serious plan—much government planning is unserious—would not only designate the emergency commander and his staff but also specify how the various responders would be deployed and supplied and communicate with each other and with the commander; it would be a mobilization plan. Prepositioning of supplies (including vaccines and chemical-protection clothing) and equipment (including means of transportation) would also be necessary, plus *realistic* rehearsals of the plan, the creation of a backup communications network, and possibly an expansion or improvement of escape routes, as well as the appointment of a standby staff to take control and direct evacuation or other response measures during the emergency.

When we turn to the question of how *much* money to allocate to each city for protection and response, we encounter once again,

---

15. The formula for the number of links required to connect all members of a set of n members is $\dfrac{n(n-1)}{2}$.

in only a slightly different setting, the baffling problems of measurement with which we began. Ideally the grant moneys should be allocated in such a way as to maximize the excess of benefits over costs. The costs are relatively straightforward. The benefits are not. They depend on (1) the target's value (not just in financial terms, of course) to the United States, (2) the likelihood of its being attacked, (3) the likely damage if it is attacked (which requires considering the range and relative probability of possible attacks on the target), and (4) the likely efficacy of a given measure in preventing the attack or in reducing the damage caused by it. Items (2) and (3) would be the most difficult to estimate accurately because estimation would call for extensive knowledge of the plans, resources, number, location, and motives of potential terrorists. But (4) is very difficult to estimate too, because the efficacy of preventive or responsive measures, such as increasing the number of policemen, installing surveillance cameras on every block, or increasing the number of SWAT teams, is extremely difficult to assess in advance.

About all that can be said with any confidence is that cities and other targets that are near the nation's borders (including coastlines) are more likely to be attacked than cities and other targets that are well inland, that larger cities with heterogeneous populations are more likely to be attacked than smaller ones because the larger and more ethnically diverse a city is, the easier it is for a terrorist to hide and move about in it without being noticed, that attacks on large cities are likely to kill more people and do more property damage than attacks on small ones, that among coastal cities New York and Washington, the targets of the 9/11 attacks, remain the prime terrorist targets because of their symbolic significance, but that to neglect the defense of the small inland cities would simply make *them* the prime targets—and an attack on such a city might sow even greater fear nationwide than another attack on a large coastal city would, by making people feel that nowhere is safe.

Unfortunately, no numbers can be attached to these probabilities.

All that is clear is that the poison of politics, mixed with regulatory inertia and general governmental incompetence, has led to dangerously unsound judgments about protection against terrorist attacks. Falkenrath, in his indispensable testimony, lists several of these:

> The Transportation Security Administration still has not deployed a system that will permit the real-time, automated checking of passenger and crew names against the terrorist watchlist for domestic flights or outbound international flights.[16]
>
> With few exceptions, major new buildings are being built all across America with almost no regard for their ability to withstand the effects of a curb-side VBIED [vehicle-borne improvised explosive device]. Cities such as New York are forced to grapple with this issue on an ad hoc basis, without any consistent national framework.[17]
>
> Since 9/11, there has been no meaningful reduction in the inherent vulnerability of toxic industrial chemicals in facilities or in transit to a terrorist attack. The Executive Branch has elected not to use its existing statutory authority to improve the security of chemicals in transit, and lacks the statutory authority to require security improvements at chemical facilities.[18]

Falkenrath expresses particular concern about the federal government's failure to regulate ammonium nitrate fertilizer, which when mixed with fuel oil—both commodities readily obtainable in the open market—becomes the powerful explosive that Timothy McVeigh and Terry Nichols used to destroy a federal building in Oklahoma City in 1995, causing 168 deaths.[19] Falkenrath also points out that the government is ignoring "the most significant port security threat," namely "an improvised explosive device borne by a small boat—that is, the precise method used by al-Qaeda in its successful attack on the USS

16. Falkenrath, note 4 above, at 22.
17. Id. at 23.
18. Id. at 24–25.
19. Id. at 25–26.

Cole in Yemen in October, 2000."[20] His biggest worry, however, is the safety of transit systems, such as the New York subway system. He points out that the federal government has invested $9.16 per passenger on airline security compared to only 6 cents per passenger on transit security.[21]

Let us step back and consider the relative emphasis to be placed on intelligence and protection. I believe that greater emphasis should be placed on the former. Protection is site specific; intelligence is not. However formidable our terrorist adversaries, they will never attack more than a minute fraction of the possible targets. Their primary aim is to punish us for what they regard as our crimes, and they can punish us severely almost anywhere in the United States. A few hand grenades detonated in the crowded area in front of the security counters of a major airport would have a serious impact on civil aviation. Should we, to prevent this, move the security counters outside the airport entrance at hundreds of U.S. airports? To harden one potential target is to make another more vulnerable, just as a homeowner who acquires a burglar-alarm system makes neighbors who don't have such a system more likely to be burglarized. We can't harden all the potential terrorist targets. The best we can do is identify a relative handful of targets the destruction of which would cause immense harm and try to secure those; we should not fool ourselves that by doing this we would be securing the nation against a devastating terrorist attack.

In contrast, if intelligence, being person-specific rather than target-specific, enables a terrorist plot to be discovered in advance, the plot can be foiled wherever and whenever it was set to go off. Attack

---

20. Id. at 26. For corroboration of Falkenrath's assessment of vulnerability to attack by small boats, see Eric Lipton, "Security Effort by Coast Guard Is Falling Short: Technology Is Faulty, and Work Runs Late," *New York Times*, Dec. 30, 2006, p. A1.

21. Falkenrath, note 4 above, at 28.

possibilities are infinite,[22] but the number of attackers is finite and information about them, if pooled, may reveal their identity. This is a compelling argument for better pooling of information—and even for guarded optimism that better pooling might have great value in fighting terrorism. Furthermore, intelligence is cheap relative to the protection of specific targets. Our intelligence capabilities could be expanded at much lower cost than would be needed to harden such targets as chemical plants and subway systems.

But one must no more oversell intelligence than protection. *All* our defenses against terrorism are porous. The hope is that if we have enough of them, and do everything we can to improve them that makes sense in cost-benefit terms, we shall have a chance to weather the storms that lie ahead.

22. See, for example, Katherine McIntyre Peters, "Volatile Mix: Deadly Chemicals and Lax Security Are a Dangerous Combination, Especially in the Post-9/11 World," *Government Executive*, Jan. 2007, p. 43; "America's Underbelly: The Virgin Islands," *Economist*, Sept. 2, 2006, p. 44.

Conclusion

Five years is an eternity in a war, and our struggle with global terrorism in an era of proliferation, whether one calls it a war or a quasi war or something else (I prefer to regard it as sui generis than to try to squeeze it into familiar preexisting categories such as "war" or "crime"), is rich in menace to the safety and prosperity of the United States. The following report of a conversation with a Pakistani who works as a cabdriver in the United States shows us what the nation may be up against:

> This man is a hard working, moderately prosperous and peace abiding person. He did not talk like a zealot. Nevertheless, he made it clear that overnight he could become a Muslim terrorist with no warning.
>
> He did not make clear how he would know when god calls him, but he was convinced it was not in what he was doing. If he received the call to jihad, he would make provision for his family, leave them and never look back . . .
>
> He considers his world view far superior to all others. Attempts

to change it are to be expected from the ignorant and unenlightened. The assumption that non-Muslims do not think as deeply about life and faith betrayed a thinly veiled mix of contempt and pity . . .

In his world view, the suicide bomber jihadists release the just to go to heaven and rid the world of sinners. No arguments or information originating outside Islam have the power to counter such views. There is no opening for a reformulation of the faith, no possibility of a new revelation and no basis to think that disputation or exposure to a better life will effect some kind of dilution of fervor. The cab driver admitted his life was far superior now to what he had in Pakistan . . . He was still prepared to kill if that was god's purpose.

These views of life and its purpose justify any kind of ruthlessness because life does not end at physical death. Armed opposition strengthens these views. Western sensibilities about compassion and humane treatment are irrelevant in winning Muslim hearts and minds and are vulnerable to manipulation by any group that lacks qualms about ruthlessness and torture.[1]

Progress in improving our national security intelligence in the five years since 9/11 has been slow; some observers sense regress. The efforts to repair the weaknesses in intelligence that were exposed by the 9/11 attacks were thrown off course by the 9/11 Commission's report and the hasty ensuing legislative reorganization of the intelligence community. The Intelligence Reform Act and another ambitious legislative response to 9/11—the creation of the Department of Homeland Security—may have retarded rather than advanced the reform of intelligence, in part because of what Congress, despite its flurry of activity, failed to do. In particular it failed to define the role of the Director of National Intelligence realistically and failed, at a time when the shock of the 9/11 attacks opened a brief window for real reform, to create a domestic intelligence service separate from the Federal Bureau of Investigation.

1. John L. McCreary, "NightWatch," Nov. 15, 2006, nightwatch.afcea.org/NightWatch_20061115.htm.

Congress was right to split the positions of Director of Central Intelligence and Director of the Central Intelligence Agency. But it should have given the DCI's successor—the Director of National Intelligence—greater power than it did over budget and personnel, so that he could be an effective manager and not go the way of the "drug czar" and other impotent coordinators of unruly agencies in our decentralized executive branch. Congress should not have designated him the President's senior intelligence adviser, armed him with analysts, and by doing these things deflected him (more precisely, *enabled* him to be deflected, on his own initiative or that of the President) from management to intelligence analysis.

Congress and the 9/11 Commission sensed organizational problems with intelligence, but neither body understood the principles of organization. They did not understand, for example in leaving domestic intelligence in the FBI, the importance of specialization, of matching task to agency culture, of denying employees a choice between an easy career track and a difficult career track, and of preventing agencies from redeploying resources from national to parochial priorities, as when the FBI reassigns special agents from intelligence to fighting crime in response to local pressures.

But the most serious mistake that Congress made, because it is the most fundamental—it undergirds most of the failures discussed in this book, including the failure to give serious thought to establishing a domestic intelligence agency outside of the FBI or at least make the bureau's National Security Branch meaningfully autonomous—was not to limit the role of the Director of National Intelligence to that of overall manager of the intelligence community, but instead to dub him senior intelligence adviser as well and arm him with analysts so that he could play the role with the requisite air of authority. The mistake, though it could have been minimized by creative executive interpretation of the Intelligence Reform Act because the act is vague and open-ended, was instead compounded by the President's appointing as the first Director of National Intelligence a diplomat rather than a professional manager. I fear that by doing so the President may have established a precedent that will force Admiral McConnell, Negroponte's successor, to assume the senior intelligence adviser's mantle as well. Exciting, time-sensitive, and time-consuming, the advisory role consumes energy that a Director of National Intelligence should devote to the formidably difficult task of actually improving the performance of the intelligence community.

The picture is not entirely bleak. The bright spots include the Open Source Center and the National Clandestine Service, though in the end these too, like the creation of the FBI's National Security Branch, may turn out to be mainly exercises in renaming. But most of the canvas is dark. The structural weaknesses of the U.S. intelligence system that argued for tighter management and thus were the raison d'être of the reorganization remain largely uncorrected: not only the disarray in domestic intelligence but also the interrelated pathologies of overclassification, inconsistent standards for security clearances, inability or reluctance to share information across agencies and with local police and other nonfederal information gatherers, and antiquated, incompatible computer systems.

Above all, the pace of reform has been too sluggish. It has taken more than two years since the Intelligence Reform Act was enacted for the horses to be led out of the paddock to the starting gate; in the case of FBI intelligence, the horses left the paddock more than five years ago but are still milling around just outside the exit. Our failed experiment of conducting domestic intelligence without a domestic intelligence agency remains uncorrected despite an emergent threat of homegrown terrorism—the terrorism we get just one shot at stopping because operations abroad and border control are helpless against the internal enemy.

To sound one last time a leitmotif of this book, the Director of National Intelligence and his staff have been trying to do too much (though with a push from Congress and perhaps under compulsion from their political superiors): trying to advise the President and other senior officials on intelligence issues, to coordinate intelligence operations, to direct some of those operations ("mission management"), and to coordinate the agencies that make up the intelligence community. Only the last is the proper role for an overall manager of the community, and it has been short-changed. This is the most important message of this book.

Granted that intelligence is only one tool of counterterrorism, the others are, it seems to me, overrated: criminal law enforcement has grave weaknesses as a counterterrorist tool, as does military action, and as does protection (hardening potential targets), which, to be effective, would require the incurring of staggering costs. (Staggering costs *are* being incurred, and with no guarantee of effectiveness.[2]) Because of the legalistic American culture and the FBI's continued domination of domestic intelligence, we are overinvested in criminal law as a weapon against terrorism. Excessive legalism, in the form of what I call "warrant fetishism," is also preventing us from dealing imaginatively with the privacy and civil liberties concerns that domestic electronic surveillance arouses. A good legislative package would combine amending the Foreign Intelligence Surveillance Act along the lines suggested in Chapter 7 (that is, substituting for FISA warrants a combination of oversight, use limitations, and penalties) with amending the Intelligence Reform Act to (1) strengthen the powers of the Director of National Intelligence (see Chapter 3) while (2) confining his role to that of overall manager/coordinator of the intelligence community; (3) create a domestic intelligence agency modeled on the British and Canadian agencies.

Protection is the domain of the Department of Homeland Security, working in (supposed) cooperation with local police and other local public safety agencies; the department has yet to gel. I have suggested some ways of improving the analysis of protection issues,

2. See, for example, Eric Lipton, "New Detectors Aim to Prevent Nuclear Terror: New York a Test Site: Devices Are Designed to Sniff Out Bombs Built within the U.S.," *New York Times*, Feb. 9, 2007, p. A1.

specifically the allocation of protective resources across potential targets and the allocation of federal grant money among local governments.

Let me wrap up by returning to the benchmarks that I listed in Chapter 2 and indicating summarily the answers to the questions posed there (a few slightly trimmed or augmented) to which my analysis points:

1. Is the reorganized structure an improvement over the previous one? If not, is there pressure for change? Are plans for change, including plans for structural change that Congress rejected (such as the creation of a domestic intelligence agency), being formulated against the day when they may be at once urgently needed and politically feasible? *The answer to the first question is probably not, and to the second and third questions, no.*

2. Has the Director of National Intelligence clearly defined his role and that of his staff? *No (though I do not seek to apportion fault— he and they are not the masters of their fate).* Are short-run concerns blotting out long-run concerns? *I fear so.* For example, is adequate attention being given to possible emergent and future threats, that is, threats other than those posed by Islamist terrorism and "rogue" nations? *No, though the prime responsibility for this may be the administration's preoccupation with the Middle East.*

3. Have the right people been appointed to the right senior jobs in the intelligence community, and are mistakes in appointments quickly corrected? *Yes and no to the first question, no to the second.*

4. Have the right priorities been set for the reorganized intelligence system? *No. Negroponte overemphasized foreign at the expense of domestic intelligence, coordination (and sometimes even direction) of operations over system-wide coordination, and substantive advice to policymakers over management of the intelligence community.*

5. Are the senior officials of the reorganized intelligence community proceeding with a proper sense of urgency or are they mired in bureaucratic molasses and "business as usual" attitudes, committed

to consensus rather than "take charge" management, and timid in dealing with the White House and Congress? *Some are, certainly, but I do not sense an adequate sense of urgency in the organization as a whole.* Are they hiding behind the comfortable evasion that Congress gave them their marching orders in the Intelligence Reform Act and march they shall—though actually, despite its excessive length and numbing detail, the act is quite open-ended? *I fear that that was Negroponte's attitude; his successor's may be different.* Has the Director of National Intelligence exercised the full scope of his managerial powers? *No.*

6. Have senior intelligence officials adopted proper benchmarks for their own performance, and if so, are they meeting them? *I believe they have not adopted proper benchmarks.*

7. Is there too much staff in the Office of the Director of National Intelligence, or too little? *Too much.* Are sound management practices being followed or flouted? Are the right lessons being drawn from the continued floundering of the Department of Homeland Security? Are officials able to step back from day-to-day management and evaluate structure and progress from perspectives informed by comparative and historical experience and by the social sciences (cognitive psychology, organization theory, statistical theory, economics, political science)? *The answer to all these questions appears to be no.*

8. Has good progress been made on other high-priority matters, such as improving information technology and the sharing of digital information, hiring linguists, standardizing security clearances to enable classified information to be easily shared within and across agencies and with experts outside government, ending overclassification, and improving "vertical" information sharing (for example, with local police)? *No, with the principal and very important exception of improved information sharing among analysts.* Do officials in the different intelligence agencies regard themselves as playing on the same team? *I doubt it.*

9. Is the community overinvested in criminal law enforcement?

In military responses to terrorism? *Yes and yes*. Do policymakers understand that intelligence methods can be used not only to detect, but also to disrupt, plots against the nation—in short, do they understand that intelligence is an alternative as well as an adjunct to law enforcement and military force? *They understand—all but the Federal Bureau of Investigation and the Department of Homeland Security*.

10. Is the intelligence community getting its message out to the general public? Is it educating the public in the need for but also the limits of intelligence? *No and no*. Is too much revealed or concealed? *Too much concealed*.

11. Is the community showing enough concern for issues of legality, privacy, civil liberties, and separation of powers? *Yes*. Do senior officials reach out to civil libertarians and other critics? *No.* Are they forthright in explaining the dangers of too expansive a conception of civil liberties? *No.*

12. Is congressional oversight of the reorganized system competent, continuous, and penetrating? *No.*

13. Are politics being kept at bay to an extent consistent with democratic governance? *I am doubtful, but I think the situation is improving*. Do policymakers sufficiently respect the professionalism and independence of career intelligence officers? *No.* To what extent are so-called intelligence failures actually policy failures? *To a great extent*.

14. Is intelligence adequately coordinated with the other components of national security? *No.*

It is tempting to blame the administration and Congress for the disarray in our systems of intelligence and counterterrorism. They have indeed made more than their share of mistakes. Basic principles of sound organization and management have repeatedly been flouted. Long-festering problems have been left to fester, such as insufficient sharing of intelligence data across federal agencies and with local police. There have been bad appointments to some key positions, notably the appointment of Porter Goss to head the CIA; and I doubt that John Negroponte, though a very distinguished diplomat, was the best possible choice to be the first Director of National Intelligence.

But the basic obstacles to improving our defenses against terrorism are systemic. It is difficult both to figure out how best to fight terrorism and to overcome institutional inertia; thus, both design and implementation are problematic. Complacency is also an obstacle, and it reinforces the problem of inertia. We cannot afford to assume that we are safe. But even if we could shake off that comfortable assumption, the ultimate obstacle to constructive reform of the intelligence system, and of counterterrorism more broadly, would remain. It is—to end with a conjecture—institutional inertia writ large. Our government has become too complex to be manageable as the challenges facing it multiply because of the size and growing complexity of American society, the breakneck pace of scientific and technological advance, and the increased number and variety of foreign threats both state and nonstate. The trend toward more complex government, bringing in its train a disastrous combination of bureaucratization and inattention (by the public and by the highest political level of government), could be a harbinger of eventual national collapse.[3]

We must not give way to pessimism, but we must be realistic. Clausewitz's dictum about war—in war everything is very simple, but the simplest thing is difficult to accomplish—applies to intelligence and counterterrorism. A critical reexamination of our practices and institutions at this time of transition, a passionate commitment to real reform, a refusal to stand pat, a sense of urgency, political fearlessness, and a burst of directed energy must be demanded of the officials in all branches of government who are responsible for our national security.

3. John A. Tainter, *The Collapse of Complex Societies* (1988).

Acknowledgments

I could not have written this book without a great deal of help. My thanks to Heather Afra, Zachary Holmstead, Matthew Johnson, Meghan Maloney, and Sam Sellers for their exemplary research assistance, and to Elbridge Colby, Jack Goldsmith, Efraim Halevy, Scott Hemphill, John Lenkart, Thomas Twetten, and Amy Zegart for a great many extremely helpful comments on earlier versions of the manuscript or parts of it. I had the opportunity to present portions of my semi-final draft in the Intelligence Forum Speakers Series of the Johns Hopkins' School of Advanced International Studies; I thank John McLaughlin for inviting me, and the audience for its intelligent comments and questions. Thanks also to Peter Berkowitz and Tod Lindberg, the general editors of Hoover Studies in Politics, Economics, and Society, the series in which this and my previous two books on intelligence have been published, and to Jeff Bliss, the Hoover Institution's associate director of communications. I have also greatly benefited from discussions of the subject matter of the book with Eli Jacobs, William Odom, George Spix, William Webster, and a number of present and former officials of the intelligence community (not limited to the U.S. intelligence community) who would prefer not to be identified publicly. Opinions and the remaining errors are my own.

Index

operations officers, 51; performance measures, 124, 128–129; politicization of, 46–49; public relations, 72, 88, 103, 234; talent drain, 20, 141; turf wars, 67, 82, 84–85; U.S. intelligence failures, 23–26; use of contractors in, 98; use of detailees, 98–99; versus target hardening, 225–226. *See also* Domestic intelligence; Fusion centers; Intelligence analysis

Iraq Study Group, viii, 62

Iraq, war in, viii, 2–3, 8–10, 62, 72, 93

Jury, trial by, in terrorism cases, 174, 178, 181

Justice Department. *See* Department of Justice

Kahan, Ephraim, 23

Kappes, Stephen, 20, 45

Katrina debacle, 11, 99, 103, 206, 208, 221–222

Kessler, Ronald, 160n

Kilcullen, David, 127–128

Lackawanna 6, 112n

Lehman, John, 19, 135–136

Levin, Carl, 47

Lie detectors. *See* Polygraph

London transit bombings, 100, 216

MacGaffin, John, 100n

McConnell, John M., viii n. 43, 45, 58–60, 230

McNamara, Thomas, 86n

MI5, xii–xiii, 110, 116–117, 138–139, 143–144, 151–153, 155–156, 158

Miami 7 operation, 111–113, 117

Military Commissions Act of 2006, 181–182, 188, 193

Millennium plot, 126

Miller, John, 111, 145n

Mission managers. *See under* Director of National Intelligence

Mudd, Philip, 118, 135n, 138–140, 143

Mueller, John, 4–6, 11, 14

Mueller, Robert, 118, 132–133, 140, 142–143, 153

National Clandestine Service. *See under* CIA

National Counterintelligence Executive, 57, 63, 66–67

National Counterproliferation Center, 44, 53, 57, 63

National Counterterrorism Center, 18, 44, 50–52, 57, 61, 82, 104, 130, 166

National Geospatial-Intelligence Agency, xi n, 49, 131

National Intelligence Council, 10, 18, 44, 53–55, 57, 73

National Intelligence Estimates, 10, 44, 53–55, 73, 93–94

National Reconnaissance Office, xi n, 49, 131

National Security Agency, xi n, 21–22, 48, 160; use by of call records, 195; warrantless surveillance program, xii, 71–72, 88, 118–119, 133, 165, 171–173. 193–202, 198–201

National Security Branch. *See under* FBI

Negroponte, John, viii, x, 18, 20, 29, 34, 54, 57–60, 62–65, 71–72, 86n, 103, 140, 229–230, 232–233, 235

New York City, vulnerability of to terrorist attacks, 215–218, 223, 225

New York Police Department. *See under* Counterterrorism; Domestic intelligence

Oberdorfer, Don, 6n

Odom, William E., 162n

Office of Strategic Services (OSS), 12, 176

Oklahoma City bombing, 224

One percent doctrine, 13–14, 112n, 162

Open source intelligence, 61, 73–81, 153; supervision of by Office of the Director of National Intelligence, 78–80. *See also* CIA, Open Source Center

Organization theory, bureaucracy, 42–
43, 99, 102–103, 113–114, 235;
control loss, 102; hierarchical versus
horizontal structure, 67–68;
organizational cultures, xi, 105, 122–
123, 129–132, 229; performance
measures, 27–28, 124, 128; "tell"
versus "sell" organizations, 125.
Overclassification. *See* Classified
materials; Security clearances
Padilla, Jose, 180n, 187
Path dependence, 99–100
Pearl Harbor, attack on, 5n, 6, 17, 23,
93n, 154
Poindexter, John, 166
Polonium 210, 10n
Polygraph, 97
President's Daily Brief, 35n, 36, 40, 44,
53–55, 57, 64–65
Privacy and Civil Liberties Oversight
Board, 198
Probabilities, cumulative, 11, 213;
importance of in counterterrorism, 1–
14, 113, 175; versus frequencies, 4.
See also One percent doctrine
Psychology. *See* Cognitive psychology
Quaeda. *See* Al Quaeda
Reid, Richard, 114, 125
Risk, bureaucratic risk aversion, 113–
114; security officers' aversion to, 95;
versus uncertainty, 210–211
Royal Canadian Mounted Police, 144,
151
Rumsfeld, Donald, 44, 131
Russack, John, 29, 85
Sageman, Marc, 7n, 171, 192
Scotland Yard (London Metropolitan
Police). *See* Special Branch
Scowcroft, Brent, 131
Search warrants, xii, 180; attenuating
the probable-cause requirement,
196–197; for electronic interceptions,
192–197, 201; Fourth Amendment's
warrant clause, 192; general
warrants, 172; under British law,

180; under Title III, 193; warrant
fetishism, 192, 231
Security clearances, 85–86, 89–90, 94–
95, 104
Security officers, 95–97
Security protocols, 85, 88
Security Service (U.K.). *See* MI5
Silberman, Laurence, 122. *See also*
Silberman-Robb Commission
Silberman-Robb Commission, 18, 46,
63, 122, 143–145
Smallpox, 13
Special Branch (U.K.), 138, 146, 151–
152, 158
Speckhard, Anne, 127n
State Department, 49
Surveillance (electronic), 231; collateral
intercepts, 194; privacy implications,
195–196, 198–199; value of to
national security, 200–201. *See also*
Data mining; Foreign Intelligence
Surveillance Act; National Security
Agency; Traffic analysis
Suskind, Ron, 13n, 108n
Taipale, Kim, 194n, 195n
Tenet, George, 43
Terrorism, "glorifying" of, 179, 181;
assessing costs of terrorist attacks,
210–218; biological, 109, 213–214,
217; homegrown, 125–128, 130,
146–149, 176, 182, 215, 230;
hypothetical attack on New York
subway system, 216–218; magnitude
of threat of, 4–5, 7–12, 35, 100–101,
114, 224–225, 227–228; social
networks of terrorists, 192. *See also*
Airline and airport safety; specific
plots
Terrorist Surveillance Program. *See*
National Security Agency, warrantless
surveillance program
Terrorist Threat Integration Center. *See*
under CIA
Tet Offensive, 6, 23
Tierney, John, 4n, 5n